A Stranger's Journey

To David
Fellow traveler
Best wishes
David A. [signature]

A Stranger's Journey

RACE, IDENTITY, AND
NARRATIVE CRAFT
IN WRITING ᔓ

David Mura

The University of Georgia Press

ATHENS

Portions of this book have appeared in the following publications:
Gulf Coast Literary Journal, Kartika Review, The AWP Chronicle,
Journal of Creative Writing Studies, 2040 Review, GrubWrites,
and on my blog, *Secret Colors* (blog.davidmura.com).

Rumi poem from *Unseen Rain: Quatrains of Rumi,*
translated by John Moyne and Coleman Barks,
© 1986 by Coleman Barks. Reprinted by arrangement
with The Permissions Company, Inc., on behalf of
Shambhala Publications Inc., Boulder, Colorado,
www.shambhala.com.

"Writing and Reading Race," RIT Scholar Works © 2016

Set in 10/13.5 Quadraat Regular
Printed and bound by Thomson-Shore, Inc.
The paper in this book meets the guidelines for
permanence and durability of the Committee on
Production Guidelines for Book Longevity of the
Council on Library Resources.

Most University of Georgia Press titles are
available from popular e-book vendors.

Printed in the United States of America
22 21 20 19 18 P 5 4 3 2 1

Library of Congress Cataloging-in-Publication Data
Names: Mura, David, author.
Title: A stranger's journey : race, identity, and narrative craft in writing /
    David Mura.
Other titles: Race, identity, and narrative craft in writing
Description: Athens : The University of Georgia Press, 2018. |
    Includes bibliographical references.
Identifiers: LCCN 2017058467| ISBN 9780820353685 (hardcover : alk. paper) |
    ISBN 9780820353463 (pbk. : alk. paper) | ISBN 9780820353456 (ebook)
Subjects: LCSH: Creative writing. | Fiction—Technique. | Autobiography. |
    Literature and race.
Classification: LCC PN187 .M87 2018 | DDC 808.3—dc23
    LC record available at https://lccn.loc.gov/2017058467

With great gratitude, for
JAMES BALDWIN,
LUCILLE CLIFTON,
EDWARD SAID, and
WAKAKO YAMAUCHI

Contents

III. Narrative and Identity in Memoir

IV. The Writer's Story

Appendix: Seven Basic Writing Assignments

A Stranger's Journey

Introduction

The earliest essays in this book were written just before Barack Hussein Obama was elected president, bringing some deluded persons to declare a postracial America. I write this introduction just after the 2016 election, in a nation where Michael Brown and Ferguson, Freddie Gray, Baltimore, and Black Lives Matter are now juxtaposed against the rampant racism, xenophobia, religious bigotry, and sexism of Donald Trump's election.

How does a book on creative writing fit into such a context? Some might believe such matters have little to do with teaching creative writing. In part, I hope what I've written here will convince such people to reexamine their beliefs.

The purpose of this book is to instruct writers about their craft, particularly fiction writers and writers of memoir as well as creative writing teachers. In composing the book, I've considered how writers of color have altered our literary tradition and the ways writers practice their craft. One key shift has involved an increased focus on the issues of identity.

At the same time, many of the principles in this book are timeless, particularly in terms of narrative construction in fiction and memoir. And yet, in my instruction, I've encountered many writers, even graduates from prestigious MFA programs, who have not been taught the basic elements of story.

The book also explores the newly evolved aesthetic principles of memoir, which has emerged in recent decades as an established genre. In the process, I examine how memoirists can learn from fiction and how fiction writers can learn from memoir.

To a large extent, these essays stem from my own experiences teaching at the Voices of Our Nations Arts Foundation (VONA), the Loft, and the Stonecoast MFA program. The book also reflects my work as a memoirist, fiction writer, and poet and the ways my writing has interrogated my own identity as a Sansei, a third-generation Japanese American.

In a sense, this book can be viewed as my third memoir, another recounting of my own stranger's journey, to use a term from James Baldwin. Significantly, as I have undergone my own personal journey concerning my identity, the society in which I live has also been undergoing transformations regarding the issues of race and identity, not just within politics but perhaps even more so within culture and its practices.

To explain what I mean by this, let me cite Jeff Chang, the Asian American critic who wrote the hugely influential *Can't Stop Won't Stop: A History of the Hip-Hop Generation*. In his second book, *Who We Be: The Colorization of America*, Chang examines the issues of race over the last fifty years, the post–civil rights era, within the context of cultural change. The book explores moments like the Black Arts Movement, the advent of multiculturalism, and the so-called culture wars; the election of Obama and the proclamation—and quick retraction—of a postracial America; the shifts in demographics and immigration politics; battles over textbooks and ethnic studies; and the rise of hip-hop. Chang's book is a must-read for anyone involved with the issues of race or culture. In his introduction, he writes:

> Here is where artists and those who work and play in the culture enter. They help people to see what cannot yet be seen, hear the unheard, tell the untold. They make change feel not just possible, but inevitable. Every moment of major social change requires a collective leap of imagination. Change presents itself not only in spontaneous and organized expressions of unrest and risk, but in explosions of mass creativity.
>
> So those interested in transforming society might assert: cultural change always precedes political change. Put another way, political change is the last manifestation of cultural shifts that have already occurred.

Sometime around 2040, the United States will no longer be a white majority country. No racial group will constitute the majority. Artists of color, who are re-creating the past, exploring the present, and creating the future, know what it means to be a racial minority in America. This knowledge is embedded within our identities, experiences, and imaginations; we speak and write from that knowledge. That knowledge is out there for white artists to share, but whether they will avail themselves of that knowledge is another question, one they'll have to answer if they're going to prepare themselves for the America that is surely coming and is, in many ways, already here.

The most recent U.S. election bears strong evidence that a large number of whites still desperately cling to a national identity in which racism and the assertion of white dominance and supremacy remain the norm and in which sexism, homophobia, religious bigotry, and xenophobia are not just accepted but touted. Chang wrote *Who We Be* in the time of Obama's presidency, so in late November 2016, his prophecy about political change remains that—a prophecy. But the work of artists—seeing the not yet seen, hearing the unheard, telling the untold—remains.

When I was younger, I was educated in an English PhD program where I read no writers of color, and the current literary issues arising from the increased diversity in American and world literature were not present. But as T. S. Eliot has instructed, each new work and author added to a tradition shifts our view of the whole tradition, alters our understanding of both the present and the past. This shift is occurring now both through the work of individual writers of color and through changes in our literary and intellectual paradigms.

A useful example of this shift is Toni Morrison's *Playing in the Dark: Whiteness and the Literary Imagination*, which, along with her novels, has become a seminal work. In her critique of how white American writers have depicted black characters, Morrison makes a trenchant observation about the mind-set of these white American authors as opposed to the mind-set of black authors:

> For reasons that should not need explanation here, until very recently, and regardless of the race of the author, the readers of virtually all of American fiction have been positioned as white. I am interested to know what that assumption has meant to the literary imagination. When does racial "unconsciousness" or awareness of race enrich interpretive language, and when does it impoverish it? What does positing one's writerly self, in the whole racialized society that is the United States, as unraced and all others as raced entail? What happens to the writerly imagination of a black author who is at some level *always* conscious of representing one's own race to, or in spite of, a race of readers that understands itself to be "universal" or race-free? In other words, how is "literary whiteness" and "literary blackness" made, and what is the consequence of that construction?

While white writers have not traditionally had to imagine a reader of color, writers of color have always been cognizant that their work would be judged and interpreted by white readers. This awareness did not necessarily mean that the writer of color had to write primarily with a focus on, or accommodation for, the white reader. But it did mean that writers of color understood that the very act of writing involved the divide and differences between themselves and white readers. For writers of color, race and consciousness of their racial Other has always been an issue. This was not the case, as Morrison observes, for white writers, even when they were writing about black characters.

What Morrison implies, but does not state, is a prescription for white writers: It is time for you as a white writer to begin imagining a reader of color. What this imagining does to your work and the way you go about your tasks as a writer is up to you. But it is time for the assumption of a monochromatic readership to end in the white literary imagination, which is also to say, it is time to end a view of our literary tradition as monochromatically white.

Both explicitly and implicitly, *A Stranger's Journey* addresses the contrasts Morrison alludes to. Overall, the book departs from creative writing books that leave the issues of race and ethnicity beyond the boundaries of how creative writing is taught. My aim here is to broaden the essential elements of the writer's craft. This book is for both writers of color and white writers, for it addresses issues of identity that anyone in the world of literature today needs to fully comprehend.

At the same time, the book offers practical craft instruction and advice on the writing life and the creative process. What links all the sections of the book, whether concerning identity, craft, or writing in general, is a pursuit of the truth, a hunger to break through to the complexities of our reality, and an understanding of how writing arises from the creativity and truth telling that resides in our unconscious.

I explore two central themes or questions in this book. The first involves the question of identity: how writing is an exploration of who one is and one's place in the world; how such exploration entails challenges to familial, cultural, social, or political norms and to one's own psychic defenses and blind spots. Though the question of identity is obviously a consideration that a memoirist must often grapple with, writing fiction can also entail a process through which the writer examines her or his identity. But in whatever genre, a writer's journey often requires investigating one's past and present selves to create a truer and more complex articulation of the self. It involves acknowledging one's current limitations—whether of knowledge, skill, experience, or psychic honesty—and fighting to overcome them.

The second central question of this book revolves around how one tells a story, whether in fiction or in memoir. What are the tools necessary for the writer to construct a narrative either for a fictional protagonist or for recounting a portion of the writer's life? There are obviously differences in these two tasks but also similarities. In this way, particularly when writing first-person or autobiographical novels, writers of fiction can benefit from understanding how memoir works, and memoirists can benefit from understanding how fiction is constructed.

In my experience as a fiction writer and as a memoirist, I have found that most creative writing texts fail to adequately address narrative structure. Instead, I have discovered a more fundamental understanding of story in books on myth, playwrighting, and screenplays. The essays in the second and third sections of A Stranger's Journey stem in part from my attempts to extend what I have learned from these books and from my teaching creative writers in fiction and memoir.

The title of the opening section, "The World Is What It Is," is taken from V. S. Naipaul's A Bend in the River. Early on Naipaul struggled to acknowledge that his own background and identity were essential to his growth as a writer. And yet he also came to see that his ultimate task was to know and acknowledge the whole world, not just the small population and community in which he grew up.

In this first section, I critique certain premises regarding race and the teaching of creative writing, how these assumptions presume a racial status quo that often goes unexamined and unchallenged. I begin with a précis of my own personal journey as writer through the lenses of identity, ethnicity, and race. In the second essay, I argue that for many—if not all—writers, an essential task is to question the premises and frameworks of the groups to which one belongs. In the third and fourth essays, I analyze the differences between the ways white writers and writers of color introduce and contextualize their fictional characters racially, and I investigate the implications of those differences in terms of literary judgment and of racial issues. In the remaining three essays of this section, I explore how race and literary practices play out in the teaching and practice of creative writing. In doing so, I outline how the teaching of creative writing must be transformed to address the needs of students of color and to acknowledge writers of color within our literary culture.

A central theme of this first section is that race provides an essential lens for interpreting and evaluating the work of writers of color, and that this lens has been instrumental in the development of most major writers of color. As such, racial issues cannot be considered as lying outside the boundaries of the teaching of creative writing. Indeed, the failure to question the ways whiteness has traditionally been defined and practiced in both literature and society can lead to failures in craft. Thus a consideration of race in writing and reading literature is an invaluable pursuit for all writers—not just writers of color but white writers too. To argue otherwise is simply a defense of ignorance, a refusal to acknowledge what now constitutes American and world literature. As T. S. Eliot observed, the tradition is always changing, and we must change with it.

The second section, "Story in Fiction," focuses on the basic techniques of storytelling and narrative structure in fiction. These include the positing of a goal for the protagonist and setting up the protagonist's irreconcilable conflicts; how and why protagonists lie to themselves and others; the gap between the protagonist's plans and what actually occurs. I also explore how a fiction writer functions both like God in the book of Job, raining calamities on the protagonist, and like the devil offering temptations to the protagonist.

The examples in this section are drawn from a variety of contemporary writers, but the focus on writers of color here differs from many traditional texts on this subject. (I've also constructed the book so that a reader or a teacher need refer to only a few texts as supplemental readings.) In the section's final essay, "The Four Questions Concerning the Narrator," I address a question that, given our society's increasing diversity, has become both necessary and sometimes confusing: Whom is the narrator telling the story to? This question is of a different order than the one posed by Morrison—who is the expected reader of the text?—but the two questions are certainly related.

The third section, "Narrative and Identity in Memoir," examines the basic aesthetic principles of memoir and how the narrative techniques and structures of fiction can be applied to it. Where the writer of fiction creates story, the memoirist discovers story. At the same time, the question of the writer's identity in memoir is almost always central. This section reflects my experiences as a writer of memoir and the various ways ethnic and racial identity may be explored in memoir—especially through the reflexive voice that comments on and analyzes the past experiences of the self. As the section progresses, I argue that the exploration of identity, whether in memoir or fiction, has become a central theme of our age, a theme far more complicated and layered than many realize.

The final section, "The Writer's Story," revisits the themes of the book in terms of the individual writer's own journey and story. The first essay takes up the themes of the first section in charting the development of V. S. Naipaul, who grew up in the small community of Indian ancestry in Trinidad and who immigrated as a young man to England. I posit that Naipaul's background and struggles represent an eccentric path that is, increasingly, no longer eccentric but emblematic; at the same time, especially early on as a writer, he engaged in what all writers struggle with: to see themselves and their place in the world clearly, truthfully.

The final essay in the book uses narrative and mythic structures to chart and understand the path of all writers. Whether in terms of identity or one's development as a writer or in the task of finishing a book (particularly one's first book), I see writers as constantly embarking on their own mythical journeys. Thus I view the process of writing as a call to change: *We start to write a book in order to become the person who finishes the book.*

Certainly, I myself have gone through this experience of change in writing this book. Indeed, through this writing, I have become someone I did not expect to be. That is one of the greatest joys of practicing my craft and finishing a book. It's my hope that readers will find this book a seminal guide to their own transformative journey.*

---

* To assist in that journey, I've included an appendix with seven basic writing assignments I give to my students. These assignments are specifically designed to address issues or questions associated with the techniques and literary principles explored in this book.

I

The World Is What It Is

The Search for Identity

A STRANGER'S JOURNEY

If writing is a search for language, it is also a search for identity. We write to articulate who we are, to describe our sense of the world.

For me, the requirements of this task were not readily apparent. As a young writer, I did not think of myself as a Japanese American or an Asian American or as a writer of color. The concepts and language for such an excavation were not available either in the literature I was taught or in the culture around me. Beyond this, my teachers encouraged me both actively and covertly to eschew the "ethnic route."

In this situation of silencing, I was not alone. For most Asian Americans, American culture provides two unsatisfactory identities: The first is that we are perpetually foreign, "strangers from a distant shore." True, some of us may have come here only last year, but even if our families arrived 150 years ago, we are still considered aliens. People still ask us, "Where do you come from?" and may assume English is not our native language. In other words, our difference from the white mainstream is, in certain ways, permanent and marks us forever as outsiders, unable to belong to this society (as my parents' internment during World War II and calls in 2016 for measures echoing that internment, such as the Muslim ban, demonstrate).

Our second identity is that we Asian Americans are honorary whites—sometimes the "model minority"—and in these appellations, our seeming closeness to "white" norms and standards of behavior is noted and praised. Here our differences are erased, and this erasure is seen as a necessary passport to our becoming accepted members of society. Growing up in a white Chicago suburb, raised by parents who, as a reaction to their internment, wanted to assimilate, I fervently believed this. In high school, I felt complimented when a white friend would say to me, "I think of you, David, just like a white person." When I first began writing, I embraced the writerly form of this identity—I insisted, à la Amy Tan, that I was simply "a writer" and not an Asian American writer.

Later, through other Asian American writers and writers of color, as well as through my own work, I came to realize that there is a third identity, one less often given voice to in the education system. There are two aspects to this identity. One is cultural. As an Asian American, a person or his parents or his grandparents or perhaps someone even much further back arrived in America from Asia, and part of his cultural identity involves mixing or integrating or jostling Asian cultural values with American cultural values and history. The larger culture sometimes acknowledges this "bicultural" identity, whether in popular works such as the musical *Flower Drum Song* or various portrayals of Asian Americans in literature such as *The Joy Luck Club*.

A second aspect of Asian American identity, much less acknowledged, examines our experience of race, which involves what it is like to look like me—that is, someone with Asian physical features—and live in America. In other words, it entails the discordant and troubling process of being "raced"—that is, categorized and treated by others through the various ways race is played out in our society. Sometimes this stems from encounters with stereotypes and prejudice and from the ways Asian Americans are portrayed in the culture and treated by other Americans. But at other times the effects are subtler and more complicated. For the racial aspect of our experience involves not only how others looks at us but also how we look at ourselves, particularly in terms of internalized racism; thus it also includes the various ways we try to hide or deny the differences in our experiences both from ourselves and from those of the mainstream white society.

In this third definition of our identity, which includes both ethnicity and race, we Asian Americans begin to understand that our experiences are far more complicated than white Americans understand and, indeed, than even we ourselves may understand. Often there are layers of feelings and thoughts and experiences that we have not yet examined or articulated—or that we even actively deny. Indeed, much of my writing has emerged out of this gap. But it emerged only through my acknowledging that the tools the culture had given me to express my identity and experience were inadequate, that they carried with them limitations imposed by history, politics, and culture.

The situation of Asian American writers concerning their identity possesses parallels with other writers of color and other marginalized writers. Take W. E. B. Du Bois's question in *The Souls of Black Folk*, what does it mean to be a problem? Or his articulation of double consciousness: the awareness of blacks that the ways they think about themselves differ from the ways whites view them; in order to survive, blacks have historically had to be aware not just of their own consciousness but of white consciousness and how it is constructed.

When, as a younger Asian American writer, I encountered Du Bois's double consciousness, it made absolute sense to me; it helped me understand my own identity and the construction of my own consciousness. Similarly, when I read Frantz Fanon's *Black Skin, White Masks* and its dissection of racial self-hatred, I immediately recognized myself in his analysis. In one particular passage, Fanon looks at the French colonial education system in the West Indies and how black school children read about their ancestors the Gauls and how the European hunters and explorers went into Africa to civilize the savages there. Fanon then asks: What are these black children learning? When I read his answer—self-hatred, self-alienation, and identification with their colonial rulers—I thought, "Oh shit, that's what I've been doing."

Thus, when I was younger, it was through black writers that I first began to acquire a vocabulary and framework to understand my Japanese American identity. There I found authors and critics who provided me with a language to explore and write about race, a language present in none of the white writers I read in my English undergraduate or PhD program.

The other tool I used stemmed in part from Marxist theorists and writers influenced by Marxist thought.

Certain writers, and this includes most writers of color, find an investigation into the political nature of their enterprise absolutely crucial to their growth as writers—or even to their simply being able to declare themselves writers. When a person comes from a family or a group that has been marginalized, when she is one of the "subalterns," the silence such a person confronts about herself and her experiences within the greater culture is a political condition. In such cases, the very act of writing about herself and her experiences becomes a political act.

When confronted with the proverb, "Know thyself," the Italian Marxist Antonio Gramsci thought less about questions of morality or character than more traditional thinkers might. Instead, Gramsci viewed self-examination as a call to understand the historical forces that have shaped a person; a person must understand that she and the world she lives in are neither natural nor something that appeared full blown out of nothing: "The starting-point of critical elaboration is the consciousness of what one really is, and is 'knowing thyself' as a product of the historical process to date, which has deposited in you an infinity of traces, without leaving an inventory. . . . Therefore it is imperative at the outset to compile such an inventory." The English Marxist critic Terry Eagleton implies that such an inventory means that writers must also look at the materials they have been given to work with and their historical lineage: "The author does not make the materials with which he works: forms, values, myths, symbols, ideologies come to him already worked-upon, as the worker in a car-assembly plant fashions his product from already-processed materials."

Looked at this way, the search to express the self becomes a very complex and multivoiced enterprise and involves many areas of investigation. Where the society might deem a person or her experiences as self-evident, the person discovers that this is far from the case. In the process, she ends up questioning more and more of the world around her, the accepted or received views of the culture. As Bertolt Brecht writes in his treatise *Brecht on Theatre*:

> It is taken for granted that a poet, if not an ordinary man, must be able without further instruction to discover the motives that lead a man to commit murder; he must be able to give a picture of a murderer's mental state "from within himself." It is taken for granted that one only has to look inside oneself in such a case; and then there's always one's imagination. . . . There are various reasons why I can no longer surrender to this agreeable hope of getting a result quite so simply. I can no longer find in myself all those motives which the press or scientific reports show to have been observed in people. Like the average judge when pronouncing sentence, I cannot without further ado conjure up an adequate picture of a murderer's mental state. Modern psychology, from psychoanalysis to behaviourism, acquaints me with facts that lead me to judge the case quite differently, especially if I bear in mind the findings of sociology and do not overlook economics and history. You will say: but that's getting complicated. I have to answer that it *is* complicated.

Brecht tried to develop a theater that reflected and critiqued these complications, that broke up the apparently seamless portrait of the world provided by his society; by doing so, he challenged the aesthetics of standard realism. He wanted to show the cracks in the scenery, to illuminate the ways that apparently seamless portraits on stage had been constructed. His stagecraft broke through the fourth wall in the ways he instructed his actors to perform and in direct addresses to the audience; he readily included other art forms and media: the use of slides with comments and settings and instructions, painting, film clips, song, and music. He did not want the audience to forget that just as history has been determined by the actions of human beings and not by natural causes, so too art is created by humans. At the same time, he wanted to present theater that made use of contemporary technology and whose multiplicity did justice to the complications of the modern world. He privileged hybridity over purity, questioning over acceptance, history over forgetting, the tales of the defeated over the tales of the victors. All this is why, when I was developing as a young writer, Brecht inspired me and aided me in my search for my own makeshift stagecraft, for the tools to convey my own glimpses of the world, my own inventory and tale.

The exploration of identity is, I believe, a central theme of this age.

When I think of this shift, that bland Disney World slogan comes to mind: "It's a small world after all." This interconnectedness is present everywhere—from AIDS to terrorism; from oil prices to trade imbalances; from nuclear proliferation to the threat of global warming; from immigration laws to so-called wars of preemption and their inevitable refugees and migrations; from the internet to satellite technology; from the movement from postcolonial to multicultural to global lit. In short, it's clear the world is becoming increasingly connected. We live in an era when strangers are encountering strangers daily, making each of us stranger to ourselves. And as James Baldwin has instructed us, we must confront a changing reality that calls us to question and transform our identities.

In our global village, the exploration of shattered and shifting identities leads us to the exploration of cultural and linguistic shifts, the crossing of borders by people and tongues; this exploration in turn leads us to the creation of forms that attempt to reflect and encompass our polyglot world. In the twentieth century, the Russian critic M. M. Bakhtin described the process this way:

> The new cultural and creative consciousness lives in an actively polyglot world. The world becomes polyglot, once and for all and irreversibly. The period of national languages, coexisting but closed and deaf to each other, comes to an end. Languages throw light on each other: one language can, after all, see itself only in the light of another language. The naive and stubborn coexistence of "languages" within a given national language also comes to an end—that is, there is no more peaceful co-existence [sic] between territorial dialects, social and professional dialects and jargons, literary language, generic languages within literary language, epochs in language and so forth.

Not surprisingly, what Bakhtin describes is a multiethnic, multiracial world with porous borders, a global village. In a telling dialectic, this means that those writers whose histories and selves are polyglot, who seem to possess no one place to call home, who are placed in numerous ways at the margins of cultures, who live in various forms of exile, who have traveled difficult journeys to get here are central to the world and the moment we are living in. The margins have come to the center, and the center is at the borders; as a result, while many of the powerful live in culs-de-sac—that is, sealed off in dead ends—the dispossessed live right smack at the crossroads.

I often tell students to think about where the tale of a journey receives its power. If the journey is over familiar, long-traveled terrain; if no forces threaten or thwart the traveler; if everything, as on a guided tour, goes according to plan, there is no story. The journey bears telling only when we hear of the difficulties and obstacles the traveler had to overcome, the unusual and unexpected occurrences along the way, the encounters with the unknown. We want to hear about the journey only when we know that the teller has been transformed because of her journey.

But there is more than one way to take a journey. Once a stranger has entered our village, wherever our village may be, however small or large that village may be, we all must become strangers to ourselves and must consider and configure ourselves anew. We all must begin reinvestigating who we are and where we come from and what our relationship to that stranger might tell us, not just about that stranger but also about ourselves. We all must then travel to someplace new. Whether we want to or not, we all must envision the position of the stranger, entering a village we have never entered before.

At other times, *we* are the strangers walking into a new village, and in that entrance, we begin to see ourselves in a different light even as the villagers must see themselves differently because of our presence. So much of my own writing these days explores my experiences making such entrances, being the first stranger or one of the first strangers who has walked into a previously unknown village.

As old Bert Brecht might say, Yes, it is complicated. Marvelously complicated.

The Idealized Portrait and
the Task of the Writer

Every social unit—whether a family or a community, an organization or a nation, a religion or an ethnic group—constructs an idealized portrait of itself.

This portrait is created through the official histories and the accepted monuments and works of that group, through public proclamations and pleasant pictures of the past and the present. Those who help create this portrait are deeply invested both in the portrait and in the social approval it provides. The portrait gives the people in the group the accepted view of things and helps create a desire for this view.

What do writers do? They challenge the accepted; they break the rules; they create new pleasures, new knowledge, new discourse. In the process, they attack and dismantle repression; they take things out from under the table and from the closet, throw them in front of people, and say, "Here are the things left out of your idealized portrait, here is the reality you have failed to acknowledge. Here are the lies, the secrets, the crimes, the blemishes, the wounds, the aberrations, the blasphemies and idiosyncrasies, the complications you want to keep silenced, the erasures no one talks about."

Rather than accepting the received simplified portrait, the writer hungers for reality, for its contradictions and complexities. Often there cannot help but be political implications to this hunger.

On a large social level, this struggle over the portrait of reality often involves the struggles of a repressed group to assert itself. In my lifetime, I have seen these breaks and breakthroughs in terms of sexual roles and sexual orientation, in racial and ethnic identities, in the struggles of colonial and postcolonial cultures. In "Diving into the Wreck," Adrienne Rich speaks of "a book of myths / in which / our names do not appear." Rich implies that her task is to create new myths, cultural artifacts that will reflect her experiences as a woman and a lesbian, experiences that the society has historically silenced.

Similarly, James Baldwin has argued that black writers must create a new vocabulary, a new language to reveal their experience:

> You see whites want black writers to mostly deliver something as if it were the official version of the black experience. But the vocabulary won't hold it, simply. No true account really of black life can be held, can be contained in the American vocabulary. As it is, the only way that you can deal with it is by doing great violence to the assumptions on which the vocabulary is based. But they won't let you do that. And when you go along, you find yourself very quickly painted into a corner; you've written yourself into a corner.

Baldwin observes that a difference in language cuts deeper than many realize; our American vocabulary was in part created and designed to deny and repress black experience and reality, to suppress the self-articulation of black identity. To understand the implications of this is to look beyond the way mainstream American culture understands itself.

At times, as in the history of colonialism, this attempt at self-description and assertion takes place both within a society and in opposition to a force outside that society. For instance, Edward Said characterizes the writings of anti-imperialist resistance as a "search for authenticity, for a more congenial national origin than that provided by colonial history, for a new pantheon of heroes, myths, and religions." In order to accomplish this goal, however, writers from the colonies had to write against the grain of the work they had studied in colonial schools, the precepts and masterpieces of their colonial rulers. These anti- or postcolonial writers needed to claim and find a new language for their own realities, the culture and history of their colonized nation. In doing so, they also struggled with the colonist inside their own psyches. In the works of writers such as Aimé Césaire, Chinua Achebe, Ngugi wa Thiong'o, Ama Ata Aidoo, Derek Walcott, V. S. Naipaul, Michelle Cliff, and Jamaica Kincaid, one finds evidence of this process, a process still continuing in the present. These writers also contextualize and provide the precedent for later generations of writers like Chris Abani, Marlon James, Chimamanda Ngozi Adichie, Arhundati Roy, Edwidge Danticat, Teju Cole, and Viet Thanh Nguyen.

A quality found in writers that sometimes seems odd or aberrant to nonwriters is the willingness to say things that others would be threatened by or afraid of saying. Doing so sometimes requires the writer to possess a certain political courage, an ability to stand up to the powers that be.

But a writer's attack on idealized portraits doesn't take place only at a large societal level. It can also occur in a community or, more commonly, a family. As Czesław Miłosz sardonically commented: "When a writer is born into a family, the family is finished."

When a writer breeches the family rules, certainly fear is involved, though obviously not the same fear as when a writer strikes out against societal forces. Still the threat of reprisal, of being banished from the group for exposing secrets and revealing misdeeds is always present.

Loyalty is a hard nugget to give up, and some never quite manage to do so (perhaps they just weren't meant to be writers). But often what the writer must also confront is her own embarrassment and sense of shame. John Updike remarked that it isn't that writers don't possess a sense of shame; they aren't that unlike other people. It's just that writers don't let their sense of shame stop them from revealing what they know. For this reason, writers are often accused of being shameless.

Writing comes out of the rift between what we have experienced and know about the world and the language we've been given to express it. We write to bridge this divide, to find words adequate to our sense of reality. We also write to find the language for what we know unconsciously. Only by unearthing that language can we make such knowledge conscious. This leads me to the following definition: *Creative writing is the search for and creation of a language that will express what the writer unconsciously knows but does not yet have a language to express.*

In this process, writers may at times upset any number of people and groups; idealized portraits abound. And since writers may also be intimately connected with those people, groups, and portraits, their greatest struggle is often with personal fears, personal internal silencings. Their job is to hold fast to their sense of truth and, at the same time, to challenge not just others but also themselves.

This challenge then involves two fronts: Not only do we possess a desire for an idealized portrait of the groups to which we belong; we also possess an idealized portrait of ourselves. Ironically, it is often in investigating ourselves and challenges to our own self-image that we begin to move toward a deeper investigation of the world around us.

On a practical level, I've often been asked, as a writer of memoir, how did I reconcile the constrictions of my family against what I've revealed in my writing? Of course, what the questioner is really asking is "How can I myself deal with this question?" But my answer cannot be the questioner's answer. Each writer must wrestle with the question for herself.

That said, I tell people that when I first entered therapy in my twenties, my therapist asked if I thought therapy would hinder my writing. I told him that I assumed we were to be engaged in questions seeking the truth. If I avoided the truth, I'd be running away from my task as a writer.

As time passed, I began to suspect that I had a higher tolerance than most people for revealing things about me or my life that might seem embarrassing or reflect negatively on me. At the same time, I decided that I was not only writing for myself but for certain readers, particularly other Asian Americans, who saw the same things I did and wanted reassurance that they were not crazy.

As for my family, I could not write according to their wishes and silences. I could only write from my own sense of reality. How they reacted to my writings was their choice. As it turns out, my parents did disagree with things in my memoirs, but both acknowledged that it was my story and I could write it the way I wanted.

Miłosz's observation quoted earlier implies that sometimes a writer must choose between the task of a writer and her family. He also implies that making this choice is part of the job.

I tell students who are reluctant to explore family secrets and problems that if their family history has emerged in their writing, it is something they should not ignore. In such cases, the writer's own psyche is calling him to move in this direction; thus his writing has led him to the point of crossing certain family taboos, challenging the family's idealized portrait, or violating community taboos or idealized portraits. If a person doesn't follow where the writing is leading, he will have a difficult time progressing as a writer.

Because of its creative nature, the writing process should ultimately follow the dictates of the writer's unconscious and not her conscious wishes. Inevitably, the unconscious leads us to those knots in our psyches that we need to untie, those areas we need to explore. Failure to do so will keep an aspiring writer from developing not only as a writer but as a person.

Therefore, I tell my students, push yourself, write what you need to write. But you can also tell yourself that you don't have to publish what you write. You can keep it in a drawer and publish it later. Or even not at all. But at least then you will have allowed your writing to take you where you need to go and will be able to move on.

In my own way, I did something similar when I wrote my memoirs. I told myself that in the end I didn't have to publish them. Or I could decide not to publish certain portions. Perhaps part of me knew this probably wasn't going to happen, but it allowed me to go forward with the project; it allowed me to complete the books.

My final word on this fear of family reprisal is related to how we view those reprisals. Seen in a certain light, the challenges I faced as a memoirist in regard to my family were relatively minor. If I compared them to those faced by writers who work under repressive regimes where their writing may land them in jail or even lead to torture or death, I had relatively little to fear. Indeed, I should be thankful that my dilemmas as a writer were so unthreatening.

My writing did lead to other difficulties, particularly in my relationships with white friends and colleagues because of the racial issues in my work. And that has even affected other aspects of my life, such as possibilities of employment or publication in some places. But again, such consequences seem minor when compared to the difficulties many writers face daily around the globe.

In the end, I find the process of writing fascinating, and I am probably most energized when my writing leads into places where difficulties abound and I feel threatened in some way. Sometimes this threat seems to come from without, from how I know I'm supposed to regard the world outside me. Sometimes the threat comes from within, from how I wish to regard myself. Sometimes it comes from the possibility of upsetting the various communities I belong to. But it is the presence of that threat that I look for. It helps me know that I am on the right track, that I am engaged with the exigencies of my profession.

Writing and Reading Race

JONATHAN FRANZEN, JHUMPA LAHIRI,
AND SHAWN WONG

I. Louis C.K., Thandeka, and
the Question of Whiteness

In one of his routines, amid his usual kvetching, Louis C.K. stops and apologizes for being such a bummer. Admitting he's a "lucky guy," he explains:

> I'm healthy, I'm relatively young. I'm white.
> I mean thank god for that shit, boy.
> That's a huge leg up. Are you kidding me?
> O my god, I love being white, I really do.
> Seriously, if you're not white, you're missing out.
> Because this shit is thoroughly good.
> Let me be clear, by the way:
> I'm not saying that white people are better.
> I'm saying that being white is better.
> Who can even argue?

For those who find this routine funny, the humor, as with most humor, arises from stating a truth that many people—in this case, white people—would rather not say out loud.

But even aside from whatever benefits they accrue from their whiteness, most white people would prefer not to refer to themselves as white. The reasons for this preference are multiple and often in part unconscious. Many whites consciously believe that any reference to race is itself racist, so the practice of avoiding identifying themselves or others as white is supposedly race neutral.

But the deeper reason that whites avoid racial identification involves the point of Louis C.K.'s routine: whites enjoy certain privileges for being white. To identify themselves as white hauls up the question of such privileges, and that is something most whites would rather avoid.

In *Learning to Be White: Money, Race, and God in America*, theologian and college professor Thandeka starts by giving accounts by white people of key moments in their childhood or youth when they learned they were "white" and what being white meant. A white man speaks of telling a black student that the student is being expelled from his fraternity in a clear move of racial exclusion, a move the white man disapproved of but still went along with. A white woman describes a childhood experience when she invited a black friend to her birthday party and was then chastised by her mother for doing so. Most of these accounts cover similar incidents; none of them are particularly unusual.

Indeed, though the white persons telling these stories to Thandeka were sometimes surprised by the import or pain of such a moment, I myself have heard similar accounts. They mirror those of the white students in my "Writing on Race" workshop in the Stonecoast MFA program, when I ask them to write about when they first discovered their racial identity. In almost all their tellings, there is surprise—"oh, I am white"—accompanied by pain and/or feelings of shame; often something they've repressed surfaces as they do the exercise. When my students of color do this exercise, they are generally less surprised by what they write about. They've lived their lives knowing consciously that they have a racial identity, and they know that identity affects the ways they interact with the world and how they are perceived.

In *Learning to Be White*, what did surprise me is the reaction of whites to an experiment Thandeka devised called the Race Game. The game originated from Thandeka's experience at a college where she was teaching. A white staff member asked Thandeka what it was like to be black and work at their institution. Thandeka replied that if her luncheon partner played the Race Game for one week, Thandeka would then answer the colleague's question. The game consisted of one rule: For one week the woman was to "use the ascriptive term *white*" whenever she mentioned "the name of one of her Euro-American cohorts. She must say, for instance, 'my white husband, Phil,' or 'my white friend Julie,' or 'my lovely white child Jackie.'"

The white woman never had lunch with Thandeka again. Over and over, when Thandeka presented the idea of the Race Game, white colleagues refused to engage in it. One colleague wrote her that in the future she hoped to have the courage to do so. In her gloss on these refusals, Thandeka writes: "African Americans have learned to use a racial language to describe themselves and others. Euro-Americans also have learned a pervasive racial language. But in their racial lexicon, their own racial group becomes the great unsaid."

Whether liberal or conservative, many whites believe the way to achieve racial harmony is simply to never speak about or call attention to race. This ostensible silence is practiced in regard to people of color, but it is even more strictly enforced when whites refer to themselves. Basically, the ideology can be summed up as follows: *Don't speak about race, and race will not exist. Moreover, talk about race inevitably leads to conflict or is evidence of racism. Therefore, the solution is not to talk about race. If we don't talk about race, then racism must not exist.*

This prescriptive silence is often echoed in creative writing workshops. Recently, a writer of color informed me that a white poet had said to her in class, "To tell you the truth I'm just not interested in poems about identity. Isn't the goal to be beyond race?"

For most people of color, this solution—just don't talk about race—simply doesn't work; it would render us incapable of accessing and describing both our experiences and our identity. We know racism exists as the practice of individuals and in the social systems in our society. We know we cannot fully describe the experiences of our lives without reference to race, without employing the lens of race.

This same divide also occurs in the world of literature. Most white writers can observe the rules of silence on racial discourse and still tell their stories *as they understand them*. In doing so, they think and write about their experiences with a set of lenses, a set of tools and categories of thought, that are very different from those employed by writers of color. And yet like most whites in this country, they do not think about how and why they think about race in the ways that they do. Their epistemology of race is not a subject many of them consider.

In this essay, I want to examine how race is built into the very structures through which white writers and writers of color tell their stories and describe the realities of their characters. I begin with a literary rule that white writers seldom consciously consider: if the character is white, the race of that character does not need to be mentioned or indicated in any direct way.

The absence of a racial marker means that the character is by default white. The exception to the rule is always the character of color. In considering this convention, what many often overlook is that whiteness here is instituted not only as the norm; its very existence must also be kept invisible, unremarked upon. In other words, this literary practice presupposes that white characters need not be identified racially. Race for them is *not* a significant part of their identity or social reality. Nor is it an important consideration in who they are and what they have experienced in life.

But what if we step back from this practice and see it not as natural or instinctive—that is, as it is practiced by most white writers? What if we regard this practice as socially constructed, that is, as part of the racial construction of whiteness? For this practice certainly embodies and reflects a central way that whiteness has been defined—or rather not defined—by our society.

At the same time, the practice also presupposes that characters of color must be identified racially, that race is a crucial part of their identity or social reality. This is the way race is defined for people of color.

Two different practices based on racial identity: separate and unequal.

This difference is related, of course, to Toni Morrison's declaration in *Playing in the Dark* that up until recently, white writers did not even consider the possibility of a reader of color. The absence of a consideration of such a reader was simply an unconscious assumption.

However, if one consciously considers these practices, certain questions arise: Who benefits from these different practices in regard to naming the race of a person or character? What is missing from the white definition of race that is included in the definition of race for people of color?

Does the contradiction between these two definitions of racial identity—white and people of color—make sense? That is, do whites lack a racial identity while only people of color possess one? Obviously, this notion is absurd. Is it people of color who gave themselves their racial identity? No, historically white people have done this. Is the identity and experience of people of color based solely on the practices of people of color? Again, the answer is no.

Examining the fallacies invoked here leads to several revealing questions concerning race and literature. The first is, *If the very way white writers introduce their characters and the very way writers of color introduce their characters are racialized, how is it that any piece of American fiction, whether written by a white person or a person of color, escapes being racialized?*

What would our literature look like if this rule were not the norm? How difficult is it for whites to identify themselves as white? And what exactly is the cause of this difficulty? When writers of color acknowledge their racial reality, what does this allow them to accomplish in their writing? Does the fact that most white writers don't do so indicate that these writers are simplifying or leaving out parts of their reality? How are these two different literary practices related to what we deem craft and artistic excellence?

All these are questions few white writers even acknowledge, much less attempt to wrestle with.

II. Jonathan Franzen and *Freedom*

I'll start then with a basic premise: It's instructive to explore the difference between the ways a white writer introduces a white character and the ways writers of color introduce their characters of color. Such an examination reveals far more about the relationship between literature and race than many realize.

As an example of white literary practice, here is the opening of Jonathan Franzen's *Freedom*:

> The news about Walter Berglund wasn't picked up locally—he and Patty had moved away to Washington two years earlier and meant nothing to St. Paul now—but the urban gentry of Ramsey Hill were not so loyal to their city as not to read the *New York Times*. According to a long and very unflattering story in the *Times*, Walter had made quite a mess of his professional life out there in the nation's capital. His old neighbors had some difficulty reconciling the quotes about him in the *Times* ("arrogant," "high-handed," "ethically compromised") with the generous, smiling red-faced 3M employee they remembered pedaling his commuter bicycle up Summit Avenue in February snow; it seemed strange that Walter, who was greener than Greenpeace and whose own roots were rural, should be in trouble now for conniving with the coal industry and mistreating country people. Then again, there had always been something not quite right about the Berglunds.
>
> Walter and Patty were the young pioneers of Ramsey Hill—the first college grads to buy a house on Barrier Street since the old heart of St. Paul had fallen on hard times three decades earlier. They paid nothing for their Victorian and then killed themselves for ten years renovating it. Early on, some very determined person torched their garage and twice broke into their car before they got the garage rebuilt. Sunburned bikers descended on the vacant lot across the alley to drink Schlitz and grill knockwurst and rev engines at small hours until Patty went outside in sweatclothes and said, "Hey, you guys, you know what?" Patty frightened nobody, but she'd been a standout athlete in high school and college and possessed a jock sort of fearlessness. From her very first day in the neighborhood, she was helplessly conspicuous. Tall, ponytailed, absurdly young, pushing a smaller stroller

past stripped cars and broken beer bottles and barfed-upon old snow, she might have been carrying all the hours of her day in the string bags that hung from her stroller. Behind her you could see the baby-encumbered preparations for a morning of baby-encumbered errands, ahead of her, an afternoon of public radio, the *Silver Palate Cookbook*, cloth diapers, drywall compound, and latex paint; and then *Goodnight Moon*, then zinfandel. She was already fully the thing that was just starting to happen to the rest of the street.

Walter and Patty aren't specifically designated as white, but, in absence of any markers indicating otherwise, that is the reader's assumption, and Franzen knows this. (Their last name, Berglund, reads as European American, but I know Korean adoptees with Germanic and Scandinavian last names.)

In his social portrait of the Berglunds, Franzen's task seems to be to differentiate the Berglunds from the other whites—also never racially designated—in their St. Paul neighborhood and to indicate the Berglunds' socioeconomic class. The Berglunds are not like the "urban gentry of Ramsey Hill," who read the *New York Times*, nor are they like the sunburned bikers across the alley. The Berglunds are "greener than Greenpeace," listeners of public radio, users of *The Silver Palate Cookbook*, and new yuppie parents; in terms of St. Paul's geography, they are the first college grads who have moved into their neighborhood, the first pioneers in a gentrification process. Franzen's portrait carries a good dose of social satire, which continues into the third paragraph:

In the earliest years, when you could still drive a Volvo 240 without feeling self-conscious, the collective task in Ramsey Hill was to relearn certain life skills that your own parents had fled to the suburbs specifically to unlearn, like how to interest the local cops in actually doing their job, and how to protect a bike from a highly motivated thief, and when to bother rousting a drunk from your lawn furniture, and how to encourage feral cats to shit in somebody else's children's sandbox, and how to determine whether a public school sucked too much to bother trying to fix it. There were also more contemporary questions, like, what about those cloth diapers? Worth the bother? And was it true that you could still get milk delivered in glass bottles? Were the Boy Scouts OK politically? Was bulgur really necessary? Where to recycle batteries? How to respond when a poor person of color accused you of destroying her neighborhood? Was it true that the glaze of old Fiestaware contained dangerous amounts of lead? How elaborate did a kitchen water filter actually need to be?

These questions continue for several more sentences. Part of Franzen's skill in listing such questions is to pin down with great accuracy a specific urban social class: white yuppie gentrifiers. At the same time, his version of realism also marks a limit: race is mentioned but only in passing, and of course, it is the person of color—who must be designated as such—who brings this intrusion. Thus there's one question about the effect of gentrification on the blacks who have lived in the neighborhood previously. The issues raised in this confrontation occupy the same importance in the Berglunds' consciousness as "What about those cloth diapers?" and "Was bulgur really necessary?" This implied equivalence in part satirizes the Berglunds. But at the same time, it marks a limit to how far the issues of race and whiteness will intrude on Franzen's portrait of their world—that is, race will be absent here. The Berglunds are more concerned about other matters, and Franzen, one could argue, is simply reflecting their vision of the world.

If I were to say that the Berglunds and their creator share a "white" vision of the world, what does that mean? And what does that have to say about the set of assumptions concerning race that undergird the "realist" aesthetic of Franzen's novel?

For one thing, the depicted reality of the Berglunds and thus the realism of Franzen depend in part on circumscribing and silencing the presence of race in the lives of the Berglunds. Franzen is giving us his version of reality; that is his right. But that doesn't mean I as a reader must be unconscious of what his version of reality leaves out. As David Palumbo Lieu has argued, the concept and practice of realism rely both on agreements and challenges and are far more open to the latter than many realize.* Often white writers—especially if they do not consider readers of color—assume that there is no disagreement about the nature of social reality. Most writers of color assume that there is disagreement, and race is an essential battleground within this disagreement. Unlike Morrison's traditional white author who did not envision a reader of color, writers of color are also aware their work will be interpreted and evaluated by white readers as well as readers of color.

* Liu explains in *The Deliverance of Others: Reading Literature in a Global Age* (Durham, N.C.: Duke University Press): "Analysis of literary realism allows us to diagnose the reputed commonality of behavior, how different people might act in concert with others, but also, this literature, *as literature*, contains a critical, self-reflective element. If literature has been charged with delivering the lives of others to us for our enrichment and betterment, how, if at all, does this new otherness change our assumptions about what is realistic, about what is common to all human beings in their behaviors, choices, actions, judgments?"

From this opening, Franzen's *Freedom* moves on to focus on an adulterous triangle and an affair between Patty Berglund and her husband Walter's best friend, Richard, a rock-and-roll musician. Later in the novel, Walter becomes involved in ecological issues that engender clashes with the Berglunds' son Joey. The social portrait that begins the novel and the shifting economics of the Berglunds' neighborhood are never really revisited in any detail nor are the changing demographics of that area of the city, which has included the influx of Southeast Asian immigrants as well as white gentrifiers into a historically black neighborhood.

Rather than focusing on the neighborhood, Franzen's novel is more about the breakdown of one family, and this is a perfectly fine subject for a novel. I merely want to point out that in this novel, Franzen eschews the lens of race to examine the lives of the Berglunds. They're middle-class white people. Why should race matter to them at all?

In an interview for *Slate*, Isaac Chotiner asked Franzen, "Have you ever considered writing a book about race?" Here's his answer:

> I have thought about it, but—this is an embarrassing confession—I don't have very many black friends. I have never been in love with a black woman. I feel like if I had, I might dare. . . . Didn't marry into a black family. I write about characters, and I have to love the character to write about the character. If you have not had direct firsthand experience of loving a category of person—a person of a different race, a profoundly religious person, things that are real stark differences between people—I think it is very hard to dare, or necessarily even want, to write fully from the inside of a person.

To his credit, Franzen speaks more candidly than many white writers might. Reading Franzen's remarks, I recall Major Jackson's article several years ago in the *American Poetry Review*, where Jackson asked why white poets didn't write more about race. One reason Jackson listed was that most white poets don't have many black friends.

Later in the interview, talking about his novel *Purity*, Franzen observed that having lived in Germany for two and a half years and knowing the literature was not enough to be able to write about German people. It was the fact that he started making German friends that established an entry: "The portal to being able to write about it was suddenly having these friends I really loved. And then I wasn't the hostile outsider; I was the loving insider."

To me, a logical question is why doesn't Franzen have "many black friends"? Why is it more possible for him to have several friends he loves who are German but few who are black Americans? After all, Franzen is an American and not a German. Are the barriers of race greater for him than those of culture and nationality? Franzen doesn't ask or reveal if he has unconsciously or consciously decided not to seek out friendships with black Americans. Nor does he wonder if his lack of friendships with black Americans has something to do with the way he approaches both his own identity and theirs; this reflection would involve asking whether black Americans who meet Franzen feel that he is a white man with whom they could have an authentic relationship, one where they as black Americans could feel they could be themselves and trust the other person to accept and value who they are.

Tellingly, in the interview, Franzen doesn't seem to realize that he actually has written about race. In *Freedom*, Walter Berglund, the white husband, eventually has an interracial affair with a twenty-five-year-old Indian American, Lalitha.

Does this relationship and character break or not break the personal rule Franzen seems to set up in the interview? I may be wrong, but I seriously doubt that he has a trove of South Asian friends. He may have had a love affair with an Indian American woman, though based on the evidence of this novel, I doubt it.

Whatever Franzen's personal relations, his portrait of this affair between an older white male and a younger Asian American female is problematic at best and certainly bears more scrutiny than most critics have given it. The Indian American woman, Lalitha, is portrayed as adoring Walter. She praises his "vision" for a problematic project that purports to be environmentally minded but is devised in partnership with a coal company; she tells Walter that he's clearly superior to his college friend, a famous rock-and-roll musician who is Walter's rival and who has slept with Walter's wife. After an encounter with his rival, Richard, Lalitha tells Water, "All I could see when we were talking was how much he admires you."

As a reader familiar with Edward Said's *Orientalism* and other postcolonial critical works, I can't help but be troubled by the ways such a relationship echoes various Orientalist tropes, tropes Franzen doesn't seem wary of or even aware of—the powerful, superior, and masculine West and the less powerful, inferior, feminine East. Instead, the novel takes this adoration and this affair on face value, or rather, in the way the older white male, Walter, regards it.

To be fair, the novel remains outside the subjectivity of the young Indian

American woman. Part of this stems from the fact that it is narrated from the viewpoint of Walter and his family and not from Lalitha's. Still, within a limited omniscient narrative, the novelist can make clear the limitations or blind spots of the protagonist's consciousness. But I cannot find any signals or hints that any racial reading or critique is at play in the novel.

Now it is true that Asian Americans in general, and Indian Americans in particular, are positioned differently racially than black Americans. These differences are myriad and far too complex to go into in this essay. But on a larger level, I would maintain that a young Indian American who enters a relationship with an older white American male must, at some level, consciously or unconsciously, process their racial differences in experience and identity. Moreover, these differences are at play whether or not the young Indian American woman is aware of how they have affected and shaped her sexual desires. This would seem especially true given that Lalitha gets involved with Walter right after ending her relationship with an Indian American, Jairam, who, according to Walter, "was thick-bodied and somewhat ugly but arrogant and driven, a heart surgeon in training." Note that "ugly" here is Walter's assessment, and yet the question of racialized standards of appearance never arises.

Clearly, in her idolization of Walter, Lalitha sees him as a figure of power, and this power cannot be separated from his position as a white male or in terms of how she views both Indian American men and other men of color. One would reasonably suspect that this affair may stem in part from her relationship with her family, but the issue of how her family views Jairam or Walter never comes up in the novel. As I've said, nothing in this novel critiques her relationship with Walter and its absence of racial investigation; there is no one else in Walter's world who might bring an alternative racial reading to this relationship, much less anyone who would question here the tropes of Orientalism—adoring younger Asian female, powerful older white male.

But even beyond the problematic relationship, Franzen's portrait of Lalitha lacks a specificity that can only be constructed with a lens that takes into account ethnicity and race. For instance, Lalitha apparently speaks with a "lilt" of an accent, but we are never told at exactly what age she came to America. That fact would indicate something of how she might process her identity and would affect also her knowledge and relationship to American society and culture. To arrive as an immigrant at seven or twelve or sixteen are entirely different experiences, but my suspicion is that Franzen hasn't considered such differences.

———

After Walter throws his wife, Patty, out of the house, almost immediately he and Lalitha make love for the first time. The description does nothing to dispel suspicions that the Orientalism here is not only Walter's but also the author's:

> He needed the quick fix simply in order to keep functioning—to not get leveled by hatred and self-pity—and, in one way, the fix was very sweet indeed, because Lalitha really was crazy for him, almost literally dripping with desire, certainly strongly seeping with it. She stared into his eyes with love and joy, she pronounced beautifully and perfect and wonderful the manhood that Patty in her document had libeled and spat upon. What wasn't to like? He was a man in his prime, she was adorable, and young and insatiable; and this, in fact, was what wasn't to like.

Note here how, in Walter's mind, the differences between him and Lalitha are their positions in power—she is his assistant—and age. Race is not worth remarking on. But then this follows:

> His emotions couldn't keep up with the vigor and urgency of their animal attraction, the interminability of their coupling. She needed to ride him, she needed to be crushed underneath him, she needed to have her legs on his shoulders, she needed to do the Downward Dog and be whammed from behind, she needed bending over the bed, she needed her face pressed against the wall, she needed her legs wrapped around him and her head thrown back and her very round breasts flying every which way. It all seemed intensely meaningful to her, she was a bottomless well of anguished noise, and he was up for all of it. In good cardiovascular shape, thrilled by her extravagance, attuned to her wishes, and extremely fond of her. And yet it wasn't quite personal, and he couldn't find his way to orgasm. And this was very odd, an entirely new and unanticipated problem, due in part, perhaps, to his unfamiliarity with condoms, and to how unbelievably wet she was.

As Toni Morrison demonstrates in *Playing in the Dark: Whiteness and the Literary Imagination*, the unconscious racial assumptions of white authors can reveal themselves in myriad ways. One is terrible prose. The prose is so bad here—"almost literally dripping with desire," "bottomless well of anguished noise," "In good cardiovascular shape"—I at first wondered if the passage were simply satirizing Walter, but Franzen's brand of satire is not Tom Wolfe's. Beyond the poor prose, there is an undergirding to this passage that's clearly racialized. If this were a student of mine, and not one of the most celebrated novelists of his generation, I couldn't imagine getting through a workshop without flagging this passage (though I can imagine that in certain white instructors' workshops, a student of color who flagged this passage would be called out for "political correctness").

In Walter's mind, Lalitha "needed to be crushed underneath him." Now this might be contextualized simply as a patriarchal attitude, but then what does one do with the awful "Downward Dog" reference? On one level, Walter is aware that Lalitha is of a different race and culture; indeed, a drunk white man in a restaurant has previously made crude racist remarks about the pair, using the N-word. But any deep contemplation of race never really enters Walter's consciousness. And yet what would the reader think if Lalitha were black and Walter believed she "needed to be crushed underneath him"? Racial alarm bells would go off everywhere. One surmises that Franzen hasn't imagined an Asian American reader or even simply a reader of postcolonial studies for whom *Freedom*'s interracial relationship would set off similar alarms.

Perhaps in part because Lalitha is an Indian American, Franzen can enter this territory without getting flagged—flagged for his lack of knowledge of the psychology, culture, and history of Indian Americans; flagged for his one-dimensional characterization of Lalitha and her desire; flagged for never questioning the racist assumptions that underlie the Orientalism not just in this passage but in the whole relationship and in Walter's own perceptions of Lalitha. In *Playing in the Dark*, Toni Morrison faults Willa Cather's *Sapphira and the Slave Girl* for absenting race from an examination of Cather's white female protagonist's struggle with power and sexuality. Similarly, the buried and unexplored aspect of Walter's identity here involves his being not just a middle-class, middle-aged man but a middle-class, middle-aged *white* man.

I focus on Franzen's weaknesses here and his blinders about race not because they are particularly egregious but because they are, I would assert, representative and common. Now I can understand a young white fiction writer thinking, "Well, if one of the most celebrated white novelists of his generation can't enter this territory without floundering, why would I choose to enter here?" Indeed, I've had young white writers express to me similar doubts.

Let me make clear that, contrary to what Lionel Shriver might maintain, I am not saying authors can't cross racial boundaries and write about characters not of their own race. But one can do this in a way that falsifies, simplifies, and fails to portray the complexities of a character of another race—or one can do this in a way that does justice to the reality of that character, that acknowledges the character's complexity and the full nature of his or her reality and experience. But to do so requires a greater range of racial experience and a greater knowledge of the literature, culture, and history of the racial other than most white writers possess (as Franzen himself implicitly acknowledges in his *Slate* interview).

Moreover, I maintain that as long as white writers unconsciously assume whiteness and the whiteness of their characters as the universal default, both as a literary technique and as an approach to the world, they will almost always fail when they attempt to portray people of color, whether in fiction or in nonfiction. Such a foundation to the racial thinking of white writers can render them incapable of understanding the reality of people of another race. In the rest of this essay and the following essay, I will discuss why I make this assertion.

For now, if you are a white writer writing about a character of color, here is one consideration: Do you have friends or colleagues of that race who would openly and freely tell you if you are failing in that task and how and why, and would you be willing to seriously consider their critiques? If not, then perhaps you should not go there. But if you've actually done the necessary work—both personally in your life and on a literary and intellectual level—and you are willing to keep going even if you fail in your first attempts, then, yes, go there, go there knowing that this is a worthwhile struggle.

III. Jhumpa Lahiri's "Only Goodness" and Shawn Wong's *American Knees*

To understand the deficiencies in Franzen's perspective on Walter and Lalitha's relationship, I want to examine two Asian American writers.

For some writers of color, their character's ethnic identity, rather than her or his racial identity, takes precedence. An example can be found in the opening of Jhumpa Lahiri's short story "Only Goodness" (from her book of short stories *Unaccustomed Earth*):

> It was Sudha who'd introduced Rahul to alcohol, one weekend he came to visit her at Penn—to his first drink from a keg and then, the next morning in the dining hall, his first cup of coffee. He'd pronounced both beverages revolting, preferring Schnapps to the beer and emptying a dozen packets of sugar in his coffee cup. That had been his junior year of high school. When she was home the following summer he asked her to buy him some six packs, planning to have a party one weekend when their parents were going to be in Connecticut overnight. He'd shot up to six feet, braces off his teeth,

whiskers sprouting around his mouth, dark pimples occasionally studding his cheekbones, her little brother in name only. She went to a local liquor store, helping Rahul divvy up the cans between his room and hers so that their parents wouldn't discover them.

After her parents were asleep she brought some cans into Rahul's room. He snuck downstairs, bringing back a cup of ice cubes to chill down the warm Budweiser. They shared one cupful, then another, listening to the Stones and the Doors on Rahul's record player, smoking cigarettes next to the open window and exhaling through the screen. It was as if Sudha were in high school again, doing things she once hadn't had the wits or guts for. She felt a new bond with her brother, a sense, after years of regarding him as just a kid, that they were finally friends.

Sudha had waited until college to disobey her parents. . . . They were prudish about alcohol to the point of seeming Puritanical, frowning upon the members of their Bengali circle—the men, that was to say—who liked to sip whiskey at gatherings.

From this passage, the reader intuits that Sudha and her brother are first-generation, middle-class Indian Americans; ethnically they are Bengali, and their parents observe either religious—Bengalis are more likely to be Muslim—or cultural strictures against alcohol. Lahiri seemingly cannot presume that without any ethnic markers, the reader will know that her characters are Bengali Americans from an immigrant family. She must "tell" this rather than "show," although she skillfully hides this "tell" by slipping it in when focusing on the issue of the use of alcohol, which is the anchoring theme of the story.

At the same time, Lahiri must create a portrait of these siblings and their family using various indicators, some that might be used by any American author and some particular to her specific ethnic American characters. The family's middle-class status is indicated by Rahul's braces and his going to Penn. The siblings were either born in America or came to America at a young enough age to have grown up with American drinking habits and musical tastes.

While ethnicity is present from the story's start through the names of the characters, race is not a major focus in this passage or in the story as a whole. Instead the story focuses on the sister's contribution to Rahul's eventual drinking problems, which take place within a middle-class Indian/Bengali immigrant family. The questions explored involve the family's dynamics and the way the two siblings react to their upbringing and their parents' Bengali American–centered social life.

Eventually Rahul leaves the middle-class, college-educated track his parents have laid out for him. He ends up marrying a white working-class woman and living in her town. Tellingly, his experiences with this woman and the white working-class world are beyond the parameters of the story, which is told from his sister Sudha's viewpoint. Sudha moves to London and marries a white British art magazine editor, and the story's ending centers on a visit from Rahul when his drinking issues reappear.

Lahiri does a superb job of depicting Sudha's guilt over helping to start Rahul's drinking and her reluctant realization concerning how far Rahul's alcoholism has progressed. On the surface, the story seems less about the cultural displacements of immigrant life or the tensions between the Indian parents and their American-born children than about the complicated relationship between the two siblings and how far Rahul has strayed from his parents and his sister. Though she marries a white Brit, by obtaining her degree and getting a professional job, Sudha has seemingly fulfilled her pact with her parents. If she hasn't remained within their Bengali social circle, she's observed their general economic and educational dictates. The outlier, the one who has left the family orbit, is Rahul, and this is because of his drinking problems, his lack of a middle-class job, and his marriage to a working-class white woman.

What the reader may not see, though, is that the story itself (and Lahiri's general aesthetic practices), as it is constructed, cannot contain what happens to Rahul once he has left the orbit of the family, once he has left the middle-class milieu that the family and Sudha live and work within—that is, once he enters white working-class America. For there, in his entry into the white working-class world of his wife, Rahul has surely encountered and experienced not just how he is viewed culturally by white America but also how he is viewed racially, which brings up a whole different set of realities and lenses.

Let me be clear here: Lahiri is absolutely free to present whatever part of the reality of her characters that she chooses. If she chooses not to follow Rahul out into America, it might partly be because the story is told from the sister's point of view. But it is permissible I think to note the parameters of the story, the ways it designates what elements of the siblings' world will be included and what will not. In terms of ethnicity and culture, the siblings' experience as immigrant children, as children of Bengali parents, is included. The siblings' experience of being racially categorized in America—or in England—is not.

For a more racial reading of the Asian American experience, let's look at the opening of Shawn Wong's novel *American Knees*:

Being the only two Asians at a party, they tried to avoid each other but failed. They touched accidentally several times. They watched each other furtively from across the room.

Aurora Crane had arrived first. They were her friends, her office mates, and it was their party. Raymond Ding was only a guest of her boss, who was the host of the office party. A visitor from out of town invited at the last minute. A friend of a friend in the city for only three days to do some business. When he arrived at the front door, she knew before he did that they were the only two Asians at a party. With dread she knew her boss would make a special point of introducing him to her and that one by one her friends, the loyal, would betray her and pair her with him. They would probably be introduced several times during the evening. It made sense to them. There was no real covert activity, no setup, no surprise blind date, no surprise dinner companion seated not so coincidentally next to her. She was not at home with mother meeting not so coincidentally her mother's idea of a "nice Japanese boy." She had a boyfriend (unfortunately in another city and not Asian and a lover none of the loyal had met and to add to the further misfortune, some knew she had moved away from him to define a future without him making it very complex in her mind, but simple in the minds of the now distrustfully loyal).

Prior to the impending introductions, she wondered when they would make eye contact, when he would realize they were the only two Asians at the party. She hoped to God he wasn't an insecure Asian male who would only talk to her. She hoped to God he wouldn't see her as every Asian boy's answer to the perfect woman—half-white, half Asian, just enough to bring home to Mother while maintaining the white girl fantasy. This gets somewhat complex, certainly more complex than *Love Is a Many-Splendored Thing*. Aurora Crane is a Eurasian Jennifer Jones. Is the Asian boy William Holden? He'd like to think so.

Aurora Crane and Raymond Ding are middle class—they meet at an office party—Asian Americans. Their being racially categorized as Asians is there from the start. As an Asian American, Aurora is aware of the ways her white coworkers will react to discovering that she and Raymond are the only two Asians at the party: her coworkers will try to pair up the two Asians. Clearly Aurora bridles at the assumption and impertinence of this "like with like" pairing. Why would her white coworkers assume that she and the Asian male at the party would have anything in common other than their race? At the same time, for Aurora, such a potential coaxing is not nearly as irritating as her mother's efforts to pair her with "a nice Japanese boy."

Even as Aurora balks at the racial expectations of her white coworkers, she has her own expectations and even stereotypes concerning Raymond. Raymond might be one of those "insecure" Asian males; he might have a thing for Eurasians. With the latter delineation of racial desire, Wong must have Aurora explain what causes this desire, how it is rooted in both family concerns and the racial hierarchy of desire—"the white girl fantasy." (This explanation is for the reader who is not Asian American.)

An instability is present here that is not found in Lahiri's story. There the demarcation between the cultural assumptions of both Sudha and her family and those of the rest of American society is quite clear and at least for Sudha, though not perhaps for Rudha, firm. But for the two main characters in Wong's novel, the lines between their ethnic and racial identity, on the one hand, and the mainstream white society around them, on the other, are neither firmly nor clearly etched. Aurora's mother may be Japanese (and probably not Japanese American), but Aurora's father is white. Thus she is racially and ethnically mixed. Moreover, it's clear that she sees herself less bound by her Japanese mother's expectations and thus by Japanese cultural expectations (though she may be reacting against those expectations as a form of rebellion or declaration of her own independence). Her consciousness and her sense of identity are not placed at a far remove from her white coworkers; she is, supposedly, an American just like them. But then Raymond shows up, his presence highlighting her difference, marking her identity as an Asian American. This is not quite the same position as when one feels oneself inalterably Othered, either ethnically or racially (as say a Somali or black American might experience).

As the novel progresses, it turns out that Raymond is not an insecure Asian male, nor does he look at Aurora as the Eurasian sexual ideal. His consciousness of himself as an Asian American actually resembles hers—both inside the white world and not quite part of it—and this is one of the reasons that the two end up together; it is also one of the reasons that their relationship is fraught with complications. Both their own individual sense of identity and their position within mainstream white society are never quite stable, never quite distinctly defined in their own minds or in the eyes of those around them.

On a broader level, it's clear that Wong's vision of his characters involves not just their ethnicity—that is, the bicultural nature of Asian American identity—but also their racial category and how the characters themselves and those around them process that racial identity. For Aurora, the gaze of whiteness plays a significant role, both in terms of how whites see her—external—and how their gaze affects the way she sees herself and other Asians—internal. At the same time, what is going on in her consciousness concerning her racial identity is something that is not transparent or even evident to her white coworkers.

To a great extent, Wong must assume the same lack of knowledge in his white readers. His task is to negotiate meaning through the Asian American consciousness of Aurora and still make her consciousness clear and available to the white reader. Unlike Franzen, he writes with an awareness of his racial Other not just in terms of his characters but also in terms of the racial Other as a reader.

IV. White Characters and Characters of Color

In this essay, I've tried to provide readings of three texts through the lenses of ethnicity and race. I hope that they will enable the reader to better acknowledge the complexity of the ways writers of color use the lenses of race and ethnicity in their fiction. Indeed, in writing this essay, I myself have been surprised at the intricacies and layers of racial readings involved in just the opening of these two works by writers of color (and in the two works discussed in the following essay).

From these readings, several generalizations or conclusions can be made here. As exhibited in their use of the literary convention that allows them to not identify their white characters racially, most white writers work from certain basic assumptions about race and literature:

> The default identity of a character—that is, the identity unless otherwise indicated—is white.

> White authors thus do not have to label their white characters by race.

> In following this convention, white writers generally assent to the assumption that race is not a significant lens through which to view their characters.

> The text need not acknowledge how people of color might view the white characters or how a reader of color might view the white characters.

> Thus the gaze and judgment of the racial other will not be present or accounted for in the text.

> Overall, then, the literary judgment of a work by a white writer does not need to take into account the lens of race.

What is missing from the text because the lens of race is not employed can have no effect on our literary evaluation of that text.

For writers of color, a different set of assumptions are at work:

The writer of color must identify her characters in terms of ethnicity and/or race if the characters are not white.

In exploring the character's ethnicity or race, the writer of color must make a decision concerning the ways a white reader, a reader of the writer's own group, and other readers of color will read the text.

This decision involves an aesthetic question that most white writers do not ask themselves.

Many characters of color are aware of how whites view them and not just how people of the characters' own race view them.

Thus the character of color is aware of the gaze and judgment of the racial/white Other and the racial hierarchy that structures the society to the benefit of that racial/white Other.

For many writers of color, the lens of race is essential to understanding their characters as well as the way the writer views her characters and the larger society.

The difference in these assumptions then inevitably comes into play when a writer of color enters a writing class or an MFA program where the majority of professors and students are white—which is to say, just about any writing program in the country:

In writing programs where the professor is a white writer, he will generally be unaware of or not discuss the techniques through which a writer of color indicates and explores ethnicity or race.

This neglect is partly because the aesthetics of most white writing view such indications as unnecessary, inessential, or exceptions to the norm.

If a writer of color specifically employs the lens of race, doing so places that writer at odds with the assumptions of white writers who believe the lens of race is inessential or unimportant.

Employing the lens of race also puts the writer of color in conflict with those who argue that American society is postracial or, at the very least, that race is not a significant factor in American life.

Inevitably the clash between the writer of color and the white professor and students also affects how the writer of color's work is judged:

> The writer's ability to read her characters and the society through the lens of race and her ability to convey the complexities of that reading constitute significant criteria through which readers of color evaluate writers of color.

> For the white readers to make such an evaluation, they must be aware of the ways people of color use the lens of race to understand themselves, their communities, and the society in which they live.

> Most white readers do not possess this knowledge. It goes against the aesthetic—and political—assumption that race is not a significant and necessary lens through which to understand characters, whether they are white or people of color.

> Such differences occur because most white readers do not assume that race is a necessary lens to view their own lives. They do not often think or want to be conscious of their own racial identity (which naming white characters as white would force them to do).

> To maintain this view, white writers and readers must deem the lens of race unnecessary to an essential understanding of the society they live in or to its literature.

> It is therefore impossible to argue that race is not a factor in the aesthetic judgment of works by either white writers or writers of color.

As I've implied, the difference in aesthetics I've been exploring possesses a political dimension. That white writers don't identify their white characters racially or view race as significant to their white characters' experience stems from a specific definition of whiteness: Except in instances of obvious racial discord or crisis, race is not a central question white people need to confront. Moreover, race is *always* a less significant problem or factor than people of color maintain. To put it another way, when white people interact without people of color present, race is not a question. The question of race supposedly only resides in interactions with or between people of color.

Given this understanding, the dominant white culture's view is that only the writer of color's exploration of racial identity and experience is political. Thus writers of color in white-dominated workshops are sometimes told, "I like it better when you don't write about race" or "Why does everything have to be about race?" Or, a bit less baldly, "You"—the writer of color—"write politically while we"—the white writers in the workshop—"write aesthetically and not politically." This is a mindless critique, almost laughable if not for the damage it does to beginning writers of color. For white writers' avoidance of race is decidedly political.* This avoidance does have a political effect: It serves to bolster and camouflage rather than challenge the racial inequities and biases in contemporary society; it implicitly contradicts the assertion that race affects the interactions of everyone in this society; it embodies and upholds society's reigning racial ideology. White writers who do address race in their work very quickly discover the purpose of the taboo for doing so.

We are approaching a point when whites will no longer be the majority racial group in the United States; indeed, 2012 was the first year in which more babies of color were born in America than white babies. Is it difficult to believe that with such demographic changes, at some point the default race of an unidentified character will no longer be white? If that changes, will white writers finally be forced to grapple with the realities that most writers of color have grappled with all along? I do believe certain white writers will begin to understand that a deeper investigation into and redefining of white identity will lead to new creative energies and a wider and more complex depiction of both white individuals and the society they live in.

Finally, when will writers of color begin to be read with an understanding of the complexity and literary merit that their works deserve?

---

* I wrote this essay well before Donald Trump was elected president. But Trump's election makes the points I'm making here both more obvious and more complicated. As Nell Irvin Painter, Ta-Nehisi Coates, and others have pointed out, Trump campaigned and was elected as a white president for white America; this marks a shift from a submerged or hidden white identity to a self-proclaimed white identity. The research of social psychologists indicates that the more whites are aware of America's shifting racial demographics, the more they embrace whiteness as a conscious identity and the more conservative they become in their thinking, even with nonracial issues. What this means for progressive white artists is a question still to be answered by white artists themselves.

Existential Threats

ZZ PACKER'S "DRINKING COFFEE
ELSEWHERE" AND SHERMAN ALEXIE'S
THE TOUGHEST INDIAN IN THE WORLD

In judging literary works, we take into account what is at stake both for the writer and for the characters the writer creates. Ignoring the stakes or inaccurately assessing them can lead to a critical appraisal that is incomplete or inaccurate. Such misappraisals often occur with the works of writers of color, either in workshops or in the greater literary world. But I would also assert that this faulty evaluation works both ways—that is, in terms of how the works of white writers are perceived and what of their own reality they are shutting out.

To unfold my argument, let me start with a basic premise: implicit in the lives of most—if not all—people of color in America is a constant and real existential threat. In many ways, writers of color and/or the characters of color must address this threat, both at the level of actual survival and on the psychological, cultural, and even ontological level. By the very nature of these threats, writers of color and characters of color must take into account the power that whiteness and white people exert over their existence.

Unfortunately, many white writers and critics fail to acknowledge such power or such threats since their view of whiteness rarely includes the existence of the racial other, much less the threats the racial other faces. White writers often refuse to consider that their identity as white and the ways society regards them have always been predicated on the presence and declaration of the racial Other(s). Whiteness in this country has never existed simply as its own entity, dwelling in some Platonic realm outside history or politics and power or apart from the presence and treatment of people of color.

To understand whiteness then requires one to examine how whiteness was created and why—to establish racial power. For white writers, this examination entails investigating the history of race in this country and how that history still informs not just the present in general but white identity specifically. This is a large task of great importance, and it involves not just intellectual or literary work or a rethinking of one's politics. In the end, as Baldwin often implies, such work is spiritual.

But it is not only white writers who must undertake such work. Writers of color must also do this work, in investigating their own identities and histories but also in contextualizing their identities and histories within the identities and histories of other communities of color.

Intuitively, though, most writers of color know that race is essential to understanding who they are and how they came to be. What may not always be apparent, though, is how deeply the origins of people of color are written inside them, how their histories and the complications of their identities can reveal themselves very quickly and even in the most seemingly casual encounters.

In various ways, then, when race enters the work of writers of color—and almost always it is there, if not on the surface, then within its depths—the political enters. This does not mean, of course, that every writer of color needs to consider his characters or writing politically; it does mean that the antagonisms of race are often undergirding and contextualizing that writing. To ask people of color to write outside politics is, in many instances, to ask them to write in a way that denies who they are, that denies their people and those who came before them.

In this essay, I use the openings of two short stories by two writers of color to examine not only how the racial identities of their protagonists are presented but also how these identities allude to and reveal deep historical, political, and ontological roots. For the protagonists of both stories, whiteness is neither invisible nor separate from who they are, as much as they might wish otherwise.

An example of a racial approach to identity without a reference to ethnicity is the opening of "Drinking Coffee Elsewhere," the title short story of ZZ Packer's collection:

> Orientation games began the day I arrived at Yale from Baltimore. In my group we played heady, frustrating games for smart people. One game appeared to be charades reinterpreted by existentialists; another involved listening to rocks. Then a freshman counselor made everyone play Trust. The idea was that if you had the faith to fall backward and wait for four scrawny former high school geniuses to catch you, just before your head cracked on the slate sidewalk, then you might learn to trust your fellow students. Russian roulette sounded like a better way to go.

"No way," I said. The white boys were waiting for me to fall, holding their arms out for me, sincerely, gallantly. "No fucking way."

"It's all cool, it's all cool," the counselor said. Her hair was a shade of blond I'd seen only on *Playboy* covers, and she raised her hands as though backing away from a growling dog. "Sister," she said in an I'm-down-with-the-struggle voice, "you don't have to play this game. As a person of color, you shouldn't have to fit into any white, patriarchal system."

I said, "It's a bit too late for that."

In the next game, all I had to do was wait in a circle until it was my turn to say what inanimate object I wanted to be. One guy said he'd like to be a gad-fly, like Socrates. "Stop me if I wax Platonic," he said. I didn't bother mentioning that gadflies weren't inanimate—it didn't seem to make a difference. The girl next to him was eating a rice cake. She wanted to be the Earth, she said. Earth with a capital E.

There was one other black person in the circle. He wore an Exeter T-shirt and his overly elastic expressions resembled a series of facial exercises. At the end of each person's turn, he smiled and bobbed his head with unfettered enthusiasm. "Oh, that was good," he said, as if the game were an experiment he'd set up and the results were turning out better than he'd expected. "Good, good, good!"

When it was my turn I said, "My name is Dina, and if I had to be any object, I guess I'd be a revolver."

What I will say here about this passage will underscore the racial context here, but I want to emphasize that the surface of this story isn't explicitly about race. At the same time, I want to open up some questions about how readers perceive this racial context and to what extent they can do so.

Rather than openly declaring her identity, the narrator of Packer's story slips in clues to indicate who she is. As college freshmen typically do, the narrator is engaged in the process of discerning her difference from the other students who have chosen to go to the same school. This school, Yale, calls up certain images of class, intellectual abilities, and educational background—and of course, race. The narrator's response to the game of Trust indicates her wariness toward the other students. But the reference to Russian roulette also reveals more about her state of mind—not simply that she feels antagonism toward the other students but also perhaps that she might be depressed. The fact that the narrator uses the phrase "white boys" indicates, of course, that she is not white. It's not simply the fact that she regards them as an Other; it's also that white people do not generally refer to other white people as "white people" unless race has already been placed on the table.

In contrast, for the narrator, once she finds herself at Yale, race is always on the table. The idea of falling into the arms of four white boys is not Dina's idea of a fun let's-get-acquainted game, and the blond—and therefore white—counselor awkwardly tries to acknowledge this. Though the counselor is attempting to show empathy toward the narrator, her remark puts the narrator in exactly the position that the whole set of games is meant to alleviate. The purpose of the games is to encourage unity; "we" are all here as Yale students and thus can trust one another. But the racial divide between the narrator and the white boys precludes such trust. Similarly, the counselor's use of "Sister" would seem to say, "Well, we can at least bond as women," but her words have just the opposite effect on Dina, the narrator.

The narrator's answer to the counselor's proposition to opt out of the "white patriarchal system" is a witty "It's a bit too late for that." The remark references the fact that if she's chosen to go to Yale, she's chosen to enter a white patriarchal institution. The deeper implication is that she can never escape the white patriarchal system; she was born into it. (But then, so was the white counselor.)

Self-consciously, the narrator compares herself with the other member of her racial group in a white crowd. By the way that she notes his Exeter T-shirt, she indicates that she probably went to a public school. The other black student's enthusiastic response to the games signals his desire to fit in and a comfort with this crowd of white students that the narrator does not feel. That she is quick to judge him indicates that perhaps she's also not prone to assume that she has a bond with him simply because they are both black.

Finally, when asked what inanimate object she would be, the narrator picks up on her mention of Russian roulette and says, "I guess I'd be a revolver." In other words, "I know I'm in danger here and in a site of racial antagonism, and no games of trust are going to change that."

Eventually, Dina emerges as a singularly ironic, witty, and intelligent character, someone who rejects attempts by both blacks and whites to connect with her. It's clear that there are reasons for Dina's anger and isolation other than race. One major reason is that her mother has recently died, a loss that Dina tells no one about at the college, even the white therapist she is assigned to after her revolver reply. Another reason for Dina's behavior stems from her sexual orientation. Early on she begins an ambiguous relationship with a white female student, Heidi, a relationship that ends in part because Heidi comes out as a lesbian, and Dina wants nothing to do with such an identification. Also a couple of small scenes of Dina's life back in Baltimore indicate that she has grown up in a particularly impoverished black neighborhood and feels shame about that (she hides the exact location of her house—and the extent of her poverty—from a black boy about her age whom she meets).

As the story progresses, the issues of race seem to recede from the prominence they carry in these opening paragraphs. Of course, the poverty Dina has grown up in cannot be separated from race, and her general wariness and anger toward the world cannot be separated from her being a poor black female student at Yale. But Packer knows she doesn't have to emphasize this perspective once she's established it in the opening paragraphs.

What these paragraphs do, though, is instruct the reader on how to read Dina and her story through the lens of race. Once Packer has set this up, it is up to the reader to carry on this reading. The reader should understand that race informs Dina's reading of the world, despite the fact that she is loathe to connect with other black students simply on the basis of race. At the same time, this contradiction is part of what makes Dina such a fascinating and distinctive character. Because of Dina's personality, the presence of race is everywhere in the story; yet it is never articulated directly—except in this opening. But how deeply the reader understands the racial context of this story depends, I would argue, on how deeply the reader understands the function of race in American society.

To conclude, let's revisit Dina's choice of what she would be—"a revolver." When I read this response, I immediately think of the school of theory called Afro-pessimism. Afro-pessimists argue that the ontology of slavery continues into the present. In this ontology, whiteness is defined as human, blackness as nonhuman. Whiteness is thus equated with being a citizen, part of a nation; blackness, as the attribute of a slave, is equated with being a noncitizen, part of no nation. As nonhuman and noncitizen, blackness can be subjected to violence without the need of provocation or justification; violence on the black body requires no declaration of war or sanction by law. Further, blackness is fungible—that is, it can be bought and sold; blacks are property.

When I was first introduced to Afro-pessimism in the brilliant book by my friend Frank Wilderson, Black, Red and White: Cinema and the Structure of U.S. Antagonisms, my initial reaction was somewhat skeptical. Since then, partly through discussions with Wilderson, I've come to understand these theories on a deeper level. Moreover, given the overwhelming evidence of racial inequities in the U.S.

justice system and the deaths of black women and men involving police, I've come to feel that such a reading explains the American justice system far more adequately than a more benign ontology (much less the idea that we are post-racial). In such a world—that is, still existing within the ontology of slavery—perhaps Dina's response here is not a sign of her neuroses or mental problems but a reflection of the very real struggle she finds herself trapped in, a reflection of the forces arrayed against her. Dina is surrounded by an institution that has been historically white and is still culturally white; she's interacting with fellow students and a therapist who have little idea of who she is, much less the ways their very existence challenges her own existence. As such, Dina understands that she is in mortal danger, and this danger is always present, if not bodily—though that may very well be the case at any moment—then in terms of her psyche and soul. Her response, "a revolver," goes to the heart of a division that clearly exists in our society: how power is structured racially.*

Let's now turn to the opening of *The Toughest Indian in the World* by Sherman Alexie:

> Being a Spokane Indian, I only pick up Indian hitchhikers.
>
> I learned this particular ceremony from my father, a Coeur d'Alene, who always stopped for those twentieth-century aboriginal nomads who refused to believe the salmon were gone. I don't know what they believed in exactly, but they wore hope like a bright shirt.
>
> My father never taught me about hope. Instead, he continually told me that our salmon—our hope—would never come back, and though such lessons may seem cruel, I know enough to cover my heart in any crowd of white people.
>
> "They'll kill you if they get the chance," my father said. "Love you or hate you, white people will shoot you in the heart. Even after all these years, they'll still smell the salmon on you, the dead salmon, and that will make white people dangerous."
>
> All of us, Indian and white, are haunted by salmon.
>
> When I was a boy, I leaned over the edge of one dam or another—perhaps Long Lake or Little Falls or the great gray dragon known as the Grand Coulee—and watched the ghosts of the salmon rise from the water to the sky and become constellations.

* And yet it is this response that leads the Yale University to assign her a "suicide single" and require visits with a white therapist. This white therapist is as unprepared to deal with Dina and her racial realities as many white writing instructors are with their students of color.

> For most Indians, stars are nothing more than white tombstones scattered across a dark graveyard.
>
> But the Indian hitchhikers my father picked up refused to admit the existence of sky, let alone the possibility that salmon might be stars. They were common people who believed only in the thumb and the foot. My father envied those simple Indian hitchhikers. He wanted to change their minds about salmon; he wanted to break open their hearts and see the future in their blood. He loved them.

As is often the case in his stories, Alexie's narrator places his Indian and tribal identity right up front—Spokane and Coeur d'Alene. The narrator then contrasts his Coeur d'Alene father's pessimism with the hope evinced by the Indian hitchhikers his father would pick up. In his father's view, neither the salmon nor the Indians would come back in the way they once were, and the reason is clear: white people will not permit it. The father doesn't attempt to ameliorate the basic antagonism between whites and Indians: "They'll kill you if they get a chance."

The father's words bring up a history that, as an Indian, he cannot forget. In this history, the whites are the "Settlers," the Indians the "Red Savages." The Red Savages can never own the land; their presence on the land was a mere inconvenience. They and their tribes did not constitute a sovereign nation. They were not regarded as human in the same way as the White Settlers. To the White Settler, genocide against the Red Savage did not present an ethical dilemma in the past nor does it in the present; it does not constitute a war crime since wars involve conflicts between nations. Genocide is a term reserved for nations and humans, not the Red Savage.

Such racialized antagonism still lies at the core of white identity and its relationship to Indians. Thus placing this antagonism at the beginning of the story marks a distinct racial boundary; no amount of love or goodwill can erase this.

Whom is the narrator speaking to here? In my view, it's not clear. He isn't speaking directly to whites, yet he is explaining things about Indians to an audience that is not familiar with the view of history espoused by his father or the disagreements concerning "hope" among Indians, or more specifically, the hope evinced by Indian hitchhikers. At the same time, the narrator posits a basic racial antagonism between him and the white reader.

The narrator's intimacy with the world of Indians and the way he speaks about them indicates his acknowledgment that a potential listener—or reader—might be Indian. Most Indian readers would readily understand the father's stance toward whites, would recognize the fear the narrator expresses concerning whites, just as the Indian reader would respond in a very personal way to the father's avowed love of Indians, particularly Indian hitchhikers.*

In any case, a white writer or white narrator would almost never posit a reader or listener who is an Indian—nor, for that matter, do most writers of color. For once that occurs, the antagonism between the White Settler and the Red Savage must either be avoided or acknowledged in a *conscious* way. Therefore, most white writers or white narrators must be *unconscious* of the Indian Other, as are many writers or narrators of color. But since white writers generally avoid any connection with race or racial issues, their unconsciousness concerning Indians is particularly intrinsic to the way the white writer and a white narrator generally define their reality and identity. Their consciousness stops before the entrance or existence of the Indian. In this way, the Indian Other is dead to the white writer or the white narrator—thus the basic truth of the father's warning, "They will kill you if they get the chance."

But for the narrator and his father—and for Alexie—the White Settler is very much alive and always present, and the narrator knows he must cover his heart in any crowd of white people. In other words, for Alexie and for his protagonist, the racial antagonism between the White Settler and the Red Savage continues into the present. Whereas in the White Settler's ontology, only the White Settler can have survived this history of genocide. The Red Savage has been erased, no longer exists, and so cannot make a claim on the land.†

---

* But what of a reader like me, who is neither white nor Indian? When the narrator states, "All of us, Indian and white, are haunted by salmon," such a reader is not included. Or it could be that the narrator's and his father's view of whites must include other people of color who are also, from the view of the Indian, settlers, namely, people who have stolen Indian land and bear the benefits of the genocide against Indians. Or it could be that the reader of color sides more with the Indian father in his view of whites—that they are dangerous, that they will kill you. Or the reader of color may reside in both of these categories at once.

    In any case, it is not possible to posit a universal reader for this story or a unitary interpretation and relationship to the story. If the reader is an American, his or her position in regard to the basic historical, cultural, and political assumptions of the narrator will differ depending on the reader's race. Alexie inscribes race into the very heart and voice of his narrator and therefore, in the reader, whether the reader is Native American, white, or some other person of color.

† In *Red, White & Black: Cinema and the Structure of U.S. Antagonisms*, Frank Wilderson provides the following anecdote: "When I attended the University of California at Berkeley, I saw a Native American man sitting on the sidewalk of Telegraph Avenue. On the ground in front of him was an upside-down hat and a sign informing pedestrians that here they could settle the 'Land Lease Accounts' they had neglected to settle all of their lives. He . . . was 'crazy.' . . . And to what does the world attribute the Native American man's insanity? 'He's crazy if he thinks he's getting any money out of us'? Surely, that doesn't make him crazy. Rather it is simply an indication that he does not have a big enough gun." This is an argument that ZZ Packer's Dina might recognize.

Alexie and his protagonist know that an ontology outside the White Settler's exists, just as Alexie and his protagonist know that they are alive. To write the protagonist's story then is an existential act, but it is also inherently a political act (as well as an ontological act). It is impossible to view the writing of Native Americans otherwise.

After this introduction, the narrator of *The Toughest Indian in the World* reveals himself to be a reporter and a middle-class Camry-driving Spokane who picks up Indian hitchhikers whenever he sees them. He has recently broken up with a white girlfriend, Cindy, a fellow reporter who only dates "brown-skinned guys." Note that to make sense of Cindy's dating preference requires that Cindy be identified as white, whereas when white writers introduce a white woman who does not date men (or women) of color, that woman's whiteness or her racial preferences in partners would remain invisible and unremarked upon (even though her not dating men or women of color would involve a racial component).

In the story proper, the narrator picks up a Lummi Indian who is a traveling fighter. The narrator and the fighter share a motel room. In the middle of the night, the fighter makes a sexual move toward the narrator, and the narrator, although remarking, "I'm not gay," responds. Their coupling is, in part, a recognition of the bond they share and the existential threat bequeathed to them both by history. It helps the narrator to see that despite their differences in class and occupation, they are both engaged in a struggle to survive in a world where the White Settler still wages a constant war against their being. In the morning, after the Lummi leaves, the narrator concludes with thoughts of those who came before him and his ties to their past:

> I wondered if I was a warrior in this life and if I had been a warrior in a previous life. . . . I woke early the next morning, before sunrise, and went out into the world. I walked past my car. I stepped onto the pavement, still warm from the previous day's sun. I started walking. In bare feet, I traveled upriver towards the place where I was born and will someday die. At that moment, if you had broken open my heart you could have looked inside and seen the thin white skeletons of one thousand salmon.

The Student of Color in the Typical MFA Program

I

In the landscape of the literary world, one dramatic shift has been the rise of MFA creative writing programs. There are now more than three hundred in the United States and Canada. Back in the late eighties, the first Associated Writing Programs annual conference I attended had about 350 attendees. This past year, the attendance was over 13,000.

Despite these numbers, if a student of color enters one of these MFA creative writing programs, he or she will be in a small minority. The director of the program will most likely be white, as will most of the professors. Of course, this situation isn't very different from that of most undergraduate colleges. But by its nature, creative writing is subjective and personal; so is the judgment of that writing. This makes it a far different course of study than math or science, where the correct answers are objective and have been objectively proven.

Since writers are a liberal lot, the white faculty and students in these institutions profess progressive views on race. Generally, they see themselves as without racial bias. Racism and racial bias might still be found in the United States, but it would be in the Republican Party or the Tea Party or the alt-right, not in a population of liberal white artists.

Unfortunately, that is not the experience of many MFA students of color. Personally, I have heard dozens—if not hundreds—of stories from individual students of color that would indicate otherwise. So have colleagues of mine.

Although the essay below focuses on MFA creative writing programs, the issues and arguments it depicts occur everywhere in American society, in educational institutions, in businesses, in political institutions, in the justice system.

When issues of race come up in these other areas, the treatment of the person of color by whites in that institution is not essentially different from what happens in an MFA program.

There are, though, a couple of telling differences: In an MFA program, the unconscious ways that whites perceive people of color are more likely to appear, since creative writing comes out of the unconscious. In other classes, race and racial issues can sometimes remain hidden or silenced. That is, it is more likely that problematic racial perceptions will emerge in student writing than in assignments undertaken in math class.

In American society, the divide between the way whites and people of color see the social reality around them is always present. Often, though, this divide remains invisible or obscured, especially in places where issues of race are often avoided rather than discussed. But creative writing involves the very description of social reality, so the gulf between the vision of whites and that of people of color is present right there on the page. Moreover, the judgment of these descriptions can also reveal a gulf between whites and people of color. Conflict then ensues. Such conflict is societal, not individual, though creative writing's focus on the individual writer may camouflage or obfuscate this.

In other words, I will argue here that what the MFA student of color experiences in a predominantly white institution is not simply an obscure or numerically insignificant occurrence. Instead, it is symptomatic and revelatory of the ways the voices and consciousness of people of color are suppressed in our society.

This essay was written specifically for student writers of color, to let them know they are not crazy, that what they perceive concerning the ways they and their work are received is real. It was written to let them know that what they experience as an individual is both a social practice and a political practice that involves a clash of power between two groups, whites and people of color. It was written as a manual for battle and survival.

II

Here is an all too common scenario MFA students of color face in their mainly all white MFA programs:

A white student brings in a piece with racial stereotypes or which presents people of color in a manner that negates their humanity as three-dimensional individuals. Later, in the same class, other students, usually white, also present pieces with similar problematic representations of people of color.

Confronted with such a piece—or pieces—the writer of color must decide whether to voice an objection to the stereotypes or two-dimensional portraits of people of color or the problematic racial approach of the white student's piece.

Since such situations have played themselves out for so many MFA students, we know that invariably neither the white professor nor the other white students will formulate and express a critique of the piece like that of the student of color.

Thus the student of color will be the sole person voicing her critique—if the student chooses to do so.

If, and when, the student of color voices her objections to the piece, more often than not neither the white professor nor the other white students will respond to the actual critique, nor will they inquire further into why the student of color is making that critique.

Instead, the white professor and the other white students will generally first invoke some notion of the freedom of the imagination (perhaps echoing something like Henry James's *donnée*: one must grant writers their starting premises). They will emphasize the subjectivity of all responses both to the reality around us and to a specific text.

At best, the white professor or other white students will argue that the problems with the white student's piece may be caused by technical deficiencies—namely, it is not really a racial issue.

At the same time, what is actually going on in the class is the following:

The white professor and the white students start with the assumption that none of the white people in the class are racists and none consciously or unconsciously subscribe to any elements from an ideology of white supremacy. To challenge this assumption is treated as blasphemy, as an act of aggression or delusion.

To maintain this belief in the absolute absence of white racism, *what must be defended is the freedom of white writers to write about people of color without taking into account the critiques of people of color.**

As part of this defense, the student of color is subtly or openly charged with acting as a censor—despite the fact that the student of color obviously has no or very little power to affect the freedom of anyone in the room to write. If the student of color is identified as a censor, then of course her or his critique must be suspect, since censorship is always the enemy of any writer.

To help in this defense, the debate will then be formulated as occurring between the individual subjectivities in the class, which means that it is framed as the subjectivity of the one person of color against the seven, ten, twelve white students along with the white professor. Framed in this way, the outcome of such a debate is already predetermined.

Thus the argument will not be formulated as *a struggle between groups*—between whites and people of color. It will not be placed within a history of the racial debate, literary, political, and otherwise, over the nature of our social reality. It will not be placed within the context of arguments made by *other* writers of color concerning the depictions of people of color by white artists. Instead, the focus will be limited to the subjective vision or opinions of the individual student of color.

Another tactic the white professor and white students might take is designating the argument as political and thus beyond the bounds of a literary class.

Yet only when the argument is considered a racial antagonism between whites and people of color can the true nature of the conflict be revealed.

But unfortunately the discussion in many MFA classrooms is deliberately constructed and guided so that this never happens.

---

* As I've pointed out in my introduction, Toni Morrison argues that historically white fiction writers have not imagined a nonwhite audience for their work, even when that work involves characters of color. Hence, it isn't surprising that white writers might not imagine the critique by people of color of their work or what that might entail.

⌒

At the same time, on an emotional and often unconscious level, something else is occurring in the class.

To entertain that the white student's work might contain racially problematic or racist elements is to entertain the possibility that the work of other white students and even the white professor might contain such elements.

Therefore, the white professor and the other white students will feel at some level that they too are being critiqued by the student of color.

Given this feeling of threat, and given their investment in the racial status quo, the whites in the class, on a conscious and/or an unconscious level, will react to the student of color's critique of the racial bias in the white student's piece with fear and/or anger and outrage.

How does this process occur?

Some white members of the class will feel that the student of color's critique is simply wrong; these members will dismiss the student and his or her critique without much thought. If the student persists, these white students will feel annoyed, then angry.

But some white members of the class may begin to feel guilty, may find a part of themselves wondering if the student of color is right. They may even sense that by critiquing the racial portrait in a white student's work, the student of color is also challenging the general portrayal of people of color in the society, the negative stereotypes that the individual white student has never had to deal with.

These feelings of guilt will conflict with the white students' belief that they are not racists. Rather than explore the possible reasons why they might feel guilty, most whites will cling even harder to the belief that they are not racists and, therefore, should not feel guilty. This is unfair, they will say to themselves and perhaps to fellow classmates. *I am being accused of something I did not do.* (Such thoughts can occur even if the student of color never mentions the word *racist* or makes any such accusation.) The white student will begin to feel angry at the student of color for treating the white student unfairly, for making the white student feel guilty. The white student—or the white professor—may even begin to feel that he or she is the victim of the student of color.

Thus the white professor and members of the class will begin to feel antipathy toward the student of color making the critique. Either silently or vocally, the student of color will be deemed a troublemaker, someone who is overly sensitive, paranoid, or overly aggressive. A political agitator. A censor. Or worse.

Occasionally the white professor and other white students might possibly admit on a theoretical level that the student of color might have a basis for critique that the white people in the class may not have sufficient knowledge to understand. But very rarely will the white professor and other white students take this critique as a springboard to consider further how the student of color's critique is connected to the tradition of literature, literary theory, and political thought of people of color—a tradition that the white professor and white students are often unaware of or have never sufficiently studied.

Very rarely will the white professor and other white students begin to examine the limitations of their own experiences. Very rarely will they begin to inquire what it means for them to be "white"—that is, rarely will they take the student of color's critique as a call to examine their own ignorance of the way racism and white supremacy function in society. They will not ask themselves, "What does it mean for me to be a white person in this society? How did I learn I was a white person? How did I learn what whiteness means to me and to others? How is the way I am feeling or acting toward the critique expressed by the student of color shaped by unspoken definitions/constructions of what it means to be white? What are the practices and beliefs that undergird a certain construction of white identity?"

Instead, the focus of emotion and discussion will center on the student of color; this focus will soon begin to spill over into a critique of the student of color's character and her motives for "disrupting" the class. It will also focus on the student of color's challenge to the white professor's authority and superior knowledge, the student's "attitude" toward the professor and fellow students.

If the student of color persists in making such critiques, she will develop a reputation in the MFA program as a troublemaker, a malcontent, perhaps even someone with psychological problems, as someone who is not supportive of the other students, as disrespecting her professors.

If the student of color persists in making such critiques, she will find herself increasingly isolated socially and shunned in various ways by the other students and professors in the department—and this may very well also include even other professors of color, who often feel that their own position in the department is quite precarious and open to challenge. These professors of color are then cited as evidence that none of these matters involve actual racial antagonisms.

After two or three years of such treatment, if the student of color persists and graduates, she will have fought a literary, psychological, and political battle that none of her white counterparts have had to face. The price of the student's ticket is not the same as theirs; the toll she has paid is far higher.

All this negative focus on the student of color, all the forces arrayed against her, is rarely seen for what it is.

It is one example of how American society fights to maintain the racial status quo. It demonstrates how this society maintains the privileges that whites enjoy by virtue of their whiteness, how it polices any threats to the system of white privilege and white supremacy. Such policing is far easier if whiteness, as a group identity, is never acknowledged or even allowed to be discussed. This is a tactic and approach often employed more consciously in the political realm.

In other words, while each individual in this scenario believes he or she is acting as an individual, the actions of the white professor, the white students, and the MFA program toward the student color have been *preprogrammed*.

That is why this scenario takes place over and over in MFA programs all across the country.

At the same time, in most MFA programs, the subject of race and writing about race is never considered an essential area of study for all writers in the program regardless of color. It is never a requirement, always an elective—that is, if it is even mentioned.

This is not surprising since the majority of the white faculty do not believe that such a study is essential to their own writing or to their own pedagogical practices.

This ignorance regarding the lens of race or the works of writers of color does not occur by accident. It is both a result of the racial inequalities of power in our society and a cause of it. It is part of the way the system of racial inequality maintains itself.

If all this is preprogrammed, if the events of this scenario inevitably play themselves out in so many MFA programs, what is the student of color to do?

That is, should she voice her criticism or not?

And if she does voice her criticism, how often and how vocally and to whom should she voice it?

What danger does she put herself in by making such a critique? What strategies should she employ in dealing with the social and power structures designed to protect white privilege and supremacy?

The answers to these questions in part depend on the individual and individual choice.

But I cannot emphasize strongly enough that the scenario I've described is not an individual scenario but a societal one—that is, it is a scenario dictated by the race and racial position of the actors within it, dictated not by individuals but by society's imperative to defend the racial status quo from any direct challenges.

Because of the nature of this struggle, I believe there are certain things the student of color should consider. One is *The Art of War* by Sun Tzu:

> Now the general who wins a battle makes many calculations in his temple before the battle is fought. The general who loses a battle makes but few calculations beforehand. Thus do many calculations lead to victory, and few calculations to defeat: how much more no calculation at all! It is by attention to this point that I can foresee who is likely to win or lose.

> It is the rule in war, if our forces are ten to the enemy's one, to surround him; if five to one, to attack him; if twice as numerous, to divide our army into two.

> If equally matched, we can offer battle; if slightly inferior in numbers, we can avoid the enemy; if quite unequal in every way, we can flee from him.

Thus the student of color might consider whether this is a battle she can win. Given the forces and numbers of the opposition and given the fact that she is a student, the student of color is clearly not in a position of superior numbers or superior power. This battle is therefore probably one that the student will lose if she continues to fight.

One problem for the student of color is the feeling that if she is silent about a piece of writing that is racially problematic or insensitive or simply racist, she will be condoning such writing.

Moreover, the student may believe that to be silent is to be a coward.

At the same time, if the student of color persists in her critiques, she will be increasingly attacked and begin to feel isolated and powerless. The student may feel then that to persist with her critiques is an attempt to maintain or regain power.

But Sun Tzu teaches that to retreat or lay low in times when one does not have power or sufficient numbers is not weakness; it is wisdom.

Sun Tzu teaches that taking time to build allies and gather forces is not weakness but wisdom.

Sun Tzu teaches that taking time to obtain information about the enemy and identify the enemy's weaknesses is not weakness but wisdom.

Sun Tzu cautions people not to fight battles they know they are going to lose. The object is not to win a particular battle but to win the war.

Or as I wrote to one such student, being an activist artist is not a sprint. It is a marathon. Artists need to plan and strategize and build their forces for the larger battles to come, to fight from strength not weakness.

At the same time, there is the option of organizing, of making these issues public in a larger way. But such an option does put a burden on the student of color that she or he should not have to deal with. Moreover, one's talent as a creative writer does not necessarily translate to political organizing. The two tasks require different skills.*

What I am saying here ought to be clear by now: Students of color, you are not crazy or misperceiving what is before and around you. You are in hostile territory. You are in a battle. In many MFA programs, your presence, your mind, and your creativity represent an alien presence, at odds with the powers that be.

You can choose not to fight certain battles. You can wait until you are in a more secure position or a position of power.

In the meantime, keep writing. Stay strong. You're not alone.

---

* I say this as someone who has done his share of political organizing, especially around cultural issues and issues of racial equity.

Writing Teachers

OR DAVID FOSTER WALLACE
VERSUS JAMES BALDWIN

I

A couple of years ago, a black writer friend recounted to me an experience in her MFA program. On the first day of class, the white professor took my black friend aside and advised my friend that she should go to the remedial English center for instruction since there were grammatical errors in her poems.

My black friend explained that the poems were written in black vernacular. The white professor, tenured, with a distinguished chair, responded that if my friend continued to write in that way, her poems would not be published.

I shouldn't have to add this, but my friend not only went on to publish poems and complete her MFA; she also earned a PhD in English literature, later worked internationally for the U.S. government, won literary prizes, and is now a college professor. My friend was acutely aware of the differences between black speech and the conventions of white literary and professional language. On the other hand, her white professor's ignorance of the tradition of African American literature or, say, critical works like Henry Louis Gates's *The Signifying Monkey* or Toni Morrison's *Playing in the Dark* was not an issue that my friend, as a student, felt she could bring up.

In his introduction to *Dismantle: An Anthology of Writing from VONA* (a conference for writers of color), Junot Díaz critiques the damage done to student writers of color in MFA programs and critiques the racism and ignorance of their professors and fellow students:

> I've worked in two MFA programs and visited at least 30 others and the signs
> are all there. The lack of diversity of the faculty. Many of the students' lack
> of awareness of the lens of race, the vast silence on these matters in many

workshops. I can't tell you how often students of color seek me out during my visits or approach me after readings in order to share with me the racist nonsense they're facing in their programs, from both their peers and their professors. In the last 17 years I must have had at least three hundred of these conversations, minimum. I remember one young MFA'r describing how a fellow writer (white) went through his story and erased all the 'big' words because, said the peer, that's not the way 'Spanish' people talk. This white peer, of course, had never lived in Latin America or Spain or in any U.S. Latino community—he just knew. The workshop professor never corrected or even questioned said peer either. Just let the idiocy ride. Another young sister told me that in the entire two years of her workshop the only time people of color showed up in her white peer's stories was when crime or drugs were some-how involved. And when she tried to bring up the issue in class, tried to sug-gest readings that might illuminate the madness, her peers shut her down, saying Our workshop is about writing, not political correctness. As always race was the student of color's problem, not the white class's. Many of the writers I've talked to often finish up by telling me they're considering quitting their pro-grams.

When Díaz placed a shortened version of this introduction on the New Yorker website, the responses in the commentary section revealed a barrage of ad ho-minem attacks and responses from white writers denying the truth of Díaz's MFA experience as well as the experiences of other student writers of color. There was also the usual response by white writers: Well, I haven't seen this or that form of racial bias or insensitivity or ignorance—that is, only if white writers them-selves have seen things with their own eyes can they actually believe the ac-counts of people of color. Such a response is not, in its essence, that different from the response of white Americans to past black accounts of police brutality and injustice. The words of black Americans were not enough because, well, just because; there needed to be video proof that whites could see (and often even that is not enough).

Writers of color don't have video proof of their reality, just their words. That their words and sense of reality continue to be dismissed, excluded, marginal-ized, and distorted links them to a struggle taking place everywhere in Ameri-can society, the struggle for their communities to be heard and their truths to be acknowledged. Writers of color are engaged in aesthetic issues and battles, yes, but it is no contradiction to say that those issues and battles also include a polit-ical dimension. Certainly, they do not have to assent to assumptions about the nature of this conflict that exclude the very basis through which they make their case.

What would it take to prepare professors and students to critique the writings of students of color?

Obviously, part of this is a matter of reading. In "POC vs. MFA," the condensed version of his introduction to Dismantle that appeared in the New Yorker, Díaz describes the dominant literary tradition in his MFA program: "From what I saw the plurality of students and faculty had been educated exclusively in the tradition of writers like William Gaddis, Francine Prose, or Alice Munro—and not at all in the traditions of Toni Morrison, Cherrie Moraga, Maxine Hong Kingston, Arundhati Roy, Edwidge Danticat, Alice Walker, or Jamaica Kincaid." Díaz provides here a contrast between a list of white writers and a list of writers of color. If you're a white writer and have not read the names on the second list, you need to start reading.

Even in 2015, you can become a very famous and accomplished white writer without feeling that you must be familiar with writers of color. I know a writer of color who told a white writer friend, "If you don't read Baldwin, we can't be friends anymore." This white writer was in his forties and had won major book awards; he's someone who could quote poems from any number of East European poets, who had studied Latin American writers. But this same white writer considered himself well educated without having read Baldwin.

One can do reading lists, and they are useful. But what is more difficult to change is the basic mind-set of many white writers, one with both conscious and unconscious components. That mind-set assumes that the reality of people of color, their lives and their consciousness, are secondary and minor, are not universal, are not required understanding, are optional. Obviously, when my writer of color friend demanded that his white writer friend read Baldwin, that white writer was making a conscious choice not to read Baldwin, a choice based on the belief that Baldwin was not a canonical writer and thus inessential.

This same mind-set is what Toni Morrison refers to when she writes in Playing in the Dark: Whiteness and the Literary Imagination, "For reasons that should not need explanation here, until very recently, and regardless of the race of the author, the readers of virtually all of American fiction have been positioned as white. I am interested to know what that assumption has meant to the literary imagination. When does racial 'unconsciousness' or awareness of race enrich interpretative language, when does it impoverish it?" Though Morrison qualifies her statement by the phrase "until very recently," one wonders how many white writers today actually wrestle with how their work might be received by readers of color. Every writer of color is certainly aware that white readers will be reading their work, just as writers of color are aware that the evaluation of their work in the so-called mainstream literary world will, to a large part, be influenced by what white readers make of it.

In viewing the difficulties of her position in terms of writing about race, Morrison asks: "What happens to the writerly imagination of a black author who is at some level always representing one's own race to, or in spite of, a race of readers that understands itself to be 'universal' or race-free?" As Morrison points out, the danger for her is not in resorting to the tropes white writers have used to construct "literary blackness":

> Neither blackness nor "people of color" stimulates in me notions of excessive, limitless love, anarchy, or routine dread. I cannot rely on these metaphorical shortcuts because I am a black writer struggling with and through a language that can powerfully evoke and enforce hidden signs of racial superiority, cultural hegemony, and dismissive "othering" of people and language which are by no means marginal or already and completely known and knowable in my work. My vulnerability would lie in romanticizing blackness rather than demonizing it; vilifying whiteness rather than reifying it. The kind of work I have always wanted to do requires me to learn how to maneuver ways to free up the language from its sometimes sinister, frequently lazy, almost always predictable employment of racially informed and determined chains.

This passage brings up a key issue regarding the teaching of writing: What if the work of a student writer of color displays some of these missteps Morrison alludes to here? In typical MFA programs, would the white professors be aware of these "racially informed and determined chains" Morrison refers to? To achieve such awareness, white writing professors would have to educate themselves in the same tradition that Morrison writes out of and is thoroughly familiar with. And if white professors are going to prepare themselves and their classes to deal with works by students of color, they would also have to educate the white writers in the class in the traditions of writers of color. But even with all that, neither white writing professors nor white students would bring to the class a lifetime of experiences living as people of color in this society and interacting with a community of color.

But let's say a white writing professor has done at least this literary and intellectual work, and let us acknowledge that a white writing professor might have educated himself enough to read the work of students of color within the broader context of both white writers and writers of color, of American writers and global writing. Other questions still remain to be asked. First, would the white writing professor feel comfortable critiquing the student of color? Second, would the white writing professor be able to provide his critique in a way that the student of color would trust and respond to positively?

II

To answer these questions, let me start with a "talk" David Foster Wallace would give to certain black students. This talk didn't involve creative writing specifically, but it does reveal certain racial dynamics that occur between a white professor and a student of color, dynamics Wallace seems unconscious and ignorant of.

In the essay "Authority and American Usage," in *Consider the Lobster*, Wallace gives a written version of his specialized talk on Standard Black English versus Standard White English.

> I don't know whether anybody's told you this or not, but when you're in a college English class you're basically studying a foreign dialect. This dialect is called Standard White English. From talking with you and reading your first couple essays, I've concluded that your own primary dialect is [one of the three variants of SBE common to our region].

Wallace goes on to explain some differences between Standard White English and Standard Black English. He then concludes:

> I'm respecting you enough here to give you what I believe is the straight truth. In this country, SWE is perceived as the dialect of education and intelligence and power and prestige, and anybody of any race, ethnicity, religion, or gender who wants to succeed in American culture has got to be able to use SWE. This is just How It Is. You can be glad about it or sad about it or deeply pissed off. You can believe it's racist and unfair and decide right here and now to spend every waking minute of your adult life arguing against it, and maybe you should, but I'll tell you something—if you ever want those arguments to get listened to and taken seriously, you're going to have to communicate them in SWE, because SWE is the dialect our nation uses to talk

to itself. African-Americans who've become successful and important in U.S. culture know this; that's why King's and X's and Jackson's speeches are in SWE, and why Morrison's and Angelou's and Baldwin's and Wideman's and Gates's and West's books are full of totally ass-kicking SWE, and why black judges and politicians and journalists and doctors and teachers communicate professionally in SWE. . . . And [STUDENT'S NAME], you're going to learn to use it, too, because I am going to make you.

Wallace then comments about this "spiel" and the way it was received by his students of color:

I should note here that a couple of the students I've said this stuff to were offended—one lodged an Official Complaint—and that I have had more than one colleague profess to find my spiel "racially insensitive." Perhaps you do, too. This reviewer's own humble opinion is that some of the cultural and political realties of American life are themselves racially insensitive and elitist and offensive and unfair, and that pussyfooting around these realties with euphemistic doublespeak is not only hypocritical but toxic to the project of ever really changing them.

For certain readers of color, one of the clues that this is a white guy talking is the phrase "This reviewer's own humble opinion." There's nothing humble at all about how Wallace addresses these students of color and critiques their English. Wallace not only knows that he's an expert in discussing the academic arguments surrounding SWE and SBE; he is also convinced he knows the way the world works, and he knows what respect is, and he knows what it is to tell the "truth." He assumes there is one version of the "truth" and that he has simply laid down that "truth" to the student of color—and to whichever colleagues find him "racially insensitive." He is giving the student of color a gift, and the student ought to see that. If the student rejects his gift, it's all on the student; the student simply doesn't want to hear the "truth." Similarly, his colleagues who call him "racially insensitive" are wrong. He, Wallace, cannot be "racially insensitive" since he is not a hypocrite; he is not "pussyfooting around" but instead is supposedly keeping it real.

In all his nonfiction, this passage is possibly the only instance where Wallace says anything significant about any writers of color. But the problem here is not that Wallace has not read black writers. Rather, it's that Wallace seems to think that his allusions to Toni Morrison and Gates—that is, his seeming knowledge of black literature—provides him with free reign to say whatever he wants to his black students. But it's difficult, if not impossible, for me to imagine Toni Morrison or Jonathan Edgar Wideman giving a talk exactly like this to a black student—which is not to say that Toni Morrison or Wideman would not want the student to learn SWE. Nor does Wallace imagine how even the same speech he makes might be heard differently by a black student if Toni Morrison were giving that speech and why that might be.

Wallace maintains that he is not engaging in anything "toxic," yet not for an instant does he entertain the possibility that his position as a white male professor might make his student regard him as potentially "toxic." He's speaking to an African American student who comes from a community where SBE is the dominant language, and he exhibits no understanding of what that student's life might have been like, the distance she might have traveled, to get to his office. He clearly has no idea how much she might distrust both him, the white male professor, and the institution he represents, or how his very words might simply confirm and echo the stereotypes she suspects are in the minds of the white people she encounters at this predominantly white institution.

Wallace presumes he knows what the student of color needs—that student needs to hear and heed Wallace's spiel on SBE and SWE. Moreover, that student of color should know that Wallace means her well because Wallace knows he means that student of color well. Any doubt on the student's part of Wallace's intentions or his truth is irrelevant. The only reality—and "truth"—that matters is Wallace's. In other words, for Wallace his own epistemology must be the only relevant epistemology. He doesn't consider that in his encounter with his black student, Wallace is encountering a very different epistemology. He doesn't understand that the less than satisfactory reaction to his talk might stem from this clash of epistemologies.

I showed Wallace's talk to a black poet friend. He said that his parents did instruct him that he should learn Standard White English, that he should be familiar with both SWE and SBE. But then he said that if David Foster Wallace had talked this way to him, my black poet friend—one of the gentlest and most congenial people I know—would have wanted to strangle Wallace.

In short, aside from some of its faulty premises, Wallace's whole spiel is wrong-headed in tone and approach. Yet he is completely unaware of the possibility of this.

Wallace makes a fundamental mistake by ignoring a principle that is part of any basic instruction in rhetoric: you must be aware of your audience and how that audience will receive your message. Wallace has no idea how what he is saying and the way he is saying it will be received by a black student whose first dialect is SBE—a student who is in her first or second year at a university where the standard language is SWE and where the faculty and students are overwhelmingly white; a black student who is listening to a white male professor tell her what the social reality of this country is and what that student will need to get ahead in this country no matter what her path will be in life. In other words, Wallace has no idea how his "truth" will be heard by his black students.

Oh, wait. He does. He's offended them.

But wait. Their sense of offense doesn't matter. He, Wallace, is telling the truth. That's all that matters. He knows he is not racially insensitive. And that's that.

It's clear Wallace never stopped to ask his black students: "Why do you think I'm being racially insensitive? Is there something here I'm missing?"

What would I do with a student like the students Wallace addresses in his spiel? First, I would try to be cognizant of the fact that SBE has been the language of this student and her community; any hint of disrespect of that language from me would be taken as disrespect toward not just that student but the student's entire community. I would understand that SBE is the language spoken by those who love this student and whom this student loves, those who brought her up and those in the community in which the student grew up. So I had best tread lightly lest I insult those the student loves, who raised, supported, and helped make her who she is. I would recognize that the elephant in the room is the assumption that those who speak SBE are less intelligent, less complex human beings, and that they are marked for second-class status as citizens. I would understand that even if I do not share this prejudice, the student has little reason to believe that is the case. Indeed, there are many good reasons for the student to suspect that I do hold such prejudices—and this would be even more so if I were white like Wallace.

At the same time, I would understand that SBE has been used by American blacks for centuries and has enabled them to survive slavery, Jim Crow, and contemporary American racism, and under those conditions, American blacks have used SBE to create aspects of American culture that are essential to all Americans, no matter their color. I would acknowledge that all Americans owe a debt to SBE and those who have spoken it for their contributions not just to American culture but to American history and justice. While someone like Martin Luther King Jr. learned SWE, there were thousands of his followers whose primary language was SBE and without whom King would not have been able to accomplish what he did; the civil rights movement was not just the SWE-speaking King but unsung blacks who spoke SBE and who faced down death threats and jail and the KKK in order to rid America of Jim Crow segregation.*

Taking all this into account, in relating to this student, I would assume that because I'm an Asian American, that student might have some distrust of me. Certainly, the student would regard whatever I say differently than if a black professor or her parents were saying something similar about SWE and SBE. I would assume that I needed to know more about the individual student. I might have pockets of ignorance concerning who that student is and what that student's experiences have been and what his or her particular truths might be. I would know that until I earn the student's trust, I would have to proceed with caution. I cannot presume from the start that the student should trust me and what I say. I would know that in the interchange between the teacher and the student, it is not just the student who should be critiqued. The student is critiquing me. And I would understand that the society the student lives in has probably given that student a lot of reasons to regard me with wariness. Many people of color, for instance, are aware that Asian Americans are viewed as the model minority, and that certain Asian Americans have chosen to play the "honorary white" status in order to be accepted by the white majority.

Finally, I would have to learn more about the student as an individual—his background, the student's self-perception and view of his place at the university, what has motivated the student to work to get to this point, for clearly he hasn't gotten here without overcoming any number of barriers I might not be aware of. I would take clues from the student as to what he thinks he might need from me, and this might not be, at this moment, a spiel about SWE and SBE. Instead, the student might need simply to feel as if he just might be able to

---

* Wallace's talk presumes not just the preeminence of SWE but an unquestioned preeminence, and it's hard for many writers of color to accept this premise. I could point to various works of literature that do use SBE, such as *Their Eyes Were Watching God*, as evidence of Wallace's myopia. Or I could point out that when he says, "If you ever want those arguments to get listened to and taken seriously," he's presuming an audience that accepts SWE as the standard and uses SWE. Implicitly, he's also saying that an audience that speaks primarily SBE cannot possibly change things. The fact that hip-hop, a form in which SBE predominates, has altered not just American culture but world culture totally challenges such an assumption. In obvious and not so obvious ways, Wallace is speaking the language of white supremacy, even as he seems to disavow any racism on his part. Apparently, he doesn't think Audre Lourde's famous observation might be relevant here—the tools of the master will never dismantle the master's house. In other words, his very language relegates the community of the student who speaks and writes in SBE to a secondary status—not just politically or culturally but on a basic human level. And Wallace doesn't see that he's doing this.

trust me, that I'm there to help him, despite our racial difference and the differences in our backgrounds. The first thing I would have to do with this student would be to establish an authentic relationship with him based on who I am and who the student actually is.

In his essay and his spiel, Wallace does not feel the need to understand his black student's reality or to empathize with how the student views the world and his place in it—not that he should become the student, which he can't, but that he should try at least for a moment to understand what it is like to walk in the student's shoes. He can't or won't let himself imagine why his black students might distrust him or what experiences have reinforced that distrust. Nor does he think it his job to try to earn their trust.

But, after all, why should he do this? He's a white male professor. The student is supposed to listen to him, submit to his superior knowledge.

Here we come to a requirement that is not often discussed in the teaching of creative writing and perhaps cannot be adequately discussed in that realm, but I'm going to talk about it anyway: spiritual humility.

For me, perhaps the basic text for the spiritual examination of race is the writing of James Baldwin. "The Black Boy Looks at the White Boy," an essay in *Nobody Knows My Name*, contains a key section where Baldwin lays out his differences with Norman Mailer as a typical white man:

> There is a difference, though, between Norman and myself in that I think he still imagines that he has something to save, whereas I have never had anything to lose. Or, perhaps I ought to put it another way: the things that most white people imagine that they can salvage from the storm of life is really, in sum, their innocence. It was this commodity precisely which I had to get rid of at once, literally, on pain of death. I am afraid that most of the white people I have ever known impressed me as being in the grip of a weird nostalgia, dreaming of a vanished state of security and order, against which dream, unfailingly and unconsciously, they tested and very often lost their lives. It is a terrible thing to say, but I am afraid that for a very long time the troubles of white people failed to impress me as being real trouble. They put me in mind of children crying because the breast has been taken away.

The contemporary version of these last sentences is "white people's problems," and this contemporary term connotes a certain awareness—or is it deflection?—on the part of white people toward the privileges bestowed on them as white people. But the protection of white innocence? That continues to this day.*

White writers who still resist the inclusion of the writings of people of color or who relegate such writings to a secondary status are indeed "in the grip of a weird nostalgia, dreaming of a vanished state of security and order" in which their lives and works are primary and unchallenged in their primacy. But this belief in the primacy of white writing is slightly different from the belief that no matter the challenge or charge of racism or racial bias, the white writer or the white writing professor must always be innocent. David Foster Wallace's self-absolution against the charges of racial insensitivity is just one example of this.

In Baldwin's essay "Stranger in the Village," published in *Notes of a Native Son*, he observes: "People who shut their eyes to reality simply invite their own destruction, and anyone who insists on remaining in a state of innocence long after that innocence is dead turns himself into a monster." But throughout Wallace's interchanges with his black students, he insists on his innocence. What buoys this insistence is ignorance: Wallace does not know what he does not know. He has never questioned if the ways he regards his black students might still be shaped by an ideology and psychology of white supremacy, since Wallace thinks he, like so many white liberals, has escaped all that. Similarly, your average white writing instructor just knows he or she cannot be guilty of racial bias; that is impossible.

And yet lingering within the consciousness of white writers and whites in general resides the suspicion that they are guilty of such charges. What happens then if they allow that guilt to rise to their consciousness? How will they be able

* One sees manifestations of this not just in white conservatives but in white liberals, of which, perhaps the writers at the Associated Writing Programs conference is one the epicenters. In certain ways, I am never more aware we live in this country in segregated racial realities than I am at the AWP conference. At the recent conference in Minneapolis, I went to an off-site group reading each of the four nights. Three were readings by writers of color—Cave Canem (the African American poets conference), The Loft EQ Spoken Word Reading (mainly local Twin Cities poets of color), and VONA (a writers of color conference). In these readings, race, politics, history, and community all came up and of course all the events of the past year that have prompted the Black Lives Matter and the Million Artists movements. But on another night at AWP, I went with a black poet friend who was appearing at a reading with about twenty-five white poets and one Asian American poet. Other than my black poet friend, none of the poems engaged race, politics, history, or community; none of the poets made any reference to the killings of blacks by police in the past year. These white poets—and the Asian American poet—seemed to live in a very different country than the poets of color I'd listened to on the other three nights at AWP.

to look at or live with themselves? How will they then proceed in their interactions with people of color?

As Baldwin observes, it is not people of color who are fooled by protestations of white innocence. It is white people who are fooled—or rather, who fool themselves.

What if Wallace had said to himself, "Maybe I *am* being racially insensitive. Maybe the anger and hurt expressed by my black students at my spiel is, at least in part, justified. Where is the truth in my black students' reactions against me that I don't see? What are the limitations in my understanding of who they are and how they see me? What if my words have an effect I am not aware of? And what if my blindness to all that is my own racism?"

If Wallace had asked himself such questions, he might have opened himself to a whole new way of thinking about the world. Certainly, his exchanges with his black students would have produced very different and perhaps more positive results (he implies that many of his black students did not go back to him to learn SWE). He might have then allowed the possibility of engaging his black students on a level where they were both equal. In such an equality, his own ignorance and his own guilt would need to be seen not in a white context but a black context.

That ignorance would include the weight of negative racial stereotypes that society has placed on his black students, stereotypes that have implicitly and explicitly denigrated these students; these stereotypes and the culture in general have hoisted onto these black students a weight that they are told they must carry—while Wallace and other white liberals can feel excluded from any responsibility for the negative effects of these stereotypes. Thus Wallace would have to take responsibility for the ways he and other whites are buoyed by these negative racial stereotypes—they know they are not *that*—and can easily ignore the effect of these stereotypes on people of color. Perhaps then there would be many things about this system that his black student might teach him; perhaps there is a huge portion of our social reality—the lives of people of color—that Wallace might be relatively ignorant of.

Such a stance on Wallace's part would have required humility, true spiritual humility. But his insistence on his own innocence prevents that.

What would Wallace have had to give up to question his own innocence? Partly he would have to subdue his pride and embrace a sense of humility; he would have to entertain the fact that this black student in his office, this stranger, might teach him something about himself. In such a state of transition, as Baldwin so eloquently expressed in *The Devil Finds Work*, a person recognizes that her own identity is constantly in progress, constantly in the process of revision and reformulation:

> The question of identity is a question involving the most profound panic—a terror as primary as the nightmare of the mortal fall. This question can scarcely be said to exist among the wretched, who know, merely, that they are wretched and who bear it day by day—it is a mistake to suppose that the wretched do not know that they are wretched; nor does this question exist among the splendid, who know, merely, that they are splendid, and who flaunt it, day by day: it is a mistake to suppose that the splendid have any intention of surrendering their splendor. An identity is questioned only when it is menaced, as when the mighty begin to fall, or when the wretched begin to rise, or when the stranger enters the gates, never, thereafter, to be a stranger: the stranger's presence making *you* the stranger, less to the stranger than to yourself. Identity would seem to be the garment with which one covers the nakedness of the self; in which case, it is best that the garment be loose, a little like the robes of the desert, through which robes one's nakedness can always be felt, and sometimes, discerned. This trust in one's nakedness is all that gives one the power to change one's robes.

"This trust in one's own nakedness"—that is Baldwin's phrase for spiritual humility. We are not all-knowing creatures. If we live in a village—and most white Americans live in an all-white village—we think that everyone thinks like us; we think our truth is the only truth; we think the way we see ourselves is the only way to see ourselves. But if a stranger walks into our village, or if we—god forbid—walk into a village of strangers, we are suddenly aware that there are other ways of looking at the world; there are other ways of looking at ourselves, at who we are, at our place in the world, at the ways we identify ourselves.

At that moment, to challenge the way one thinks about oneself, to contemplate transforming one's identity is, as Baldwin observes, "a terror as primary as the nightmare of the mortal fall." And so you can either refuse that new knowledge—by labeling it secondary or minor or subjective or nonuniversal—or you can admit that your view of reality is neither completely objective nor universal. And you will then have to change your robes—meaning your robes are not as splendid as they seemed a moment earlier; meaning you are not your robes, however magnificent and natural they have seemed; meaning you are, as Shakespeare observed in Lear, "a poor bare, forked animal," a naked soul.

David Foster Wallace never let himself truly learn from the black students who walked as strangers into his white village. That is partly because he never saw what it truly meant for him to live inside his white village. Wallace never understood that he refused to accept his black students as equals, even though he thought he did. Because if Wallace had accepted his black students as equals, he would have learned something from them, and nothing in his essay indicates any such learning. For as implied in Baldwin's words above, this shift of identity depends on your seeing that the stranger possesses a knowledge you do not possess; accepting that involves acknowledging that there are ways in which that stranger is knowledgeable and you are ignorant.

Admitting one's ignorance is as formidable a task as admitting one's guilt. That is why it is so difficult for white writing instructors to teach students of color. To truly engage in such teaching is to approach a terror primary as that of the nightmare of the mortal fall.

But suppose one entered that terror and began to investigate and explore its nature and then to write about it? That is one way for white writers and white writing teachers to move beyond where we are now, to prepare themselves and their writing for the America that is here all around them, and even more so, for the America arriving very soon in our future.

On Race and Craft

Years ago, in a positive review of my first poetry book, a critic cited the long lines in a poem as influenced by the long lines of Allen Ginsburg. Titled "Song for Uncle Tom, Tonto and Mr. Moto," the poem referenced anticolonial and antiracist positions around the globe, and the long lines were actually influenced by Aimé Césaire's *Cahier d'un retour au pays natal* (*Notebook of a Return to the Native Land*). Had the reviewer been aware of Césaire and the Négritude movement in Francophone literature, the literary influence would have seemed obvious.

A couple of decades later, Junot Díaz published *The Brief Wondrous Life of Oscar Wao*, a novel chronicling the misfortunes of a Dominican family both in the Dominican Republic under Trujillo and in America. One of the novel's minor features was an extensive use of footnotes. In a couple of reviews, the influence for these footnotes was cited as David Foster Wallace. But Díaz himself has explained that the use of footnotes was influenced by Patrick Chamoiseau's *Texaco*, a novel set in Martinique at the time just before and after slavery was abolished. That Díaz would have been influenced by a fellow Caribbean writer is quite understandable, especially given Chamoiseau's focus on Creole linguistic and cultural practices and the shared themes of political repression, colonialism, and racism in both works.

Both of these misreadings of influence are relatively minor. Still they point to the ways that ignorance of the traditions of writers of color and the history of colonialism and racism can easily lead to a lack of understanding in how writers of color practice their craft and how their work should be contextualized literarily. In both instances, a white male American writer is deemed as possessing a greater influence and universal relevance than is actually the case. Just as significantly, the influence of a writer of color goes unnoticed. I would add that while Díaz and I have read Ginsberg *and* Césaire, David Foster Wallace *and* Patrick Chamoiseau, our respective critics had only read the white writer of each pair.

Several times in the past few weeks, I've encountered instances where discussions of literature and race have been placed in opposition to considerations of craft or the "true" concerns of literature. Such critiques also take the form of a supposed opposition between the political and the aesthetic. Within institutions, an increase in the number of writers and artists of color can also be met with similar grumblings or critiques: X is supposed to be an educational or an arts institution, not a political or social service organization; the purpose of X should be art and not political correctness. In these instances, it's almost as if the writing, critical theory, and presence of writers of color are viewed as infecting the house of literature and must be quarantined and excluded.

Many writers of color and white writers understand that such arguments are specious and that such oppositions are attempts to keep writers of color from challenging the aesthetics and power of white writers in the literary world. But those who believe in a greater inclusivity are sometimes at a loss as to how to argue against such opposition. In contrast, those who oppose investigating issues of race within the house of literature—whether in terms of craft, evaluation, tradition, and canon or in the workings of institutions—often seem quite certain of the basis of their positions. They state their beliefs as if pronouncing eternal verities handed down from Parnassus and the literary gods of the past. They invoke seeming universal truths as if self-evident.

But such truths are not self-evident—as sometimes becomes apparent when you ask such critics, How do you define craft? By whose authority? Do you think craft is simply about the structure of sentences or the teaching of poetic forms? Wouldn't a better and more realistic definition of craft include whatever tools a writer needs to improve her work? The modernist critic Kenneth Burke—whom even Harold Bloom approves of—defined literature as "equipment for living." Could it be that the equipment white writers think they need to conduct their lives might be different for writers or readers of color? If I am a writer of color, why do you the white writer get to determine what "equipment for living"— what literature—I need?

Similarly, if you are a white writer, by what basis of knowledge do you claim to know all the tools that a writer of color requires to improve her craft? Might it even be the case that some tools that a writer of color uses could be either outside the common knowledge of white writers or even in opposition to some of the tools offered in a white-dominated workshop—especially taking into account Audre Lourde's famous observation, "The tools of the master cannot dismantle the master's house"? And if you the white writer have never examined in any concerted way the traditions of writers of color, what they have said about their craft, how do you know that if you yourself didn't do such study, your own writing might not improve?*

If literature involves creating language not simply to describe but to understand one's reality, why wouldn't a deeper understanding of race in your present and your history expand your ability to write about that reality? If literature is a search for the truth, how is it that exposure to the ways that America has lied about the realities of people of color—and thus of white people too—would harm that search? Do you understand that the same arguments about craft and technique were used to delegitimize other cultural productions by black Americans such as blues, jazz, and rock and roll (it's not music; it takes no skill, technique, or learning; it's not aesthetically valid; it's just noise)? If the neglect of writers of color in the past and the present involves, at least in part, racial bias, as it has in other cultural exclusions, how can one confront that bias without a reference to race?

Do you understand that in almost any political situation, the status quo is invariably defined as nonpolitical and neutral while any threat to the status quo is deemed political and partisan? That such a difference is not a real difference but one of semantics? Do you understand that the status quo in any cultural field has a political effect, just as a change in the literary status quo will also have a political effect?

By whose authority do you claim your definition of the aesthetic as excluding race or the political to be universal? What arguments can you make to support that universality? Does such universality include all writers and artists or only some? Have you, consciously or unconsciously, made an a priori assumption that most of the writings and criticism of writers of color aren't worthy of study? And if the vast majority of the writers and artists you cite are white, how can you prove that your views are not based on the racial segregation of your reading and learning? How can you prove that your criteria do not originate in a

* In the workshop "Writing on Race" that I cotaught in the Stonecoast MFA program, we found that such study and investigation not only improved the work of writers of color but also of the white writers. The white writers became more fearless, more willing to explore difficult or painful issues, expanded their understanding of their lives and history, discovered gaps in the ways they understood themselves and their identity, their families, as well as society and history in general. The realities and narratives they explored in their work became more complex, more expansive, more inclusive, and more ambitious. They also became more literate and better read, and discovered not just one or two new works, but sometimes a whole tradition of new literary works and thought.

history of racist practices that have been used to exclude people of color not just from literature but from all areas of society, particularly positions of authority and power?

Finally, have you considered the principle that diversity—not monoculturalism—of thought, of people, of cultural influence, increases creativity? That a wider range of reading, of literary practices, will open up possibilities and new insights, much more so than a segregated white-dominated literary bubble?

To those writers of color confronted with white critics who oppose the issues of race as part of craft, I offer these questions as a way of starting—or perhaps ending—the conversation. Note that many of my questions begin with asking for a definition of terms. Once the definitions of the opposition are established, you can then question by whose authority those definitions are given universal application and meaning. Invariably, the opposition has not proven this universality—since, in actuality, it does not exist—but simply asserted it. The opposition has never truly considered that other definitions and terms and tools are possible and that people of color do not have to accept the universality of white definitions and terms that form the bases of white racial arguments. Of course, invariably, the refusal of people of color to accept this presumed universality infuriates their opposition, not simply because they have refused the (il)logic of their opponents but because they have refused the opposition's power over them.

But to answer such critiques completely, I would need a whole book at least. Or I could begin with a reading list with works many conservative literary folk may not have read: Toni Morrison's *Playing in the Dark*, Edward Said's *Orientalism* and *Culture and Imperialism*, James Baldwin's *The Price of the Ticket*, Henry Louis Gates Jr.'s *Signifying Monkey*, David Palumbo-Liu's *The Deliverance of Others*, Kevin Young's *The Grey Album*, Bertolt Brecht's writings on theater, the criticism of John Berger, Chinua Achebe's *Hopes and Impediments*, Martin Espada's *Zapata's Disciple*, or almost any book by a poet of color in the University of Michigan's Poets on Poetry series. Also relevant would be W. E. B. Du Bois's *The Souls of Black Folk*, Frantz Fanon's *Black Skin, White Masks*, Paulo Freire's *Pedagogy of the Oppressed*, Marxist criticism, feminist criticism, GBLT criticism, scholars like Claude Steel on stereotype consciousness and stereotype threat. . . . This list could go on and on.

I realize many of the works on my list are works of literary, cultural, and political theory, though of course the essays of Baldwin or Berger have become now as standard literary texts as the essays of Matthew Arnold or Emerson. Yet such seemingly nonliterary works certainly have helped form my own sense of what literature is, how it functions in the world, and how it is evaluated, and it has influenced how I approach my own writing; this, I would argue, is also true for many other writers of color.

We turn to literature to find expressions of our reality and our consciousness that are more complex and accurate, that expand our understanding of ourselves and our world. In this way, literature involves a struggle against the cliché, the stereotypical, against untruth and facile assumptions. Such a struggle often possesses political implications; as John Berger puts it in an essay in *Portraits*: "Reality, however one interprets it, lies beyond a screen of clichés. Every culture produces such a screen, partly to facilitate its own practices (to establish habits) and partly to consolidate its own power. Reality is inimical to those with power."

To extrapolate from a Richard Wright remark, black America and white America are engaged in an argument over the description of reality. And of course, literature is an essential element in those conflicting descriptions. To think that once that argument enters the realm of literature, we are not engaged in a conflict over race is the sort of denial on which whiteness, as it is traditionally practiced in the United States, is built. Whiteness has traditionally been regarded as the neutral status quo. Thus when writers of color and indigenous writers describe their lives and tell their stories, they are exposing a reality that a society of white supremacy has always worked consciously and unconsciously to deny. There is a significant gap in quality between *Gone with the Wind* and *Beloved*, and that gap involves differences in language and style and in the depth and complexity of characters, but that difference of quality cannot be severed from Morrison's exposure of realities Mitchell denies, particularly in regard to slavery. Such a comparison is an illustration of a more useful principle or definition of craft: *The pursuit of reality and truth is always part of the practice of craft.*

What many people also don't quite realize is that power can establish itself not simply through repression but also through pleasure. As Michel Foucault explains: "What makes power hold good, what makes it accepted, is simply the fact that it doesn't only weigh on us as a force that says no, but that it traverses and produces things, it induces pleasure, forms knowledge, produces discourse. It needs to be considered as a productive network which runs through the whole social body, much more than as a negative instance whose function is repression." Thus literature can function as a pleasure that reinforces the existing structures of power and perceptions of our reality, or it can function as a pleasure that comes from exposing those structures by expanding our sense of and understanding of our reality.*

I would argue that many of those who object to including the issues of race in discussions of literature are attempting to defend the existing structures of power and existing perceptions of reality, rather than expanding and critiquing them. When a young white male poet tells a female poet of color in a workshop, "I'm just not into identity poems," he seems to be remarking on the quality of her poem. But what he's really saying is that he gets no pleasure from *any* poems about racial or ethnic identity, no matter their quality. He is also saying, I don't want to know who you are or what your reality is; moreover, contemplating that is unpleasant for me—namely, it doesn't give me pleasure. But why would this be so? For one thing, poems concerning racial identity point to the limits of poems that this young man does receive pleasure from; in certain ways, this spoiling of his pleasure is what fuels the emotion behind his dismissive remarks: "I am comfortable being ignorant, and being forced to confront my ignorance not only causes me pain, it takes away from the pleasures in what I enjoy, and in ways I can't articulate, this enrages me."

But of course, the opposite is true for the female author of the poem about her racial identity. She finds pleasure in such poems and aesthetic worth—of course depending on their quality—and this pleasure is tied to her struggle to articulate who she is in the face of a culture of white supremacy. It is a pleasure that derives from discovering a truth denied. Obviously, the young white male poet could also receive this pleasure, but to do so, he would have to begin undergoing a transformation and interrogation of his own identity.

While this debate seems to take place in the realm of aesthetics, this opposition of pleasures is part of the struggle over race that is taking place everywhere in society, and it is both an aesthetic and a political question.

Yes, both of the above quotations come from Marxist theorists. So let me quote here from that old literary conservative T. S. Eliot:

> What happens when a new work of art is created is something that happens
> simultaneously to all the works of art which preceded it. The existing monu-
> ments form an ideal order among themselves, which is modified by the intro-
> duction of the new (the really new) work of art among them. The existing

---

*When asked if literature and writers have a political effect, Marlon James has observed: Just ask dictators. They know that writers and artists have a political effect; that's why they lock them up.

order is complete before the new work arrives; for order to persist after the supervention of novelty, the *whole* existing order must be, if ever so slightly, altered; and so the relations, proportions, values of each work of art toward the whole are readjusted; and this is conformity between the old and the new. Whoever has approved this idea of order, of the form of European, of English literature will not find it preposterous that the past should be altered by the present as much as the present is directed by the past. And the poet who is aware of this will be aware of great difficulties and responsibilities.

Eliot argues that no poet or work of art stands alone. Poets must be aware of the works that have come before them; an individual poem takes its meaning within the context or "order" of the works of the past. In my experience, writers of color never argue that they don't have to know white literature of the past, whereas white writers frequently argue that the literature of people of color is inferior or extraneous or nonessential.

At the same time, Eliot is also arguing here that the new work alters our perception of the tradition and past works; the new work forces us to view the tradition and previous works within a new order, a new context. In this process, our evaluation of older works is altered, and our understanding of previous works transformed. The tradition is neither static nor some Platonic ideal; it is always evolving, and we evolve with it.

Years ago, I taught a course titled Third World Postcolonial Literature in English. At the time, I knew little of such work, and the field of postcolonial studies was still developing. As preparation for the course, I read Edward Said's *Culture and Imperialism*; there he argues that certain canonical works cannot adequately be contextualized or critiqued without an understanding of the process and history of colonialism. Said applied these principles in analyzing canonical works, such as Yeats's poems (which Said placed within a context of anticolonialist efforts to establish the culture and history of the colonized), Austen's *Mansfield Park* (where the whole supporting infrastructure of Mansfield Park, based on colonialism and slavery, is absented from the lives and consciousness of the novel and its characters), and Conrad's *Heart of Darkness* (whose roots in colonialism and whose racism should be entirely obvious to us now).

As I designed the course, it was clear to me that Chinua Achebe's *Things Fall Apart* should be juxtaposed with Conrad's novel, and I also assigned Achebe's essay on Conrad. There Achebe spoke of first reading Conrad's novel. Having been educated in the British colonial educational system, Achebe, like a "good native," identified with the European colonizer narrator Marlowe as he regarded the unintelligible African "savages" on the shore of the river. It was only later that Achebe thought: Those "savages" were my ancestors, could have been my grandparents or great-grandparents. Achebe then asked, Do I believe they were unintelligible savages? This train of thought led him to write his seminal novel, which explores of the life of an Ibo man just before and just after the first European colonists arrived. Achebe's essay and his novel, explicitly and implicitly, critique the racism in the vision of Conrad's novel, and in Achebe's eyes, Conrad's racism must lessen our estimation of the novel (though I would also argue that Conrad's conception of what the world was and what realities the novel could contain was far larger than that of any of his English contemporaries).

Thus the new work can transform our evaluation of the past and the tradition. Just as Eliot's poetry and criticism changed our evaluation of the Victorian poets—lowering them—and metaphysical poets—raising them—so Achebe's novel and essay alter our evaluation and understanding of Conrad's *Heart of Darkness*. Similarly, the reading list for my postcolonial literature course included Jamaica Kincaid, Derek Walcott, V. S. Naipaul, Ama Ata Aidoo, Bessie Head, Michelle Cliff, J. M. Coetzee, Nadine Gordimer, and Salman Rushdie,* and it altered my sense of the tradition and its aesthetic values. By the end of the course, I realized that if I added Leslie Marmon Silko or Toni Morrison to this list, they would fit within the themes and concerns of the authors in my course. But if I added say Jay McInerney or John Updike or Anne Beattie, they would seem as if they came from another world. I was forced then to ask: When we talk of universal standards, whose universe are we talking about?

In the last fifty years, think of the writers of color who have entered the canon: Ralph Ellison, James Baldwin, Toni Morrison, Alice Walker, M. Scott Momaday, Leslie Marmon Silko, Jonathan Edgar Wideman, Lucille Clifton, Amiri Baraka, Yusef Komunyaka, Rita Dove, Joy Harjo, Edwidge Danticat, Junot Díaz, Chimamanda Ngozu Adichie, Chinua Achebe, Gabriel García Marquéz, Maxine Hong Kingston, David Henry Hwang, Sandra Cisneros, Marlon James . . . the list could go on and on. And with each addition, the tradition changes. For example, with the addition of Morrison and other black writers in the second half of the twentieth century, Zora Neale Hurston entered the canon retroactively and increased in significance. At the same time, through the inclusion of Morrison's novels and criticism, our understanding and perception of Cather, Twain, and Hemingway have been altered. Her *Playing in the Dark* demonstrates how these

---

* Neither Coetzee nor Gordimer excludes the issues of race from their work or from their critical thinking about literature. Obviously, they both understand that the history of colonialism and of their country involves a consideration of race.

authors failed to critique and go beyond received categories of white and black. This lack in turn resulted in artistic deficiencies in the way these canonical white authors portrayed both their white and black characters—in other words, clinging to a white definition of social reality was a direct cause of *a failure in craft.*

What all this means is that those who write without an awareness of how present-day writers of color are altering our perception of past literature have stuck their heads in the sand. They are calling for a defense not of learning but of ignorance.

But what does all this have to do with craft?

Again, let me resort to T. S. Eliot and two quotations, the first from his essay on the metaphysical poets:

> When a poet's mind is perfectly equipped for its work, it is constantly amalgamating disparate experience; the ordinary man's experience is chaotic, irregular, fragmentary. The latter falls in love, or reads Spinoza, and these two experiences have nothing to do with each other, or with the noise of the typewriter or the smell of cooking; in the mind of the poet these experiences are always forming new wholes.

The second quotation is from his essay on Marvell:

> We can say that wit is not erudition; it is sometimes stifled by erudition, as in much of Milton. It is not cynicism, though it has a kind of toughness which may be confused with cynicism by the tender-minded. It is confused with erudition because it belongs to an educated mind, rich in generations of experience; and it is confused with cynicism because it implies a constant inspection and criticism of experience. It involves, probably, a recognition, implicit in the expression of every experience, of other kinds of experience which are possible.

Let's first focus on the phrase "disparate experience" in the first quotation. Throughout Western history, the definition of what constitutes legitimate literary experience and what constitutes reality has traditionally been the provenance of white people in general and white writers in particular. As Walter Benjamin observed, history is the tale of the victors. But what happens when the less powerful, the defeated, begin to speak? Throughout Western history, people of color and indigenous people have challenged white definitions and descriptions of experience and reality. And as history has progressed, more and more people of color have asserted their own sense of reality and history. At the same time, people of color have always had to acknowledge and know the experiences of whites and the ways they define both their reality and the reality of whites. People of color could not have survived without doing so.

This is what Du Bois meant when he spoke of the Negro's double consciousness: Blacks have had to be aware of how the white master and white man thought of and defined both whites and blacks; yet blacks were also aware that the ways they thought of and defined themselves were different from white consciousness. Thus black consciousness was always more complex, not less, than white consciousness, since white consciousness was constructed in part on the premise that blacks were inferior and lacked a complex consciousness that required consideration. Black consciousness therefore always contained a wider and more disparate set of experiences, or at least a set of experiences that white consciousness would not even acknowledge existed. If the poet is supposed to be "amalgamating disparate experience," then, whose consciousness contains more disparate experience?

If, as Eliot maintains, an essential quality of the poet is wit, and wit involves a recognition that "other kinds of experience . . . are possible," what does this mean for white writers who write only from and of white experiences? Recently, at the GrubStreet 2017 Muse Conference, a reader for the O'Henry Prize stories remarked wearily of a preponderance of stories set in a kitchen with a white husband and white wife having an argument, usually in New York or some East Coast city. Such a preponderance bespeaks a lack of both worldliness and imagination.

In contrast, any college-educated person of color in this country understands that he must know how whites think and how the white world operates and how whites experience the world and their history. People of color are acutely aware that white people think differently and experience the world differently than they do. People of color know they will not be considered literate if they do not know white culture and specifically white literature. But they also know that they must steep themselves in the literature of their own traditions of color.

Beyond this, since many people of color have come to white-dominated countries from across the globe, they are particularly conscious of other cultures and traditions, other histories, and such an awareness informs their writing and the ways they evaluate and contextualize their own experiences and our writings. They understand that one cannot make sense of American history—and thus its literature—or world history—and thus its literature—without understanding how race affected and determined that history. Similarly, when I taught the Third World Postcolonial Literature in English course, I discovered that the conjunction of literature and politics and of literature and race was a central theme of almost all the global authors we studied, just as it is for writers of color and indigenous writers in America.

In this way, the calls for craft as excluding or being in opposition to any consideration of race clearly contradict Eliot's call for wit and for "amalgamating disparate experience." As I've said, such opposition is a defense against erudition and learning; it is a defense against encountering lives different than one's own; it is a defense of ignorance. Moreover, it is enforced not by any logic of how literature is written or what the history of the world has been or the principles of creativity. Instead it is simply enforced by an assertion of power and a definition of reality as expressed by whiteness. In that way, it excludes not just the writings of people of color and indigenous people, but their thinking, their experiences, and the ways they express and understand their lives. If that is not white supremacy, then the term has no meaning—which, for some people, seems to be the case.

II ༂

Story in Fiction

Storytellers

MYTHS AND THE TIMELESS

As Joseph Campbell has demonstrated, myths—and thus stories—are integral to all human cultures. We are storytelling creatures. We tell stories to help us make sense of our lives, to understand the human condition, our fallibility, our mortality, the motives and desires of our existence. When one analyzes these myths, as Campbell did in his *The Hero of a Thousand Faces*, one finds certain universal structural similarities, certain basic principles. These structures and principles have been used by human beings over and over throughout history. They've served our ancestors, and they will serve us, if we let them, if we have the patience and fortitude to learn our craft.

In his beautiful book-length essay *And Our Faces, My Heart, Brief as Photos*, John Berger pictures the storyteller as residing in a timeless realm and viewing the actions of her characters, who live the story in the realm of the temporal. Characters in stories cannot see their futures, cannot know their fate. They can only act and through those actions determine their fate:

> What separates us from the characters about whom we write is not knowledge, either objective or subjective, but their experience of time in the story we are telling. This separation allows us, the storytellers, the power of knowing the whole. Yet, equally, this separation renders us powerless: we cannot control our characters, after the narration has begun. We are obliged to follow them, and this following is through and across the time, which they are living and which we oversee.
>
> The time, and therefore the story, belongs to them. Yet the meaning of the story, what makes it worthy of being told, is what we can see and what inspires us because we are beyond its time.

The storyteller knows what has occurred and what the outcome of the story will be. That is why the storyteller can see what has happened as a narrative with a narrative structure: a beginning, a middle, and an end. The storyteller apprehends or discovers this structure and understands it in a way the characters in the story cannot. According to Berger, the storyteller views the characters' temporal lives through the lens of the timeless, and in the grinding of that lens, we function as Death's secretary. In that office, we investigate mortality from the realm of the immortal.

This is true even when the story is autobiographical: In that case, the author is looking at herself as a character in the past and is regarding that character from the future, as one who knows what has happened and the fate of the character (at least within the time frame of an earlier period of the author's life). We human beings live as fallible mortals who lack omniscience, who do not know what will happen next or where our actions are leading us. But once we know where a series of actions have led, we can assess which of those actions were crucial, which involved a telling decision, which revealed something about our personal character and helped determine our fate. (As I often tell my students, I can tell the tale of any failed relationship using a three-act structure that resembles Campbell's mythic structures.)

Thus story is not simply a recording of events. If a camera followed us each moment of our lives, the results would not be a film with a story. A documentary filmmaker creates a story through cuts, through focusing on certain moments or events. Only through the filmmaker's deciding what to leave in and what to leave out can a story emerge, can a structure be constructed or revealed.

In his book on narrative nonfiction, *Writing for Story*, Jon Franklin observes that when most news reporters come upon a triumph or tragedy, they think that is the story—a team wins a championship, a candidate wins an election, someone shoots and kills someone. But that is not the story, Franklin argues. That is only the end of the story. The rest of the story must be discovered through further investigation; the writer must discover the events—or more precisely, the actions—that led the character or protagonist to his particular ending. In other words, the writer must discover or uncover the story's beginning, middle, and end.

Long ago, at the end of their day, our ancestors sat around a fire and told stories. Sometimes those stories were of events they or others in their tribe had experienced. Sometimes those stories were of gods and mythical creatures. Sometimes they were about their ancestors. The stories entertained those who sat around the fire, but they did more than that. They helped the members of the tribe make sense of their world, with its terrors and enemies, with its death and destruction, with the mysteries of time and their mortal lives. The best of these stories possessed a beginning, a middle, and an end, and these were the stories that have been handed down to us. They employ the structures through which the myths of the world achieved their immortality.

To picture ourselves as part of this line of storytellers is both comforting and humbling. We are taking up an ancient craft. In doing so, it is best we learn what the ancients have to teach us.

Discovering Story

I

E. L. Doctorow has likened the process of writing a novel to driving at night on a winding road. Your headlights only illuminate the small stretch of the road ahead; that's as far ahead as you can see. You cannot view all the way to your destination. But if you just keep on going, you eventually get to the end.

Unlike Doctorow, some novelists, like John Irving, like to know the ending from the start. What Irving doesn't know is how his characters reach the ending.

Despite these differences, both Doctorow and Irving point to the exploratory nature of narrative writing and our limited knowledge as we proceed through that process. Certainly, when writers begin a narrative, whether a short story or a novel, they generally don't know a great deal about how the story is going to be structured. They're writing to discover what the story is about. That process can involve any number of misdirections and wrong turnings, driving into cul-de-sacs and backing up and reversing.

At certain points, it is useful and necessary for writers to step away from the process and look at what they've written. In working with students, who are most often writing short stories, I've found that they generally don't know what questions to ask about their material. They don't know the principles of story, so they can't apply those principles to their work.

Sometimes a simple basic question can help the student discover what the story is about: "What does the protagonist want?" or "What is the goal of the protagonist?" If the student doesn't have an answer to this question, trying to answer it can help her revise and refocus the story.

At other times, it helps to look at the story's ending and see what it reveals:

Does it involve a desire or goal of the protagonist? Does the protagonist fulfill that desire or goal or does she fail? Are the actions which led to that end result revealed in the story?

Sometimes the rest of the story is not connected to the ending, and thus either the ending or the rest of the story needs to be rewritten. Sometimes rather than the designated or nominal protagonist, another character may have a greater hand in determining the final event; perhaps then the story may be more about that character, who must then be regarded as the true protagonist.

In other cases, the goal itself may need to be evaluated: Does it connect with the themes of the story? Does it reflect tensions within the protagonist, or does reaching it signify an important shift or change within the protagonist? Is it concrete enough, rather than some vague abstraction—that is, is it potentially achievable through concrete actions? If not, then perhaps a new goal needs to be created.

II

When I confer with a beginning student over a story with structural problems, I start by asking the student what the story is about. Very often the student will provide an answer that centers on the subject or themes of the story—a failed relationship or the struggles between a parent and a child; jealousy, identity, the struggles of immigrant life; a trip to Jamaica or the death of a grandmother. Beginning writers think that their attentions should be focused here, especially if the theme involves an issue or a psychological area they are drawn to or passionate about.

But to look at the subject or theme of the story is to take too general a viewpoint. The telling of the story requires a closer, more specific focus. The storyteller needs to find a goal for the protagonist, something the protagonist desires to obtain or accomplish.

Especially with short stories, almost invariably the more concrete and tangible that goal is the better. Sometimes that concrete and tangible goal can even be surprisingly small, modest, even trivial.

If writers focus on something large and abstract, like love or reconciling with the past, that larger element may be in the material or in the experiences they're basing the story on, but these are merely themes; as such, they are much too vague. If the protagonist is after love, what is that character to do? When the character confronts this question at this level of abstraction, there's no clear action he can take. And if there's no clear action for the protagonist to take, there's no story. If the character is trying to woo a specific person, that's a little more concrete, but the question remains, how is the protagonist going to win the heart of this person? But if the protagonist is trying to become an expert at salsa to win the heart of Felicia, the Cuban woman he's met at the local salsa club, that's concrete. That is something I can write a story about.

Beginning short-story writers often fail to see that even the smallest of goals may be quite revealing. Indeed, choosing a goal that is quite simple or small and yet concrete may be far more useful than some seemingly grander—and sometimes melodramatic or abstract—goal. By concrete here, I mean something that the protagonist can take definite actions toward trying to achieve.

It's difficult to describe the protagonist fighting against time or mortality, but a writer can describe the character trying to cook a soufflé or putting up siding in an effort to remodel her house or taking her new girlfriend's five-year-old to Chucky Cheese or trying to get a creditor to give her more time to pay her debts. In this way, the protagonist's goal can involve something that seems at first quite mundane. Yet trying to fix up a house or an old car or traveling to some destination may easily carry great psychological or thematic significance.

Journeys, by their very nature, possess a very definite beginning, middle, and end and thus can readily be structured as stories. One should note though that the beginning is not so much the actual physical beginning as it is the process immediately leading up to the decision to take the journey. At the same time, any journey carries within it possibilities for metaphoric resonance and the ability to signify something larger.

In James Joyce's short story "Araby," the young narrator develops a crush on a friend's older sister. After talking with her about a bazaar that is coming to town, he promises to bring her a gift from the bazaar. This becomes, in a way, his knightly quest, one for which he must journey, both in time and distance, toward his goal. In his imagination, the older girl, the bazaar, and his quest all take on a romantic sheen: "Her image accompanied me in places the most hostile to romance."

Eventually the boy's waiting and his difficulties in getting to the bazaar start to take a toll on him (his uncle, from whom he must get permission, comes home late and drunk). When the boy finally reaches the bazaar, his failure to find a suitable gift there reveals to him something disturbing and critical about his own limitations and desires as well as the limitations of the world around him. The story's ending possesses a striking depth, yet its beginnings are quite mundane and rooted in the ordinary activities of childhood.

Taking in the gaudiness and cheapness of the bazaar and the behavior of the young man and woman flirting, the boy suddenly apprehends the falseness of his gauzy romantic picture of the world and thus himself. Even at such a young age, he comprehends the nature of his own vanity, the false pride on which he has based his ego. And all this comes from a story with a simple goal, to go to the bazaar to find a gift for his "love":

> I could not find any sixpenny entrance and, fearing that the bazaar would be closed, I passed in quickly through a turnstile, handing a shilling to a weary-looking man. I found myself in a big hall girded at half its height by a gallery. Nearly all the stalls were closed and the greater part of the hall was in darkness. I recognized a silence like that which pervades a church after a service. I walked into the centre of the bazaar timidly. A few people were gathered about the stalls which were still open. Before a curtain, over which the words *Café Chantant* were written in coloured lamps, two men were counting money on a salver. I listened to the fall of the coins.
>
> Remembering with difficulty why I had come, I went over to one of the stalls and examined porcelain vases and flowered tea-sets. At the door of the stall a young lady was talking and laughing with two young gentlemen. I remarked their English accents and listened vaguely to their conversation.
>
> "O, I never said such a thing!"
>
> "O, but you did!"
>
> "O, but I didn't!"
>
> "Didn't she say that?"
>
> "Yes. I heard her."
>
> "O, there's a . . . fib!"
>
> Observing me, the young lady came over and asked me did I wish to buy anything. The tone of her voice was not encouraging; she seemed to have spoken to me out of a sense of duty. I looked humbly at the great jars that stood like eastern guards at either side of the dark entrance to the stall and murmured:
>
> "No, thank you."
>
> The young lady changed the position of one of the vases and went back to the two young men. They began to talk of the same subject. Once or twice the young lady glanced at me over her shoulder.

I lingered before her stall, though I knew my stay was useless, to make my interest in her wares seem the more real. Then I turned away slowly and walked down the middle of the bazaar. I allowed the two pennies to fall against the sixpence in my pocket. I heard a voice call from one end of the gallery that the light was out. The upper part of the hall was now completely dark.

Gazing up into the darkness I saw myself as a creature driven and derided by vanity; and my eyes burned with anguish and anger.

III

What do I mean when I say that story is a metaphor? A metaphor has a subject, the tenor, and something the subject is compared to, the vehicle. In a way, we can consider the goal and the actions the protagonist takes as the vehicle of a metaphor. The theme or character of the protagonist is the tenor.

In our art, we construct or create a vehicle because that vehicle will allow a more complex rendering or expression of the tenor than any direct discussion or description of the tenor. Part of the reason for this, I believe, is that as the conscious mind tries to confront the problem of creating a vehicle—that is, as the conscious mind pays attention to the technical problem of constructing a story—it is the unconscious mind that finally comes up with the solution. As I repeat often to my students, *the unconscious mind is always more creative and complex than the conscious mind.* Beginning students tend to privilege their conscious intentions rather than what their writing has unconsciously revealed.

Stories where there is no concrete and tangible goal often read like a series of random events that have no clear relationship to one another and lack a sense of progression. Moreover, little is revealed about the protagonist because the protagonist has not had to take actions and struggle toward a goal.

How do the protagonist's actions in the story reveal character?

The Manicheans believed that if the world were not evil, each choice would not constitute a loss. With each action the protagonist takes, he or she also makes a choice not to take other actions. Through these choices, the protagonist creates his or her own fate.

In order for the protagonist to struggle to achieve a goal—and there should always be a struggle—the protagonist must encounter obstacles toward that goal.

These obstacles can be seen in two ways, externally and internally.

In pursuit of his goal, the protagonist can encounter outsider forces or persons who block or thwart his pursuit of the goal. The protagonist then takes actions to overcome these obstacles.

Often, though, the prime block between the protagonist and her goal is internal. That is, the protagonist is presented with two mutually irreconcilable desires: If she acts one way, she will achieve desire A; if she acts in another way, she will achieve desire B. Though she desires both A and B, it appears that she cannot take an action that will allow her to obtain both A and B.

Thus the protagonist is forced to decide whether she should take an action which will lead her closer to one thing she wants, but which will take her farther away or even eliminate her chances of achieving something else she wants. Invariably, when the protagonist sets out in pursuit of A, she does not envision that in pursuing it, she will risk losing B.

Devising irreconcilable choices or desires in pursuit of a goal is integral to the process of creating a story. If the protagonist's choices are not irreconcilable, the protagonist's decisions to act one way instead of another will lack tension. Just as importantly, nothing will be revealed about the protagonist: how a protagonist reacts and chooses to act when presented with irreconcilable desires reveals who that protagonist is.

If in the story I have suggested above, my protagonist's desire to learn salsa is accomplished easily and without conflict, there will be no story. If the instructor of the salsa class is insufferable; if the protagonist's friends make fun of him for taking up salsa; if the class conflicts with a previous commitment or something else the protagonist wants to or must do; if the class is made up only of gay men and the protagonist is homophobic; if there is another woman there he is attracted to; if the class is far away and difficult to get to or otherwise too costly; if the protagonist's mother wants to join the class too; if the protagonist must suddenly take care of his eight-year-old son—all of these bring up potential irreconcilable conflicts.

Part of the writer's job then is like that of Poseidon in relationship to Odysseus: To think of any number of ways of foiling the protagonist's pursuit of his goal. Part of the skill of the storyteller involves how inventive the writer can be in this foiling and how these blocks between the protagonist and the goal reveal the character of the protagonist.

One reason for this revelation of character involves the battle within the protagonist between delusion/illusion and reality, between a lie and the truth.

When people are presented with irreconcilable conflicts or desires, they will often lie to themselves as well as to others about the true nature of these conflicts. My job is important to me; my child is important to me. But when I am presented with an irreconcilable conflict between my job and my child, what will I choose? How will I rationalize a choice of one over the other? How will I interpret reality so as to diminish the irreconcilable aspects of my choice ("that meeting is not so important" or "the school play is not so important")? How can I try to control or negate other people's reactions to relieve my unease about my choice ("my boss won't notice" or "my son won't notice"; "I will make it up to my boss" or "I will make it up to my son")? How will I present my motives to myself and others—for instance, "By choosing my job I'm really choosing my family since my job provides for my family"—and leave out other motives—"I like the prestige my job provides me and I like what the money allows me to buy"?

Invariably, when we are faced with irreconcilable choices, we human beings try to fudge: We lie to ourselves and declare that these choices are not irreconcilable. "I can choose A and I will not lose B." In this way, we deny reality.

But if the story is constructed well, reality will inevitably confront and destroy or expose the protagonist's lies to himself and to others. In this way, the story will reveal the truth both about the protagonist and the world.

Now there are times when a protagonist discovers an action which will reconcile a seemingly irreconcilable conflict. This often happens, as they say, in the movies. But in literature which examines with a cold eye the nature of our existence, which reveals the realities we would deny, which acknowledges how limited and frail our powers actually are, such reconciliations are few and far between.

We, as human beings, come to desire things of the world around us. We make plans and take actions so that we will obtain our desires. We expect and intend our actions to achieve our ends. We wish and often believe our powers and control over the world are godlike.

But alas, we are not gods, and there is always a gap between our expectations and the reality that ensues; there is always a gap between the intent of our actions and the results.

In several of the following essays, I will explore how the principles I've just outlined work with different authors and within specific pieces of fiction.

One final note: The narrative structures and techniques I introduce in this book are tools; to instruct readers on how to use these tools I focus on works where it's easier to explore how they are being used. Once a writer grasps these techniques and structures, the writer can use them in more complicated ways or even forgo some of them. Certainly, as the writer gains in skill, the use of these tools will become more unconscious and simply part of the way that writer thinks and works. I am also aware that part of my explanation of these structures and techniques takes a more linear form than narratives from certain cultures; I use this more linear approach because it's easier for pedagogical purposes and not because linear structures are necessarily preferable or superior to more nonlinear structures.

Junot Díaz's "Ysrael"

VOICE AND STORY

For me, as for many others, the publication of Junot Díaz's book of short stories *Drown* marked the debut of a major literary talent. In the time since, I have often referred to his work and the work of Edwidge Danticat as two prime examples of a new wave of American writers who are exploring the ways recent immigrant communities are contributing to a new vision of American society and culture. Of course, it is much more than his subject matter that makes Díaz's works so singular and significant.

One critic has praised Díaz by stating that he possesses "the dispassionate eye of a journalist and the tongue of a poet." Certainly, the poetry of Díaz's voice is apparent from the very first pages of *Drown* in the story "Ysrael":

> Rafa and I stayed with our *tios*, in a small wooden house just outside Ocoa; rosebushes blazed around the yard like compass points and the mango trees spread out deep blankets of shade where we could rest and play dominoes, but the campo was nothing like our barrio in Santo Domingo. In the campo there was nothing to do, no one to see. You didn't get television or electricity and Rafa, who was older and expected more, woke up every morning pissy and dissatisfied. He stood out on the patio in his shorts and looked out over the mountains, at the mists that gathered like water, at the brucal trees that blazed like fires on the mountain. This, he said, is shit.
>
> Worse than shit, I said.
>
> Yeah, he said, and when I get home, I'm going to go crazy—*chinga* all my girls and then *chinga* everyone else's. I won't stop dancing either. I'm going to be like those guys in the record books who dance four or five days straight.

Some aspects of the poetry here are readily apparent—the comparison to compass points possesses an almost metaphysical wit—but perhaps less noticeable is the skillful way Díaz contrasts the beauty of the campo with its everyday poverty, a poverty that is more than simply economic but is also cultural and imaginative. The juxtaposition of Rafa in his shorts with the mist on the mountains and the blazing brucal trees anchors both sets of images in a subtle yet revealing fashion. But there is also the striking mix of vocabularies and levels of diction, as in the phrase "pissy and dissatisfied" or the deflation that takes place at the end of the first paragraph. Although the two boys speak in Spanish, Díaz conveys a sense of the colloquial through finding equivalents in American English and through his use of Spanish; he shifts between these registers like a master musician. (Throughout *Drown*, Spanish words are situated such that the reader often can infer their meaning even if she does not know Spanish.)

Eliot stated that "the poet is constantly amalgamating disparate experience," and this is certainly the case in Díaz's work. This disparate experience involves what these two boys are immediately going through—their boredom with the campo, their awareness of a natural beauty there that seems to them of no use— and beyond that, the sense of displacement they feel in their summer exile from their mother and the Santo Domingo barrio. But there is another level of experience working here too, for the language of the passage implies that this story is being told by someone who has left the Dominican Republic and who has not only learned English but has acquired a fluency in the American urban demotic. The usual dialectic that occurs between the older narrator and the younger self is complicated then by a dialectic that involves a layering of the languages and the cultures the speaker has inhabited.

Here we can begin to understand why Díaz's work and the experience it explores are so essential to our understanding of the present historical moment. We live in an increasingly global culture, one in which the United States has experienced a more diverse immigrant population, not just because of increased migration from Latin America but also as a result of 1965 Hart-Celler Act. Because of these changes, it's become apparent that Mikhail Bakhtin's analysis of the role of fiction in a global age has become increasingly relevant and accurate: Bakhtin argued that we are now engaged in a world where "the period of national languages, coexisting but closed and deaf to each other, comes to end."

One value of Junot Díaz's work is that it fully engages with Bakhtin's "new cultural and creative consciousness" of this "actively polyglot world." This is the world in which he has grown up; this world has shaped who he is.

The narrative structure of "Ysrael" is quite straightforward and starts with a sentence at the end of the first paragraph: "I was nine that summer, but my brother was twelve, and he [the narrator's older brother, Rafa] was the one who wanted to see Ysrael, who looked towards Barbacoa and said, We should pay that kid a visit." Later, it's revealed that Ysrael is a boy whose face was attacked by a pig when he was an infant; his face is now hidden by a cloth he wears over his head.

The story then possesses the structure of a journey; the journey's goal is simple and concrete—to see what this boy's face looks like beneath his mask.

Yunior, the younger brother and narrator, is excited about the prospect of being able to accompany Rafa on this trip. In the ensuing section after this first paragraph, Yunior delineates one main block in his pursuit of this goal: the older brother's disdain of the younger brother and his reluctance to bring the younger brother with him on any venture. When Rafa sets off to see one of his girls, the narrator tells us, "I always followed Rafa, trying to convince him to let me tag along. Go home, he'd say. I'll be back in a few hours. . . . If I kept on he'd punch me in the shoulder and walk on." Yunior knows he must be on his best behavior if he is to be able to accompany Rafa on the trip to see Ysrael.

But when they start on their trip the next morning, Yunior runs into the first of his irreconcilable conflicts. After the boys deposit some bottles at the local comaldo to obtain money to pay for their trip, Yunior wants to use some of the money to get something to eat. But Rafa insists that they need to keep the money for their trip and perhaps to get something to drink later. Thus Yunior faces a dilemma: he wants to go on the trip, but he also wants something to eat; if he uses his money to buy some food, he runs the risk of angering Rafa, and his brother won't let him come along.

But then, in a seemingly fortuitous moment, Rafa becomes engaged in looking for the next bus, and Yunior is able to sneak off and buy a pastelito, thinking he has overcome this irreconcilable conflict. In doing so, he commits a lie of omission, since he of course does not tell Rafa that he is buying the pastelito. Yunior thus tells two lies—one to himself, that he can get away with disobeying Rafa's orders, that is, that he can overcome his irreconcilable conflict, and one to Rafa.

Unfortunately for Yunior, he is about to encounter a central reality of human existence that fiction explores: the gap between what we intend our actions to achieve and what they actually achieve. On the bus, Yunior hides the pastelito in his pocket, which then creates a grease stain on his pants. As this happens, Rafa is engaging the conductor, the cobrador, in a scheme to confuse the cobrador and allow the boys to ride without paying a fare. Meanwhile, the man next to Yunior notices the grease stain on his pants and offers to help Yunior clean it up: "He spit in his fingers and started to rub at the stain but then he was pinching at the tip of my *pinga* through the fabric of my shorts." When Yunior protests, the man squeezes the boy's biceps, making him whimper and warns Yunior to keep quiet.

Of course, it is not Yunior's fault that he is molested. But what happens on the bus with this man stems directly from Yunior's actions: his attempt to overcome his seemingly irreconcilable conflict concerning his brother's admonition not to spend their money on food.

After the boys get off the bus, Yunior starts to cry. Rafa thinks this is because Yunior is scared because they cheated the *cobrador*. Yunior may want to tell Rafa about what has happened to him, but he probably thinks that if he does so, he will have to tell about the *pastelito*, and then Rafa will get angry and leave him. Of course, Yunior could tell Rafa about the incident with the molester without mentioning the *pastelito*, but I don't think this possibility enters his mind, and even if it does, he senses that his crying about his molestation, with or without mentioning the *pastelito*, will only annoy his brother. After all, his brother tells him, "If you can't stop crying, I'll leave you." So Yunior must be silent and suppress his emotions that result from his being attacked. He chooses this silence in order to continue the journey; it is the unexpected toll the journey requires.

When the two brothers finally find Ysrael, Yunior encounters another thwarting agent in the pursuit of their goal. Despite their intentions, which are based on the view of Ysrael as a freak to be gawked at and not a human being, Yunior almost immediately starts to relate to Ysrael as just another kid, someone he might be friends with. Ysrael is holding a kite, which looks to be "no handmade local job":

> Where did you get that? I asked.
> Nueva York, he said. From my father.
> No shit! Our father's there too! I shouted.
> I looked at Rafa, who, for an instant, frowned. Our father only sent us letters and an occasional shirt or pair of jeans at Christmas.
> What the hell are you wearing that mask for anyway? Rafa asked.

The mention of New York causes Yunior to recall their father, and he reacts in a way that highlights that he and Ysrael have something in common. This displeases Rafa, who quickly tries to get things back on track to their original goal: unmasking Ysrael. But again Yunior, overcome by his innate openness, starts to converse with Ysrael about wrestling. In a way, against Yunior's intention, this disarms Ysrael, and Rafa, seeing an opening, smashes Ysrael in the head.

What Yunior had not foreseen when they set out to find Ysrael was that

Yunior would make a human connection with the scarred boy and that he, Yunior, would have to throw aside this connection to complete the unmasking. It's clear this price is greater than Yunior has expected, both in terms of the way he must regard Ysrael and the violence involved in the attack. Then too there is what Ysrael's face finally reveals:

> His left ear was a nub and you could see the thick veined slab of his tongue through a hole in his cheek. He had no lips. His head was tipped back and his eyes had gone white and the cords were out on his neck. He'd been an infant when the pig had come into the house. The damage looked old but I still jumped back and said, Please Rafa, let's go! Rafa crouched and using only two of his fingers, turned Ysrael's head from side to side.

The results of their journey and the unmasking of Ysrael reveal a world of violence that surrounds the narrator Yunior and lies in wait for him in the future, as he makes the transition his brother has already made into manhood. This violence is a direct result not just of the economic poverty around the boys but also of the surrounding psychic and spiritual poverty; it is what seems to be required in order to survive—to not become even more of a victim than they are. At the same time, they have no older male authority to guide them; the fathers are absent. The incident with the molester and the incident with Ysrael seem to carry a message to Yunior: either you are attacked or you attack; that is the irreconcilable choice.

The results of Yunior's journey are numbness and emotional silence, a cynicism or harsh realism about what is to be expected from the world. At the story's end, Yunior, thinking that Ysrael's father in Nueva York will get doctors to help the scarred boy, opines, "Ysrael will be OK." To which Rafa replies, echoing his description of the *campo* that opened the story, "Don't bet on it. . . . they aren't going to do shit to him."

Rafa makes it clear to Yunior that such realism is something Yunior must accept if he's going to be able to accompany his older brother and become part of the masculine world his brother represents to him. The story is clearly centered on the loss of innocence and the acquisition of knowledge, and it invokes the irreconcilable choices Yunior faces in order to complete his journey.

Junot Díaz has remarked that he views *Drown* as a tool kit for young writers of color, especially those from an immigrant community. For any beginning writer, what "Ysrael" demonstrates is how powerful, complex emotions and concepts can be conveyed within a simple, straightforward story structure: The protagonist has a clear concrete goal, something he desires. In order to achieve this desire, he faces thwarting agents and irreconcilable conflicts. Each action he takes, each choice, moves him either closer or further from his goal. Some of his actions create results he did not foresee and thus a gap between his expectations for his actions and what actually results. Lies, such as the lie of omission by Yunior to his brother, almost always create such gaps.

Beyond its structure, the genius of the story is its multilayered voice and the imaginative and penetrating way the writer brings the narrator—and the reader—into and through the journey toward his goal.

The Storyteller as Sadist

(OR ZUCKERMAN'S COMPLAINT)

If in the world of our stories, we as authors resemble God, it is because we visit trials and tribulations on our protagonists, while we sit removed from their world, watching them suffer, investigating their suffering, rendering their suffering—indeed, causing their suffering. In short, we treat them the way God treated Job: We test their patience and their fortitude; we foil their hopes and plans; we place before them obstacles, opponents to thwart them, false comforters and flatterers, betrayers; we create for them conflicts, impossible and debilitating situations, irreconcilable dilemmas; we teach them that they are mortal and fallible, that those they love or admire are mortal and fallible; we not only watch them fail, we provide them with the means and opportunities to fail; we hammer at their pride and illusions, their achievements and beliefs; we strip them to the bone, reveal their poor, wretched, naked selves, their animal hungers and wants; we take them into despair and desperation; we lead them into situations where they will lie, and then their lies only bring on more complications and often suffering and the inevitable exposure of the lies; we deny them their desires and sit back and watch how they howl in complaint, how they choose to proceed, often in the wrong direction; we bring them to the point of giving up and see if they will do so.

In doing all this, in setting up their world of suffering and torment and temptation, of frustration and failure, we watch them respond to that world, reveal their character, and create their fate.

In *The Facts: A Novelist's Autobiography*, Philip Roth makes a key distinction between the autobiographical facts of one's life and what a novelist does with those facts. Roth does this through a clever appropriation from his fiction: The main section of *The Facts* is a memoir that provides an account of Roth's early life, but in the preface, Roth writes a letter to his fictional alter ego, the novelist Nathan Zuckerman, who shares certain biographical resemblances to his creator. In this preface/letter, Roth asks Zuckerman's opinion about the ensuing memoir.

At the end of the memoir, in a nicely postmodern move, Zuckerman writes a letter back to Roth, advising him not to publish the work. Zuckerman argues that we judge the author of a novel differently than an autobiographer; the autobiographer is judged by an ethical imperative—to tell the truth—whereas the novelist is judged by an aesthetic imperative—to tell a story well. Zuckerman argues that in autobiography the relevant question is

> how close is the narration to the truth? Is the author hiding his or her motives, presenting his or her actions and thoughts to lay bare the essential nature of conditions or trying to hide something, telling in order not to tell? In a way we always tell in order not to tell, but the personal historical is expected to resist to the utmost the ordinary impulse to falsify, distort, and deny.

Zuckerman questions whether Roth is actually accomplishing this task of the autobiographer. He wonders if Roth hasn't painted a far more benign and uncomplicated portrait not just of himself but of the other people he writes about: his parents, his ex-lovers, and his ex-wife.

In this fictional letter, Zuckerman then argues that Roth's real talent is not for "separating the facts from the imagination and emptying them of their potential dramatic energy." Instead, Roth's talent as a fiction writer involves infusing the facts with his imagination, willfully distorting the facts, inventing scenarios and alternative events, ratcheting up the emotional stakes, investigating the lies and falsifications people create concerning themselves and others and their past. In short, Roth as a memoirist or autobiographer isn't writing to his strengths. In Zuckerman's view, the results show it:

> But why suppress the imagination that's served you so long? Doing so entails terrific discipline, I know, but why bother? Especially when to strip away the imagination to get to a fiction's factual basis is frequently all that many readers really care about anyway? Why is it that when they talk about the facts they feel they're on more solid ground than when they talk about fiction? The truth is that the facts are much more refractory and unmanageable and inconclusive, and can actually kill the very sort of inquiry that imagination opens up. Your work has always been to intertwine the facts with the imag-

ination, but here you're unintertwining them, you're pulling them apart, you're peeling the skin off your imagination, *de*-imagining a life's work, and what is left even they can now understand.

Zuckerman criticizes readers who mistake the true nature and purpose of fiction, who mistake its purpose as that of autobiography, which is rendering the facts. Zuckerman argues that such a rendering is, paradoxically, a form of deception, of holding back; it doesn't get at the true complications and contradictions of our existence, which is why we resort to and need the creation of fiction, of story. What Zuckerman implies but doesn't quite say directly is that story provides us with the metaphor to explore our existence in a way that is not literal and therefore reductive. It allows the imagination—that is, the unconscious—a means of entrance and in so doing belies the limitation of our conscious mind's understanding and adherence to the facts.

According to Zuckerman, one reason fiction or stories can do this is that they bypass the various censors both within and outside us. Thus Zuckerman tells Roth that his portrait of his parents is too pious and respectful and leaves something essential out:

> In the few comments you do make about your mother and father, there's nothing but tenderness, respect, understanding, all those wonderful emotions that I, for one, have come to distrust partly because you, for one, have made me distrust them. Many people don't like you as a writer just because of the ways you invite the reader to distrust those very sentiments that you now publicly embrace. . . . Look, this place you come from does not produce artists so much as it produces dentists and accountants. I'm convinced that there is something in the romance of your childhood that you're not permitting yourself to talk about, though without it the rest of the book makes no sense. I just cannot trust you as a memoirist the way I trust you as a novelist because, as I've said, to tell what you tell best is forbidden to you here by a decorous, citizenly, filial conscience. With this book you've tied your hands behind your back and tried to write it with your toes.

Zuckerman argues that fiction allows the author a freer space, a dimension in which the blasphemous and outrageous, the forbidden and denied, the ugly and upsetting are allowed not simply entrance but given free rein. Fiction provides license; autobiography provides shackles—whether those shackles come from outside the writer or from within. (I would add, though, that many of the best memoirists break through those shackles and do not let such censorship—

self-censorship or societal censorship—prevent them from accessing difficult truths; moreover, as I argue later in this book, the line between memoir and fiction is, for some, more ambiguous than is stated here by Zuckerman/Roth.)

Zuckerman also recognizes that his author, Roth, provides him not just with attitudes or emotions or beliefs that Roth the autobiographer tends to shy away from. No, Roth the author provides Zuckerman with difficulties and trials that Roth, if we are to believe his autobiography, has been relatively free from. While Roth's parents seemingly supported and approved of his career as a writer and the work he produced, Zuckerman has suffered an irreconcilable breach with his father because of his writing. In an ironic and comic complaint, Zuckerman chastises Roth for lacking sympathy for the troubles Roth has visited on him:

> I wonder if you have any real idea of what it's like to be disowned by a dying father because of something you wrote. I assure you that there is no equivalence between that and a *hundred* nights on the rack at Yeshiva. My father's condemnation of me provided you, obviously, with the opportunity to pull out all the stops on a Jewish deathbed scene; that had to have been irresistible to a temperament like yours. Nonetheless, knowing what I now do about your father's enthusiasm for your first stories and about the pride he took in their publication, I feel, whether inappropriately or not, envious, cheated, and misused.

Zuckerman reacts here as if he were Roth's Job, but with a more critical and perhaps more human response than his biblical counterpart. I have suffered, says Zuckerman, in order to provide you with fictional opportunities, with venues for your explorations, for your profit and livelihood, perhaps even for your amusement. And it all could have been avoided.

Of course, if Roth had kept Zuckerman from his troubles and suffering, Roth would never have written his works of fiction. Nevertheless, Zuckerman helps us recognize a certain sadism in the role of the fiction writer.

And it's not just Zuckerman who bemoans this sadism. Zuckerman's fictional British wife, Maria, also reads Roth's manuscript. She complains that Roth has given her an anti-Semitic mother and inserted that mother far more deeply into their marriage than she would have wished. Indeed, Maria wishes for a life that's sane, "uninteresting, unimportant." But Roth has provided neither her nor her husband with such a life, and she fears there are signs that he will soon visit more troubles on them: "To have spent all of this evening reading

this book—and now I feel so defenseless against what I just know is coming!"
To which Zuckerman then adds:

> Is Maria right? What is coming? Why, in her England, *have* I been given this close-cropped, wirebrush, gray-speckled beard? . . . How can we really believe that this beard means nothing when you, who have rabbinically bearded me, appear in even just your first few pages to be more preoccupied than ever in your life with the gulf between gentile and Jew? Must this, my fourth marriage, be torn apart because you, in middle age, have discovered in yourself a passion to be reconciled with the tribe? Why should your relentless assessing of Jewish predicaments be *our* cross to bear!

Despite their complaints, the fictional Maria and Zuckerman never quite plead with their creator to let them off the hook, to treat them and their lives more gently (note the last sentence in the above quotation ends not with a question mark but with an exclamation point). They both know it is not in the nature of the beast. Roth is a fiction writer, and this is what fiction writers do: They make their characters suffer. Job's cries, Zuckerman's kvetchings—let them be loud and manifold and visceral.

Pride Cometh before the Fall

FLANNERY O'CONNOR AND ZZ PACKER

I

"Pride cometh before the fall."

So many of Flannery O'Connor's classic short stories illustrate this precept, one that, in our present age, can seem to some readers outmoded and overly moralistic, though obviously not to many. In "A Good Man Is Hard to Find," a grandmother accompanies her son's family on a vacation. She's a prattling fool, judgmental, willful, and full of herself, and she clearly gets on the nerves of her son and his family. As the story opens, she argues with her son, Bailey, about his decision to take the family to Florida; she wants to visit "some of her connections in east Tennessee." To dissuade him, she tells her son that she's read in the paper that a convict called the Misfit "is aloose from the Federal Pen and headed toward Florida," but Bailey simply ignores her. Her grandson says, "If you don't want to go to Florida, why dontcha stay at home?" and her granddaughter adds, "She wouldn't stay at home to be queen for a day. . . . Afraid she'd miss something. She has to go everywhere we go."

At a certain stretch in the trip, the grandmother mentions an old nearby plantation that she once visited as a young lady. She alludes to a secret panel in a wall there, and this excites her grandson, who joins her in urging the annoyed Bailey to turn off the main highway to go see the plantation.

With a biblical sense of the preordained, by taking this side trip, the family runs into the Misfit and his fellow escaped convicts. The convicts take the family prisoner. In a long interchange with the Misfit, the grandmother keeps urging him to pray and turn to Jesus. Eventually, after the Misfit's companions haul the rest of the family off into the woods, the talk turns into a debate about whether Jesus could raise the dead. There are a series of pistol reports, and the

111

grandmother cries out, "Bailey Boy, Bailey Boy!" But this does not stop the Misfit's theological ramblings:

> "I wasn't there so I can't say He didn't," The Misfit said. "I wisht I had of been there," he said, hitting the ground with his fist. "It ain't right I wasn't there because if I had of been there I would of known. Listen lady," he said in a high voice, "if I had of been there I would of known and I wouldn't be like I am now." His voice seemed about to crack and the grandmother's head cleared for an instant. She saw the man's face twisted close to her own as if he were going to cry and she murmured, "Why you're one of my babies. You're one of my own children!" She reached out and touched him on the shoulder. The Misfit sprang back as if a snake had bitten him and shot her three times through the chest.

At the end of the story, when the Misfit's companion remarks that the grandmother was a talker, the Misfit replies, "She would have been a good woman . . . if it had been somebody there to shoot her every minute of her life."

For O'Connor the Lord's judgment and mercy are always available, but in our pride and stubbornness, we humans refuse this reality. In her stories, her protagonists are trapped within their own vanity, certain of their take on the world, their evaluation of others, and their own place within the world. In these evaluations, their own place is set atop a hierarchy of values to which they fiercely hold fast.

Eventually, though, the events of the story, the conflicts they encounter, various frustrations of their will and desire come to challenge their certainties. But still they persist. It is often only in the presence of great violence or death that O'Connor's protagonists are forced to confront a reality and truth greater than themselves. Thus her characters eventually come to an epiphany, a reckoning for and a recognition of their sins. But this illumination almost always comes at a great price. This price often involves great violence, as in "A Good Man Is Hard to Find," but its essence is the destruction of self-delusion and the illusions of pride.

II

The epiphanies in ZZ Packer's stories may not possess the violence of O'Connor's, but the stories in Packer's *Drinking Coffee Elsewhere* can also be read through the palimpsest of "pride cometh before the fall." Most often Packer's protagonists are fueled by religious or moral certainties, but even when they are not, they cling to a sense of their own superiority over others, a pride that comes not so much from who they are but from not being "that"—"that" being some other character or characters or group in the story whom the protagonist judges harshly. O'Connor's stories often embody an almost Old Testament sense of judgment, as if her protagonists cannot be confounded and brought to the light by anything other than great violence, disaster, and death. In contrast, Packer tends to approach her protagonists with a series of ironical jibes and jabs, undercutting them with comic turns of events or another character's withering or bewildering retort.

Packer's protagonists are all black, but that tells us only so much about her work. What is more revealing is that Packer often chooses as protagonists characters who might be expected to display less pride or sense of importance than others in their world. Sometimes this is because of their youth and the fact that they exist in a world where others clearly possess more power than they do ("Brownies," "The Ant of the Self"). Sometimes the protagonist has entered a world—Yale, Japan—that is unfamiliar to her, where she possesses no ready-made place—the so-called fish out of water ("Drinking Coffee Elsewhere," "Geese"). Sometimes it is because of their humble position in an organization such as the church ("Every Tongue Shall Confess").

In "The Ant of the Self," Packer starts with a son bailing his father out of jail for a DUI in Louisville. The son's stated goal: "I just try to get my father, Ray Bivens Jr., back across the river to his place in Indiana."

From the start, it's clear that the son, Spurgeon, wants as little to do with his father as possible. He mocks his father's dated and rhetorical political language ("He's the only person I know who still calls cops 'pigs'") and dismisses his father's talk on "investments" as another attempt to wring money from his son; he reminds his father the he, Spurgeon, is the one who has paid the father's bail with the money Spurgeon has won from school debates. When Spurgeon ignores one of his father's questions, his father gets angry and insists he respond: "You *answer me* when I ask you something. . . . Do you know who this is? . . . Do you know who you're *talking to?*"

Now the father has, in many ways, failed his son, just as the father's insistence on being respected has clearly failed. Given these failings, one could imagine a story from the father's viewpoint, examining his doomed attempts to resuscitate his pride and to achieve respect from his son. Indeed, elements of all this are in the story, but they are not the story's focus.

Instead, Packer chooses to make the son the protagonist; this choice forces the reader to see a complexity in the son's character that might not otherwise be discernible. The reader must look beyond a view of the son simply as a victim of a father who drinks too much, who borrows money from him, and whose shortcomings have led him to be divorced from the boy's mother and estranged from his son. The story accomplishes this in part by using its events to reveal the son's own faults and failings.

As the story unfolds, it's clear that Spurgeon's attempts to get his father home and be rid of him are not going to succeed. At first the father manages to force Spurgeon to take him to the father's girlfriend's house. Previously, the father has bought a number of birds with the hopes of selling them, but failing to do so, he has been forced to keep the birds with his girlfriend.

Spurgeon then learns that his father intends to pay him back for the bail by having them both travel to the Million Man March in Washington, D.C., to sell the birds. Spurgeon thinks this is, at best, a dubious idea, but he goes along with it, in part because he still feels an obligation to obey his father and in part because he wants his bail money back. But he also wants to make things difficult for one of his school's debate team members, a black basketball player who will have to take Spurgeon's place if Spurgeon is absent (just as Spurgeon condescendingly appraises his father, so he looks down on his fellow debater, who lacks Spurgeon's verbal and logical skills and his disciplined sense of hard work).

At one point, after Spurgeon criticizes the father's treatment of his girlfriend, the father insults him, and Spurgeon kicks his father out of the car (it's his mother's car). But Spurgeon can't get rid of his father so easily (otherwise there wouldn't be a story); instead, feeling guilty about leaving his father, he turns back and retrieves him.

At the Million Man March, Spurgeon is able to separate from his father, but when one of the marchers tries to get Spurgeon to respond to the march and its proceedings, Spurgeon blurts out, "I'm just here because my father made me come." Almost instantly Spurgeon is surrounded by older black men who chastise him for not supporting the spirit of the march and forging a bond with his fellow black men. When he tells them his father's "whole damn life is as slack as a pantsuit from JCPenney!" one marcher replies, almost as if acting as a stand-in for the father, "You need to learn that responsibility is a two-way street!"

Later Spurgeon, again against his wishes, ends up in a bar with his father. He becomes even more frustrated when his father actually manages to sell his birds and come up with six hundred dollars. When Spurgeon tells the people at the bar that he's glad to be out of school, where he's the only black kid in his class, they chastise him for not appreciating the opportunity to go to school: "We the ones *fought* for you to be in school with the white folks."

Wherever Spurgeon turns, either his father or someone else is telling him to stop thinking he's so special and to stop denying his connections to other black men, especially those who came before him—like his father. And though Spurgeon prides himself on his skills as a debater, he finds himself again and again overwhelmed, outnumbered, stumbling out weak responses or simply retreating into silence.

Then, too, Spurgeon's own feelings sometimes betray him. When his father accuses Spurgeon of not loving or understanding him, he replies, "*You* don't understand *you*." But then feeling guilty for his remark, Spurgeon relents a bit:

> I grip my father's elbow and try to speak with him one on one. "I'm sorry about what I said at the March."
>
> "No you ain't."
>
> "Yes," I say, "I am. But you've got to tell me how to understand you." I feel silly saying it, but he's drunk, and so is everybody else but me.
>
> He lurches back then leans in forward again. "Tell you? I can't *tell* you." He drums each word out on the counter. "That's. Not. What. It's. A-bout. I can *tell* you about Paris, but you won't know 'less you been there. You simply under-*stand*. Or you don't. . . . You either take me, or you *don't*."

Once again Spurgeon refuses what the father is trying to tell him. Spurgeon's anger at his father and his judgmental streak keep him at a distance, even as his guilt and desire for connection keep drawing him back (all this constitutes an example of irreconcilable desires—I want contact and closeness with my father versus I'm angry at my father for all his failings and being with him only frustrates me).

By the story's end, it's unclear whether Spurgeon is ever going to understand his father. But he can't escape him, even though his father has left him, forcing Spurgeon to take a train alone to get home. The last image of the story is of a father and a son whom Spurgeon happens upon at the train station. The boy's happiness while riding on his father's back so unsettles Spurgeon that he feels a wave of emotion he still wants to deny: "And though the urge to weep comes over me, I wait—holding my head in my hands—and it passes."

The reader understands that for Spurgeon to actually weep, he must acknowledge his connection to his father. But, of course, that connection is filled with a pain he wishes to deny; that connection is denied by his sense of pride in what he's done and who he is away from his father—a champion debater, a good student, someone extremely disciplined who doesn't make mistakes. And so Spurgeon remains aloof, not just from his father or even the other men at the bar or the Million Man March, but also from himself. Despite all the blows he has received, all the signs that he cannot ever separate from his father, his pride rests both on his difference from and his indifference to his father—that is, in his isolation, in what sets him apart. Yet the reader senses there is a reckoning to come; eventually bearing his burden of pride, Spurgeon will either fall weeping or he will fall from the weight of his years of numbness, but he will surely fall.

Irreconcilable Conflicts, Lies, and Character

When things go wrong with your fiction, you may need to ask yourself: What do the principles of story tell me about what's missing in this story or novel? What do those principles tell me about what needs to be changed or added? How do the principles suggest ways I could rethink and reconceive the basic starting points or parameters of the story?

The following is a brief description of what this process might entail.

Let's start with the basic facets of story: A protagonist discovers a goal or a desire and takes actions to achieve that goal or desire.

But this is just a starting point. A story must involve more than the protagonist's pursuit of a goal. Every day we wake up, and we formulate in our minds a set of actions, and these actions are related to various goals. But if there is no difficulty or problem with our pursuit of the goal, there really isn't a story. If I commute to work every day over the Bay Bridge and the trip takes thirty minutes, and yesterday morning, I took that trip to work and it took thirty minutes, I don't tell a story about it to others. Now if there's an earthquake or a huge traffic jam and the trip takes two hours, well, I might tell a story about it. But even out of the ordinary circumstances or extraordinary difficulties don't really make a story, other than perhaps some little anecdote that I might tell people I know.

Why is this so? For one thing, the difficulties so far are merely external—the earthquake or traffic jam. Those difficulties affected thousands of other commuters on that day. In dealing with those events, my story so far doesn't differ from that of the other commuters in any significant way. Moreover, the difficult circumstances of my morning commute don't yet reveal anything about my character.

So how is character revealed in story? In the pursuit of her goal, a protagonist may encounter outside forces that prevent her from obtaining her goal. These outside forces may be other characters or various other sorts of hindrances—physical, financial, social/communal, legal, political, and so on. In action films like *The Terminator* or a James Bond movie, the main focus is on these outside forces. Very few of the struggles the protagonist goes through in such films end up revealing anything new about him. He is roughly the same at the end of the movie as at the beginning and so is our knowledge and opinion of him.

In David Mamet's critique of the problem play or film in *Three Uses of the Knife*, he argues that a lesser work will somehow keep the protagonist from really being forced to wrestle with irreconcilable conflicts. This type of film or play, says Mamet, may move us for a few moments, but we forget it almost immediately afterward. Nothing about it sticks with us. Partly this is because we know, deep in our hearts and minds, that the world doesn't work this way. One way that a "romance" or "problem play" keeps the irreconcilable conflict from actually being irreconcilable is that the valence between the two terms shifts. Often a type of deus ex machina swoops in and, poof, the conflict disappears (someone else pays a debt, your fiancé did not sleep with someone else, a chance meeting provides the key clue that frees the client).

But in a serious literary work, the writer's job is to set up the circumstances of this irreconcilable conflict so that it is indeed irreconcilable. If it's not, the writer needs to shift the valances of the conflict so that it is irreconcilable.

So how does the writer shift these valences?

Here's one example of the process a writer might go through in doing so: Imagine a story about a marriage. If the protagonist's husband and her mother are arguing, and the protagonist is thinking of divorcing her husband, then that doesn't present her with an irreconcilable conflict. The same is true if she's always had difficult relations with her mother and is no longer seeking her approval.

In reconceiving this story, the writer needs to make the protagonist's choice of either her husband or her mother truly a conflict, truly irreconcilable. To accomplish this, other factors may have to be shifted. Say the protagonist hasn't gotten along that well with her mother, but her father has just died and her mother is grieving for him. That shifts the valence more toward the mother. Or say that the protagonist has found herself faced with a huge debt, and she plans to ask her mother for a loan. Again that changes the valence and makes the conflict in choosing between her husband and her mother more irreconcilable.

Shifting the valences of the conflict does not always require a huge change; sometimes it merely entails changing or adding one or two elements to the story or reshaping/reconceiving some aspect of a character or situation. But once the conflict reaches a balance of irreconcilables, there will be an increase in narrative and dramatic tension; this increase stems from the pressure such a conflict puts on the protagonist.

Let us say that the writer has created a situation where in pursuit of her goal, the protagonist faces an irreconcilable conflict. The protagonist chooses to pursue one competing goal at the expense of another. The question then becomes, what happens next?

Often, as I've said earlier, we lie to ourselves about the irreconcilability of the conflict. To pick a current obvious lie: we want fossil fuels, and we want to be safe from global warming. Solution: there is no such thing as global warming. A more common example: we want a new computer or new iPhone, and we don't want to go in debt. Solution: we'll buy the goods on credit; we'll pay it back later—surely we will. In both instances, the lie involves our ignoring or wishing away the consequences of our actions.

Why does a lie invariably call forth the gap between our plans and expectations for our actions and what actually results from our actions? For one thing, lies to ourselves and to others are a denial of the truth, of reality. Therefore, if a lie is the action that we take, that action almost inevitably does not succeed because it is not based on a true assessment of our situation. Indeed, in difficult tasks or situations, we may find that the action we took to pursue our goal actually lands us even further from the goal than before. Thus the lie reflects a mindset that believes that we have more control over ourselves and our environment than we actually do.

In this way the lie arises from hubris, from excessive pride, and as we know from the Greeks, pride always leads to a fall. We think we are gods and can act like gods. The gods—who are incarnations of fate and reality—tell us otherwise. They remind us of and instruct us in our fallibility, our less-than-godly understanding of the world and ourselves, our inability to control completely the results of our actions and thus our fate.

Beginning writers sometimes stumble off track by becoming too involved in thinking of the story from the point of the view of the protagonist. Frequently, this is because the protagonist is a representative of the author—that is, the author identifies herself with the protagonist. Since she approaches the protagonist as a version of herself, the writer consciously—or unconsciously—does not want anything bad to happen to her protagonist or, even more so, for her protagonist to act badly.

At other times the author is so concerned with creating and describing the consciousness and identity of the protagonist that he tends to think of the pursuit of the goal in terms very similar to those of the protagonist. When the protagonist makes an assessment of a situation and creates a course of action, when the protagonist takes an action and expects a certain result, the author thinks only in terms of what the protagonist expects and desires.

One solution for these tendencies is for the writer to identify with and explore the desires and plans of characters who may be in conflict with the protagonist. These characters can act as hindering forces; they can also elicit other desires in the protagonist that might conflict with her pursuit of a goal. I tell my students to think of the director's instruction to Cuba Gooding Jr. in *Jerry Mc-Guire*: Cuba, your job is to frustrate Tom Cruise's character as much as possible. In other words, as a fiction writer, think a bit like Cuba Gooding Jr. Find ways of annoying, goading, wreaking havoc with your protagonist.

The writer's identification with the protagonist may also lead to the writer wanting to protect the protagonist not just from others but from herself—that is, from the protagonist's failings and character flaws—or the writer may conceive the protagonist as possessing no or just a few failings or character flaws. Here again, if this is the case, the writer must detach herself from the protagonist and work to create situations where the protagonist may be in such internal conflict that she *does* act badly, that she does lie to herself and/or to others.

The writer must then see that once the protagonist lies—either to herself or to others—the lie will create its own repercussions, its own penalties and circumstances of revelation. One lie so often leads to another and another. The writer's job then is to pursue these repercussions, to find or create these penalties and the ways through which the lie is revealed.

A simple principle therefore is *create situations where the protagonist is forced to lie.*

To devise situations where the protagonist is forced to tell a lie, a useful figure for the writer is the Devil. Like the Devil, the author actively searches for flaws in a protagonist's character and seeks to exploit those flaws. If the character possesses a hair-trigger temper, the Devil author seeks to create situations where that temper can explode. If the protagonist is particularly susceptible to one of the seven deadly sins, the Devil author seeks to create and put a vehicle of temptation right smack dab in the path of the protagonist—a chance for money, power, sex, social status, revenge.

Rather than punishment, the Devil often offers pleasures; rather than working through humiliation, the Devil works through exaltation. Thus, unlike God in the book of Job, the Devil might increase Job's abundance and feed his ambitions in order to puff up his sense of himself, in order to let Job inflate his own sense of self-worth to a point where he will invariably fall; where an overblown or overconfident Job will create his own enemies or turn others against him.

As in the story of Adam and Eve, once the Devil has successfully tempted his prey, once the protagonist has committed a sin, once again the inevitable occurs: the protagonist lies about the sin. As a result, the consequences of this lie must follow, and a path opens up to the end of the story, where the lie is ultimately exposed. Pressure should be applied then, questions asked or situations created that force the protagonist to either reveal the truth or lie further.

As an author, your job is to find ways of exposing the lies of your protagonist.

In doing this, you are invoking an age-old dramatic structure. As David Mamet has observed: A play begins with a lie. When the lie is revealed, the play is over.

Why frustrate the protagonist in his pursuit of the goal? Why create situations where she must face irreconcilable conflicts and desires? Why tempt her to sin? Why lead her to tell a lie?

There are many answers to these questions. Some involve narrative drive. Only if a writer does these things will the protagonist's pursuit of the goal be difficult enough to create tension and anticipation. Only through such means can the writer create a series of rising and falling, so that the question of whether the protagonist will reach her goal is, in the mind of the protagonist and in the mind of the reader, a real question. Or one could say simply: These things make the story more interesting

But of course, in addition to the dictates of story, there is also the question of character. It is through these tribulations and trials, these frustrations and conflicting desires, these stumblings and mistakes, sins and lies, that the character of the protagonist is revealed.

If the protagonist were in complete control of her life and her environment, if she pursued her goal with no frustration or possibility of failure, she would never have to question herself, nor would others question her. She would never be forced to make a choice that might hurt or betray someone, whether another person or herself.

But if the journey to the goal is sufficiently difficult and set up correctly, key dramatic questions arise: Does the protagonist deny the irreconcilable conflict? Does she lie about it—to herself or to others? Does she make a choice between two irreconcilable desires? Then clearly her choice of one over the other reveals something essential about her that was not apparent at the beginning of the story. The protagonist—sometimes consciously, sometimes unconsciously—must reckon then with a new understanding of her character and who she actually is and her place in and relationship to the world.

Destroying the Imago of the Protagonist

SHERMAN ALEXIE'S "CLASS"

One way to consider the ego of a protagonist is what I call the imago. Each of us creates a self-image, or imago, of ourselves, which includes both how we would like to look at and identify ourselves and how we would like others to look at and identify us. This self-image is intimately tied to our ego, to our sense of self-worth. It tends to dominate our presentation of ourselves in public or social interactions and, to a certain extent, in our private interactions. Most of us also have a secret life or self, one that often contradicts, in very interesting and revealing ways, the self-image of our public and private life.

Seen in this light, our public self-image is a facade, a simplification. It hides key aspects or facets of the self. Some of these things one consciously hides. But there are also facets of the self that one does not know one is consciously hiding.

As the protagonist pursues the goal and runs into failure and frustration and difficult choices, these blows of reality make the protagonist aware of his limitations, his foibles and faults. Each blow then chips away at the protagonist's imago, at his projected self-image.

Here's one way to picture this process: The protagonist goes around carrying a cardboard projection of his ideal self and presenting this projection to the world. As the story progresses, the events of the story, the reaction of the world to his plans, his internal struggles all serve to chip at and tear away this cardboard projection.

In various great works of fiction, by the ending, that cardboard projection has been utterly destroyed and what is revealed is the naked self, so that the reader or audience sees, as Lear puts it, the "poor, bare, forked animal." If most successful stories or plays do not reach this tragic nadir—or zenith—most will still generally succeed in presenting the reader with an understanding and portrait of the protagonist that goes beyond or behind the protagonist's imago and, by the end, reveals new truths about who the protagonist truly is.

Sherman Alexie's "Class" is a useful example of a story where events chip away at the imago of the protagonist until he is forced to admit who he truly is and not who he wishes to be. The story also demonstrates how, in a short story, the use of a three-act structure does not mean that all three acts are presented in equal detail.

In myth and the classic three-act play structure, the first act involves the protagonist's introduction to and taking up of the goal—or, as Joseph Campbell calls it, "the hero's journey." This journey usually starts with the hero living in a kingdom or land where something is amiss, where things are fallow or not flourishing—a plague, corruption, an evil king. Such a situation can also serve as a metaphor for the hero's psychic stagnation, from which the hero is called on to undertake a journey or task, a heroic goal.

Campbell says that in many myths it takes two invitations or calls before the hero assumes his task. In psychological terms, the first call loosens the hero's psyche and prepares him to be ready to take up the task at the second call (the unconscious hears the call even if the conscious puts it aside). Once the hero undertakes the task or journey, the first act ends.

The second act involves struggle and doubt as the hero makes progress toward the goal. There is often a point in the second act where the hero fails and/or falls into darkness and despair.

The third act is the final battle, the setting or situation in which it becomes clear whether the hero will succeed or fail in reaching the goal.

Often, short stories retain their brevity by focusing mainly on the third act, the final battle. This is true of Alexie's "Class."

In the opening section of "Class," Edgar, the protagonist narrator, meets a woman at a white middle-class party—they've just been discussing the shrimp appetizers and whether cayenne goes with lobster—and the woman asks him if he is Catholic. The two flirt and dance around this question, and in the process, it's noted that the woman is blind in one of her blue eyes; this blind eye is a result of a childhood accident in which her brother attempted to stab another sister with a pencil and the sister ducked and the brother struck her instead.

At one point the narrator reveals that the woman is also blond and, more importantly, is "the tenth most attractive white woman in the room." He then explains the relevance of this fact: "I always approached the tenth most attractive white woman at any gathering. I didn't have enough looks, charm, intelligence, or money to approach anybody more attractive than that, and I didn't have enough character to approach the less attractive." (Note here that the narrator has found a solution to the conflict between two desires: I want to be with the most attractive white woman versus I don't want to face rejection.) In mythic terms, Edgar's kingdom is fallow because he is not in a relationship.

Shortly after the narrator lets us into his thoughts on his choice of women, the woman says to him, "You're Indian." The scene at the party ends with this conversation:

> "I'm Edgar Eagle Runner," I said, though my driver's license still read Edgar Joseph.
> "Eagle Runner," she repeated, feeling the shape of my name fill her mouth, then roll past her tongue, teeth, and lips.
> "Susan," I said.
> "Eagle Runner," she whispered. "What kind of Indian are you?"
> "Spokane."
> "Never heard of it."
> "We're a small tribe. Salmon people."
> "The salmon are disappearing," she said.
> "Yes," I said. "Yes, they are."

In the very next paragraph Edgar tells us about getting married to Susan McDermott in a Catholic ceremony. Three dozen of Susan's friends and most of her coworkers attend. But her brother and parents, Edgar informs us, "stayed away as a protest against my pigmentation." Members of Edgar's law firm, who are seemingly all white, attend, and one of them, whom Edgar knows only through work, comes up just before the ceremony and announces, "Hey Runner . . . I love you, man." The only member of Edgar's family he has invited is his mother, who, he explains, "was overjoyed by my choice of mate. She'd always wanted me to marry a white woman and beget half-breed children who would marry white people who would beget quarter-bloods, and so on and so on, until simple mathematics killed the Indian in us."

Though my students sometimes do not see this, the wedding is the end of the first act, which involves the announcement of the goal. The goal Edgar engages is his wedding vows: to stay married to Susan.

Often when the hero takes up the goal, it entails leaving the old kingdom for the new. In many mythic tales, this transition is easily marked because the tale involves a journey. Having gone beyond the borders of the old and entered the new kingdom, the hero experiences a sense of exhilaration. He discovers new powers inside himself, powers that had lain dormant while he was in the old kingdom. He encounters new perceptions—a new landscape—and his various senses are heightened and his experiences intensify, as often occurs when we travel.

Alexie's story skips this period, the honeymoon (or perhaps the premarital courtship). Instead, within the first year of being married, the protagonist discovers that his wife is having an affair with one of his coworkers; while searching her closet, Edgar finds a box of love letters and reads one of them. The story itself doesn't examine in any detail how Edgar chooses what to do next. He simply decides to keep "the letters sacred by carefully placing them back" and not reading the rest of them. Seemingly for this reason, he chooses not to confront his wife directly about the affair. Instead he decides to seek revenge. He offers that he could have sought revenge by sleeping with one of her coworkers, as she has done, but instead, as a form of retaliation, he starts sleeping with prostitutes when he goes on business trips.

All this information is conveyed very quickly within about a page. From the standpoint of story structure, it's useful to understand that for Edgar the discovery of his wife's affair presents him with a dilemma, a choice between irreconcilable desires. His wife has had an affair and kept it secret. He finds out about the affair by accident/stealth, and he keeps that knowledge secret. He says that he doesn't talk to her about the letters because they are sacred, so, in his mind, the irreconcilable conflict is between talking with his wife about the affair or violating something sacred.

But in my view, Edgar is lying to himself: he simply doesn't want to talk to his wife because doing so would force him to confront in an intimate way how he feels—"brokenhearted, betrayed"—and because he'd rather not go through the painful and difficult process of trying to communicate with her. At the same time, he still feels betrayed and angry so he acts on those feelings by sleeping with prostitutes; he then helps himself ameliorate his own violation of trust and intimacy by deluding himself that he's been more honorable than she has because he doesn't embarrass her by sleeping with one of her coworkers.

Edgar tells himself several lies here: the surface lies are that he cares about the sacredness of his wife's letters, and he's trying not to embarrass his wife. Even if he does care about the sacredness of his wife's letters, however, he's using those feelings to tell a lie to himself about what he wants to avoid. Thus the deeper lie is that he would rather avoid talking honestly with his wife about how he feels about her affair; he would rather eschew the painful difficulties of trying to work toward a new intimacy. In short, he would rather avoid the labor necessary to make his marriage work.

I realize that what I've just said sounds a little psychobabblish. But what Edgar probably ought to do, what might be the therapeutically sound choice, isn't the most crucial point here in terms of the creation of story. Debating what Edgar ought to do is more the stuff of English lit. classes and not the focus of a fiction writer.

But it is important to keep in mind how Edgar's lies reveal his character. If Edgar had read all his wife's letters and confronted his wife, he would be someone else. If he hadn't decided to seek revenge through sleeping with prostitutes, he would be someone else.

But this all seems fairly obvious. For a writer, what's more useful is how all this illustrates a basic principle of story. As I've said earlier: faced with irreconcilable desires, a protagonist will want to deny the irreconcilability of those desires, will want to deny the reality those irreconcilable desires represent. To do this, the character will lie, first to himself and then to others, about the irreconcilability of these desires. Once a lie is told, it automatically sets up a mechanism of tension and forward narrative movement: How will the lie be revealed and what will happen as a result of this revelation?

Again, it should be noted that Edgar's decision to sleep with prostitutes takes place quickly and without the extensive analysis I've just done. Alexie decides instead to focus more attention on the second act of his story—the sleeping with prostitutes. In this section, most of the writing centers on the occasion when Edgar decides he has reached the point where he will sleep with one last prostitute. Revealingly, he wants this last prostitute to be an Indian woman.

In terms of pacing, the portion of the story about Edgar's wife's affair and his decision to sleep with prostitutes takes one page and the procuring of the last prostitute and his experience with her takes three pages. Rather than in narration, this latter section is executed in a scene mode. In other words, from a pace of narration that covers a couple years in a page, Alexie switches to a mode where most of the movement is moment by moment. This allows him to focus very specifically on the ways Edgar is both humiliated and frustrated in his quest for an Indian prostitute:

> "A-1 Escorts," said the woman. A husky voice, somehow menacing. I'm sure her children hated the sound of, even as I found myself aroused by its timbre.

"A-1 Escorts," she said again when I did not speak.

"Oh," I said. "Hi. Hello. Uh, I'm looking for some company this evening."

"Where you at?"

"The Prescott."

"Nice place."

"Yeah, they have whirlpool bathtubs."

"Water sports will cost you extra."

"Oh, no, no, no. I'm, uh, rather traditional."

"Okay, Mr. Traditional, what are you looking for?"

I'd slept with seventeen prostitutes, all of them blond and blue-eyed. Twelve of them had been busty while the other five had been small-breasted. Eight of them had claimed to be college students; one of them even had a chemistry textbook in her backpack.

"Do you employ any Indian women?" I asked.

"Indian? Like with the dot in the forehead?"

"No, no, that's East Indian. From India. I'm looking for American Indian. You know, like Tonto."

"We don't have any boys."

"Oh, no, I mean, I want an Indian woman."

In certain stories, a protagonist will start out with a conscious goal. Then, through the course of a story, a previously unconscious goal emerges. The most obvious form of this is the traditional wedding comedy where the groom or bride-to-be discovers, as the person proceeds toward the wedding, that he or she is actually in love not with the betrothed but with someone else. In a way, that too is the surface plot of Alexie's story. Edgar starts out at a party trying to bed the tenth prettiest white woman in the room. He then marries her and thus sets himself the new goal of remaining married to this white woman. But along the way he discovers that he also desires to sleep with an Indian woman.

Again, following the principle of frustrating the protagonist, Edgar doesn't succeed in his initial attempt at fulfilling the goal. The prostitute A-1 Escorts sends turns out to be "a white woman wearing a black wig over her short blond hair."

Thus ends the second act, which occurs after eleven pages. The next eleven pages describe the third act of Edgar Eagle Runner, the final battle. It turns out that "Class" is a short story that runs very quickly through the first two acts and then is most detailed in its depiction of the third act. In several Raymond Carver stories, particularly those focused on relationships, such as "Chef's House," the first paragraph or page will run through the first two acts; then the story itself focuses on the third act, the final battle, the time when it will be finally clear whether the protagonist reaches his goal or not.

The setup for the third act of "Class" is the dark night of the second act, but that dark night takes place briefly in a page, that is, at a fast narrative pace. Edgar and his wife conceive a child who dies "ten minutes after leaving Susan's body." Eventually they resume having sex until one night, while making love, Edgar discovers that Susan's one good blue eye is as dead—devoid of any spark of interest—as her blind one. Edgar gets up from the bed and goes out for a drink and ends up at an Indian bar. The story's third act begins at the bar, and the narrative pace slows to a moment-by-moment account.

In the nearly empty bar, Edgar encounters two characters: Sissy, the bartender, and Junior, who is playing pool and who, to Edgar, looks like Chief Broom from *One Flew over the Cuckoo's Nest*. Edgar assesses Junior as someone who "could have killed [him] with a flick of one finger." Almost immediately Junior confronts and sizes up Edgar as an unwanted intruder: "I'm sick of little shits like you. . . . Fucking urban Indians in your fancy fucking clothes."

At first Edgar tries to placate Junior, until Junior goes into a diatribe against Edgar that ends, "Go back to your mansion and read some fucking Teletubbies to your fucking white kids." Partly in reaction to his lost child, Edgar comes back at Junior with a "Fuck you" and only Sissy's hopping over the bar and coming between them with a pistol temporarily stops them from fighting. She explains to Junior that she's intervening not to save Edgar but to save Junior, who will go to jail "forever" the next time he is arrested.

But Edgar persists in his desire to fight, and he steps out into the alley where Junior is waiting and promptly gets knocked out. He comes to in the storeroom with his head in Sissy's lap and finds that his nose is broken and that Junior has cut off one of his braids.

When Edgar makes a pass at Sissy—recall his goal to sleep with an Indian woman—she is insulted and attacks his sense of presumption: "I just want to know, man. What are you doing here? Why'd you come here?" To which he feebly replies:

> "I just wanted to be with my people," I said.
> "Your people?" asked Sissy. "Your people? We're not your people."
> "We're Indians."
> "Yeah, we're Indians. You, me, Junior. But we live in this world and you live in your world."

"I don't like my world."

"You pathetic bastard. . . . You sorry, sorry piece of shit. Do you know how much I want to live in your world? Do you know how much Junior wants to live in your world?"

Of course I knew. For most of my life, I'd dreamed about the world where I currently resided.

In the bar, Junior functions as an obvious antagonist for Edgar and there is literally a final battle (one of the seminal characteristics of a classic third act). Junior serves to humiliate Edgar's wounded sense of manhood, but he also serves as a figure in a triangle between Edgar, Junior, and Sissy (triangles are often inherently more dramatic, unstable, and tension filled than dyads). At one point Junior tells Sissy, "In another world, you and I are Romeo and Juliet," and Sissy replies: "But we live in this world, Junior."

Sissy's role is to point out to both men the reality of who they are and their place in the world. She is, to use a term from Saul Bellow, a reality instructor, and this is another useful element in thinking about how, as a writer, one can think about the relationship between other characters and the protagonist: the other characters can teach the protagonist about the nature of reality, can show the protagonist who the protagonist truly is (and not who he thinks he is).

In the course of the story, Edgar has come to understand the truth of his marriage and what his desire to enter the white world and to be married to a white woman will cost him: his connections to other Indians and the community which he has been working so hard to escape.

Rather than confronting this irreconcilable conflict of desires—I want to enter the white world and be at home there versus I want to remain an Indian and be connected with other Indians—Edgar has deluded himself into believing that he could pursue one side of these conflicting desires without losing the other or without having the other matter. That is the lie he has been telling himself. Thus the unconscious goal, which emerged in the second act—to sleep with an Indian woman—remains unfulfilled. In his failure, Edgar is revealed as a man unable to live with the choices he has made. He has lied to himself about the requirements of his quest: to stay married to Susan, the tenth most attractive white woman in the room.

It could be argued that the bluntness of Sissy's dialogue with, and chastisement of, Edgar is a little too on point. There's not a lot of subtext here. But I would argue that Alexie succeeds partly because the comedy of Edgar's humiliation is so funny and on point and partly because he's pointing to class divisions and contradictions within communities of color that are often ignored. Then, too, perhaps it's hard not to feel that a certain amount of self-criticism and self-investigation occurs through the character of Edgar—after all Alexie himself now lives the middle-class life of a very successful writer as opposed to anything resembling the lives of Junior and Sissy.

If there is a certain resemblance between Edgar and Alexie, clearly Alexie is able to separate his identification with the character from his job as a writer. That job is to expose what lies beneath the imago of his protagonist by creating impediments and conflicts in the protagonist's quest to pursue his goal. Indeed, one senses a certain delight on the part of the writer in the ways he humiliates and humbles his protagonist, in the ways he takes apart Edgar's imago.

At the end of "Class," Edgar goes home and crawls into bed with his wife, and when she asks, "Where did you go?" he replies, "I was gone . . . But now I'm back." Through the events in the story, through the difficulties he has faced in both his conscious goal—to be married to Susan—and his emerging unconscious goal—to sleep with an Indian woman—Edgar has been forced to recognize who he has become and what his pursuit of his conscious goal must and has cost him. He has stopped lying to himself, at least for now, and his story therefore has reached its conclusion.

The A-B-C of
Multiple Story Lines

JUNOT DÍAZ'S "FIESTA"

In many short stories, the protagonist often pursues a very concrete goal: to teach a class, to take a trip, to separate herself from someone, to get a job, and so on. The protagonist then takes concrete actions to achieve that goal.

This pursuit of the main goal is what I call the A line of the story. There may also be a B line, which is sometimes a subplot—contemporaneous—or at other times background, say, a past narrative. Generally, the A line is told in a linear temporal fashion and is more extensive than the B line. If the B line is a subplot, it can move in a linear temporal fashion or not. It is usually shorter than the A line.*

Thus a story might have a teacher and her relationships with a class or a particular pupil as the A line. The B line might be a relationship with another teacher or the teacher's marriage. The B line could also be background, say, the history of the character.

There is sometimes a C line, what I dub the deep background—for example, some horrible incident the teacher experienced when she was a student. Or

* In some works, the A line is less dominant at times than the B or C line. In Marguerite Duras's autobiographical novel, The Lover, the story starts out simply with the image of the young Duras on a ferry crossing the Mekong. It is on this ferry that Duras will meet the Chinese banker who becomes her lover. The trip on the ferry is told in images, and it takes thirty-five pages before she finally meets the Chinese man. In between these images, Duras provides all sorts of background material—on her family, on who she was at sixteen (there are two adjoining paragraphs at one point, designating "what I know" and "what I don't know"), flashing forward to the future, talk about writing, love. The trip on the ferry becomes the clothesline on which she hangs a number of other things. But always it is clear that the through line of the novel is charting the progress of her affair with the Chinese banker.

The point I'm making is that the A line, the primary through line, generally needs to be clear and prominent. Then the other elements can be added. Remember that the central function of the B and the C line is to teach us how to read and interpret the A line.

something in the teacher's past that affects her teaching and how she views it. In short stories, this C line is generally not very expansive. It's merely the information the reader requires in order to contextualize the A line, to interpret its metaphoric and thematic resonances.

A perfect example of such a structure takes place in Junot Díaz's "Fiesta." In this story, a young Dominican boy and his family are going to visit relatives for a day of socializing and eating. But the boy has been prone to carsickness and often vomits on car rides if he has eaten beforehand. His short-tempered father has ordered him not to eat before the visit to his aunt's and especially during the visit.

The A line of the story covers the events of the day of the fiesta. In this A line, the goal of the protagonist is not to throw up. This means that he is supposed to resist the temptation to eat at the fiesta. The A line takes up the bulk of the story. There's also a B line involving events before the day of the fiesta and the protagonist's previous struggles not to throw up. The B line is there as a background.

Then there's the C line. While driving his son around to get him used to the car, the father stops a couple times at the house of his mistress. These visits introduce the theme of the father's adultery and how the father makes the protagonist a witness to his adultery.

In many ways, psychologically and thematically, the C line of "Fiesta" is the center of the story. So why does it occupy only a small section of the story?

There are two reasons for this, one structural, one aesthetic. In terms of structure, the obvious problem Díaz confronted when trying to write about the father's adultery is that it is the father who actively pursues the adultery, who takes actions to achieve a goal. In contrast, the boy in the story is merely a witness to the adultery; he is caught in a situation rather than attempting to achieve a goal. Thus, in regard to the adultery, the father takes actions and could be the protagonist, but the boy, who is in a passive position, could not.

Now the boy is supposed to remain silent about the father's adultery and that could be a goal, but that goal requires that the boy take passive actions. If the boy were trying to find a way to tell an adult, particularly his mother, about the adultery, a story might result from that situation, but that development probably is not in keeping with the autobiographical origins of this story.

Instead Díaz had to search for a goal that would better befit his protagonist's position as a child. Here the temptation of food, of refusing to obey the father's injunction not to eat, seems more appropriate to a young boy. Throughout the party at his aunt's house, the boy doesn't eat. But then his aunt takes him aside and offers him food, and the boy succumbs. The aunt then asks the boy about his father:

> How is it at home, Yunior?
>
> What do you mean?
>
> How's it going in the apartment? Are you kids OK?
>
> I knew an interrogation when I heard one, no matter how sugar-coated it was. I didn't say anything. Don't get me wrong, I loved my tia, but something told me to keep my mouth shut. Maybe it was family loyalty, maybe I just wanted to protect Mami or I was afraid that Papi would find out—it could have been anything really.

Yunior gives in to one temptation—to eat—but he refuses another—to tell about his father's adultery. So again, why not make the story about the latter?

The aesthetic answer is the same as that old screenwriter adage: if the scene is about what it's about, you're in deep shit. Art is metaphor; it is the discovery of the concrete representation of the abstract, whether that abstract be thematic or psychological. By focusing the story on the A line and the first temptation— to eat (and thus to vomit)—Díaz creates a metaphor for the C line and the second temptation—to tell about the father's adultery. The C line comes in only two brief sections, just a few paragraphs, but by the end of the story it tells the reader how to read the A line. The reader realizes that Yunior's nausea and vomiting are metaphors for the truth about his father, which he wants to reveal but knows he cannot.

At the end of the story, having eaten the food his aunt tempted him with, the boy fails to keep from vomiting, but he keeps what he knows about his father to himself. Though the presence of the father's adultery haunts the final passage of the story, the surface of the last line focuses on the A line and Yunior's failure to reach his goal:

> In the darkness, I saw that Papi had a hand on Mami's knee and that the two of them were quiet and still. They weren't slumped back or anything; they were both wide awake, bolted into their seats. I couldn't see either of their faces and no matter how hard I tried I could not imagine their expressions. Neither of them moved. Every now and then the van was filled with the bright rush of somebody else's headlights. Finally I said, Mami, and they both looked back, already knowing what was happening.

Of course, from another angle, Yunior does finally tell the truth about his father; that truth is the story, "Fiesta."

The Four Questions
Concerning the Narrator

FROM CONRAD'S MARLOW
TO DÍAZ'S YUNIOR

I

In terms of narration, a series of crucial and complicated questions confront any fiction writer:

Who is the narrator?

Whom is the narrator telling her story to?

When is the narrator telling the story?

Why is the narrator telling the story?

What is remarkable is how often beginning fiction writers do not ask these basic questions.

In my work with beginning fiction writers—and memoirists—I have found that confronting these questions is often essential to successfully moving forward with their work. In recent years, it's become clear to me that the increasing diversity of young writers has only made these questions more essential and relevant.

To put this in perspective, consider the original storytellers who sat around a fire after the day's activities and told their stories to their tribe. For such tellers and their audience, the answers to these questions—who is the narrator, whom is the narrator telling the story to, when is the narrator telling the story (relative to the events in the story)—would be readily apparent. The why of the story would be revealed in the telling.

But unlike with those gathered around the original campfires, we storytellers now come from many tribes, and our potential readers also come from many different tribes. The situation of our telling has changed. And yet what I am doing as a fiction writer still comes out of those original campfires and their stories. Storytelling is storytelling, yes. But the dialectic between the storyteller and the listener/reader is far more complicated now. Today's writer faces a far greater range of potential answers to the question, "Whom is the narrator telling the story to?"

When I gave a version of this essay at the Stonecoast MFA program of the University of Southern Maine, I started with a demonstration. I asked someone in the audience from Maine to explain where she lived to someone from San Francisco. I then asked the person from Maine to do this with someone from Maine.

Of course, the two explanations were quite different. The explanation to the person from San Francisco was more generalized; it took longer for the speaker to orient her listener, and she never did get very precise. With a fellow Mainer, the speaker used the names of towns and highway numbers. The cadence of her speech was quicker, punchier, the tone more familiar and intimate.

This demonstration was an example of two different economies of explanation between the speaker and the listener. In our conversations, we are constantly gauging how much our particular listener needs to know in order for us to be understood. In other words, we intuitively calculate what *the economy of explanation* will be for that particular listener. Such an assessment is even more crucial when one is telling a story.

II

To investigate this point, let me start with what is a relatively straightforward example, the 2008 Booker Prize winning novel, *The White Tiger*, by Aravind Adiga. Here's the opening of that novel:

For the Desk of:

His Excellency Wen Jiabao
The Premier's Office
Beijing
Capital of the Freedom-loving Nation of China

From the Desk of:

"The White Tiger"
A Thinking Man

And an Entrepreneur
Living in the world's center of Technology and Outsourcing
Electronics City Phase I (just off Hosur Main Road)
Bangalore, India

Mr. Premier,

Sir.

Neither you nor I speak English, but there are some things that can be said only in English.

My ex-employer the late Mr. Ashok's ex-wife, Pinky Madam, taught me one of these things; and at 11:32 p.m. today, which was about ten minutes ago, when the lady on All India Radio announced, "Premier Jiabao is coming to Bangalore next week," I said that thing at once. . . .

I have something important to tell you. See, the lady on the radio said, "Mr Jiabao is on a mission: he wants to know the truth about Bangalore."

My blood froze. If anyone knows the truth about Bangalore, it's *me.* . . .

When you have heard the story of how I got to Bangalore and become one of its most successful (though probably least known) businessmen, you will know everything there is to know about how entrepreneurship is born, nurtured, and developed in this, the glorious twenty-first century of man.

The century, more specifically, of the *yellow* and the *brown* man.

You and me.

It is a little before midnight now, Mr. Jiabao. A good time for me to talk.

By the fifth page of the novel, certain basic questions concerning the narrator have been answered. Balram Halwai, a Bangalore entrepreneur, is writing to Wen Jiabao, the premier of China, to tell Jiabao the truth about the Bangalore economic boom. Balram will do this by telling his own story of how he rose from humble origins to become a successful businessman.

In a review in the *New York Times*, Akash Kapur describes the novel's opening:

Balram's triumphal narrative, framed somewhat inexplicably as a letter to the visiting Chinese premier, unfurls over seven days and nights in Bangalore. . . .

As a parable of the new India, then, Balram's tale has a distinctly macabre twist. He is not (or not only) an entrepreneur but a roguish criminal with a remarkable capacity for self-justification. Likewise, the background against which he operates is not just a resurgent economy and nation but a landscape of corruption, inequality and poverty.

Kapur here summarizes the tale but finds the way the tale is told to be inexplicable. Why does Adiga choose this letter form? And why a letter to Wen Jiabao?

The answer to these questions can be derived by considering the economy of explanation. Through the letter, the reader knows that the narrator, Balram Halwai, is telling his tale to Wen Jiabao, the premier of China. If Balram were telling his story to one of his cousins in his home village, the story he tells would take a very different form. Balram could refer to members of the family, places in the village, without any need of explanation or even description. His cousin would know these same family members, would know these same places.

But in addressing the premier of China, Balram knows that there will be many things in his tale—people, places, customs, beliefs, social conventions, historical events—that Wen Jiabao will probably be unfamiliar with. To make the story comprehensible to the premier of China, Balram will have to define or provide a gloss to these elements that are unfamiliar to Wen Jiabao. When Balram works as a driver, he explains to Wen Jiabao the nonlinear way street numbers are placed in New Delhi. When Balram is sent to buy liquor for his employer, he provides his epistolary partner with the following sociology: "I should explain to you, Mr. Jiabao, that in this country we have two kinds of men: 'Indian' liquor men and 'English' liquor men. 'Indian' liquor was for village boys like me—toddy, arrack, country hooch. 'English' liquor, naturally, is for the rich. Rum, whisky, beer, gin—anything the English left behind."

By choosing the particular audience of Wen Jiabao for his tale, Balram establishes a precise economy of explanation. It is clear he must explain any reference that the premier of China might not be familiar with.

On a different plane, in choosing the narrator and the audience that he does, Adiga also chooses his relationship to his readership. His novel is designed and designated for an audience beyond an English-speaking Indian readership. Of course, Adiga knows English-speaking Indians will read this novel; after all, it's a picaresque tale about an exuberant and ambitious Indian villager who experiences the economic changes taking place in India in recent years. Moreover, many Indian readers are interested not just in what is happening in their country but also in how the rest of the world perceives what is happening in their country, and the letters from Balram to Wen Jiabao play on the increasing international business concerns of India. But given the particular audience that Balram chooses to tell his story to, the novel's events are presented in a way that will be understandable to readers who are not very knowledgeable about India and Indian culture. An English-speaking reader in Liverpool or Topeka can make her way through this novel without constantly having to refer to Google and Wikipedia, without constantly feeling that there are cultural references and subtleties that she might be missing.

Balram is addressing not just a stranger but a foreigner, and a foreigner who is privileged and powerful and probably did not start from the bottom as Balram has. Thus the tone of the novel will be more formal than informal, more extroverted than introverted, more in the tone of a guide rather than an emotional intimate, more about surface events than deep psychological explorations. The author tries to ameliorate some of these losses by having Balram emphasize his connection to Wen Jiabao as two men of color and to a certain extent two men of Asia. The fact that Balram wants to help the Chinese premier understand the how and why of the Indian economic progress lends an urgency and purpose to his narrative. This is the why of his telling of Balram's tale. At the same time, it's obvious that if Balram were addressing a cousin in his village or say his wife, the voice and tone of the novel would be entirely different, and what the novel would explore would, most likely, be entirely different, even with the same set of events constituting the story. If the writer chooses one aesthetic path, other paths become closed.

But that is precisely why it is useful for a writer to be aware of these choices and their implications, especially when addressing these basic questions about the narrator.

III

Let me turn now to a work of fiction where the narrator addresses his story not to a stranger but to a group of intimates, men much like himself—Conrad's *Heart of Darkness.**

To understand Conrad's aesthetic choices in this work, it is useful to recall his biography and his position as an immigrant writer. Conrad was born and raised in Poland, then traveled the world as a young man as a sailor; in his thirties, he came to write his books not in his first language or even his second, French, but in his third language, English. In various ways, he felt as if he were an outsider within English society, a stranger in its midst. Moreover, as a result of his world travels, the subjects he was writing about—the colonial ivory trade in Central Africa, a revolution in a South American country, a disgraced seaman

---

* I'm aware of the objections to this work, which have focused on its racist elements and its convoluted defense of colonialism. I refer readers to Chinua Achebe's *Things Fall Apart* and Achebe's essay critiquing Conrad's portrait of the relationship between colonists and Africans.

who takes up residence in Malaysia—were not the traditional subject matter or experiences depicted in the English novel. Conrad's version of *Great Expectations* might have told the story of Magwich in Australia rather than the adventures of Pip.

For someone in Conrad's unique position—a Polish ex-sailor and colonial traveler writing in English—his relationship to his audience presented a constant question, on both a practical and an aesthetic level. It's no accident that Marlow first appears in "Youth," which Conrad wrote just after he had signed a contract with the literary journal *Blackwood's Edinburgh Magazine.* Ian Watt explains the connection between *Blackwood's* and the way Marlow is set up to tell his tale in *Heart of Darkness:*

> The first Marlow story, "Youth," was also the first story which Conrad ever wrote with a particular group of readers—that of *Blackwood's*—in mind. This defined audience may have given Conrad the initial psychological impetus towards dramatizing a fictional situation in which a narrator rather like Conrad addresses an audience rather like *Blackwood's*. Marlow's listeners comprise a company director, an accountant, a Tory lawyer, and a primary narrator, all of them ex-seamen; in effect they are a composite of the two audiences Conrad had himself encountered—those at sea and those he now visualized as his readers. . . .
>
> At all events, through the presence of Marlow's companions on the *Nellie*, the old friendly commerce of oral storyteller and the listening group is restored.

For an outsider like Conrad to determine the range of knowledge and expectations of the general reading public in England was a difficult task. And yet without a firm grasp of who his readership might be, he would have been hard pressed to determine the economy of explanation for the story and material in *Heart of Darkness.*

I believe Conrad reached an aesthetic solution to this problem by considering certain factors and influences that were available to him. First, *Blackwood's* was the type of journal that would be found in the lobby of English men's clubs, which were a prominent aspect of British society in the nineteenth and early twentieth centuries. There was a minor tradition of men's club novels—novels in which a member of the men's club told a story to other members of the club in a sitting room or over dinner. It is easy to see how Conrad might have connected this literary tradition with the Polish oral storytelling tradition of the *gaweda*. This men's club novel gave Conrad a firmer grasp of who his audience might be. But then, by setting Marlow's telling on a ship on the Thames amid a group who might belong to the same men's club but who are also all sailors, Conrad further homogenized and particularized the group to which Marlow would be telling his tale. This gave Conrad a much firmer grasp of what Marlow's—and thus Conrad's own—economy of explanation might be.

Beyond this, the use of Marlow and the storytelling tradition returns the quality of orality to the text. As the first unnamed narrator makes clear, he—and hence the reader—was listening to an oral version of the story of Marlow and Kurtz.

> The traffic of the great city went on in the deepening night upon the sleepless river. We looked on, waiting patiently—there was nothing else to do till the end of the flood; but it was only after a long silence, when he said, in a hesitating voice, "I suppose you fellows remember I did once turn fresh-water sailor for a bit," that we knew we were fated, before the ebb began to run, to hear about one of Marlow's inconclusive experiences.
>
> "I don't want to bother you much with what happened to me personally," he began, showing in this remark the weakness of many tellers of tales who seem so often unaware of what their audience would best like to hear; "yet to understand the effect of it on me you ought to know how I got out there, what I saw, how I went up that river to the place where I first met the poor chap."

This orality, this teller of a tale, stands in contrast to Flaubert's aesthetic of a cooler—less emotional, less subjective—and writerly (recall Flaubert's concentration on style) text. In a way that isn't quite apparent in *Heart of Darkness*, Conrad points to a very different direction in writing from that of Flaubert.

For an American audience, this direction becomes clearer if we recall the difference between Twain's *The Adventures of Huckleberry Finn* and James's *Portrait of a Lady*. Hemingway once pronounced *Huckleberry Finn* the seminal work in American literature, and to a large extent, it's the colloquial style of Huck's storytelling, the presence of the spoken voice as opposed to the Jamesian written text, that lies at the marrow of this judgment.

But there are other ways in which Conrad's use of Marlow stands in contrast to the more neutral stance of Flaubert. Unlike Flaubert's projected godlike author who never announces his presence, Marlow is everywhere present; he is the lens through which we are told, and through which we view, the story. As readers, we must be actively engaged in judging his telling, in assessing where Marlow's subjectivity might be coming into play. Indeed, Marlow never pretends to be objective. He's telling the story of Kurtz for a purpose, one that he himself· has a stake in.

Here it might be useful to bring in the third question concerning the narrator: When is the narrator telling this story? From Marlow's rendition, it's clear he's a few years removed from his experiences in Africa. But not so much time has passed that he feels these events are beyond disturbing or engaging him; he still doesn't possess enough distance in time to view the events objectively. No, he remains passionately connected to Kurtz, to the desire to redeem or at least ameliorate Kurtz's actions. That is part of the why of his storytelling.

At the same time, Marlow is still trying to properly assess Kurtz's character, to discover or decipher just where and how Kurtz moved away from the path of light into darkness. Marlow clearly feels both a certain affection for Kurtz and a certain loathing of him; he is attracted to the man and repelled. He seems to be telling the story again with the hope that he might finally settle on an interpretation of his experiences in Africa and of Kurtz. Yet in the telling Marlow finds that nothing has been settled, that his questions and doubts about himself and the man still remain. It is partially because Marlow is so engaged with Kurtz and his history, because Marlow cannot seem to let Kurtz go, that we the readers become similarly engaged. In this mode, a subjective and partial narrator involves us with his story in ways that a more neutral third-person telling—like Flaubert's neutral godlike narrator—might not.

Because Kurtz remains beyond Marlow's understanding and Marlow's ability to capture him in his telling, Kurtz and his story possess dimensions and reverberations that a more straightforward, realistic third-person version of his story would not. As some writers have observed, for certain larger-than-life, many-sided characters, it is often best that the character be observed by others, that is, that the reader never be provided a direct glimpse into the character's consciousness afforded by an omniscient third-person voice. Thus, Ahab is seen from the point of view of Ishmael, Kurtz by Marlow, Gatsby by Nick Carraway. The protagonist doesn't tell his story; it is told by a secondary character, by the one who survives.

IV

On a more practical rather than literary-history plane, how are these four basic questions concerning the narrator useful for your practice as a writer of fiction or memoir?

The tradition of Flaubert's omniscient godlike, nonintrusive, everywhere-present, but not detectable author still guides many of our fiction-writing practices. As a result, when you write in the third-person, omniscient voice, you might not ask yourself who the narrator is or whom the narrator is telling the story to.

And yet whether you ask yourself this question or not, in your novel—and in your memoir—you are narrating a story. Thus, you are choosing a "you" to tell the story, even if you don't think about who this narrator might be.

But if you do ask yourself who the narrator is, you must ask: Is this narrator a person like myself? And what properties of this narrator make her like me? Does that include my ethnic and/or racial identity? What are the narrator's linguistic tendencies or skills or range of languages or reference? Or am I consciously or unconsciously assuming a persona as a narrator of this story (some developing writers of color feel a pressure to assume the voice of a white middle-class narrator)? And if this is a persona, who is this persona? Which linguistic tendencies or skills or range of language or reference does this persona possess? If I am writing of a world outside a narrowly defined white middle-class range of experience—whether in terms of ethnicity or race or sexuality or class or in terms of science fiction or fantasy—is the narrator part of the world she is narrating about or is she not from that world?

Of course, if your narration is in a first-person voice, you will inevitably ask, Who is this narrator? And who is this narrator's voice going to speak or write like? You realize that you are not just positing a narrator; you are creating a character with a voice.

But the question of who is the narrator also bears a relationship to the question of whom the narrator is telling the story to because any narrator adjusts the telling of her story to the audience she is telling the story to. If she does not know the audience she is telling the story to, she does not know what knowledge and experience she can assume on the part of her listeners/readers and what knowledge she needs to provide for her listeners/readers to understand the story she is telling.

As a way of demonstrating and explaining my point here, I'll describe an exercise my friend, the writer Chris Abani, conducts with his students. In this exercise, Abani asks a student to tell the class a five-minute story about anything the student chooses. He records the student telling the story.

Invariably, the student tells a clear and coherent story, one that no one in the class has trouble understanding. Yet that clarity and coherence may actually be missing from the student's written stories. In those stories, there are often points where readers find themselves confused, where they find themselves asking, What is this story about? Often, for instance, the student's language when she writes a story has little resemblance to the language she uses to tell her oral story. Abani also maintains that the narrative structure of the oral story is probably closer to the narrative structure that is most natural to the student.

In this exercise, why is the student's oral story so clear and often so much more engaging on a basic level than her written work? One reason is that when the student is telling the oral story to the class, she is constantly considering what her listeners need to know in order to understand the story. To use my term, she has a fairly clear vision of what her economy of explanation needs to be.

Indeed, in all our conversations with various people, we are constantly gauging what our economy of explanation must be—that is, what we can assume our listener knows or understands and what requires further knowledge or explication. Each of us tells a story differently depending on who is listening to the story—for example, if the listener is an intimate or a stranger, part of our tribe (however we define it) or not.

But often when we sit down to write, we don't think of ourselves as addressing a reader or, if we do, we have a very generalized or vague notion of who our readership might be. As a result, we don't have a clear idea of what our economy of explanation will be. At times we may overexplain, use more words than we need. At times we will underexplain or omit information that the reader needs. The result is a text that is confusing not just for the reader, no matter who the reader might be, but also for the reader who wonders, Just who is this writer writing to and for?

I know, I know. In some quarters, you have been told not to think of the reader or your audience. If you do so, supposedly you'll just lose your way or begin to write for the concerns of others or in reaction to the pressure of others.

But what I'm talking about here is not a commercial consideration. It's the consideration that storytellers have been making since the very first human beings started telling stories. You are telling stories to an audience; you are trying to communicate, so wouldn't it make sense that you decide who your audience is, whom you are trying to communicate with?*

---

* The question of whom your narrator is telling the story to certainly doesn't mean that you should consider the broadest possible audience or that you should make this question a commercial consideration. No, this question is an aesthetic question, and the more precisely the writer answers it, the more precise his writing can be and the clearer the purpose for that writing.

V

Let me conclude with an example that is the opposite of Aravind Adiga's *The White Tiger*: Junot Díaz's *The Brief Wondrous Life of Oscar Wao*. This novel is told by Yunior, a Dominican American, about his friend Oscar and Oscar's family. At the novel's start, Yunior says that the story of Oscar, Yunior's college roommate, which is also Oscar's family's story, is a *fukú*—a curse—story. The story spans three generations, and the curse starts when the dictator Trujillo imprisons Oscar's grandfather. The novel follows Oscar's mother's life, her immigration to America, and her starting a family and then how the nerdy, overweight Oscar falls in love with and persists in an ill-fated affair with a Dominican prostitute.

To contextualize Yunior, the narrator of *Oscar Wao*, it's useful to look at Díaz's first book, a collection of short stories, *Drown*. A few of the stories there are written from the point of view of Yunior, a young Dominican American, who came to the United States as a child. In the stories, Yunior has arrived at a young enough age that he probably doesn't speak English with a Dominican accent and has gained mastery of the language used by urban kids of color. At the same time, given his roots in the community and his mother's limited English, Spanish remains part of his daily vocabulary. The language of *Drown* is a mixture of these languages. Though the reader senses that Yunior is a bright kid, there's no evidence of any intellectual or literary language in *Drown*. Nor are there many references to American pop culture.

But for *The Brief Wondrous Life of Oscar Wao*, Díaz presents a Yunior who has gone to college, who's an intellectual and a budding writer, who is familiar with the theories of postcoloniality and race; at the same time, this Yunior is someone who grew up during the era of hip-hop and possesses a knowledge of the American culture of that era, including an encyclopedic acquaintance with the genres of science fiction and fantasy:

> No matter what its name or provenance, it is believed the arrival of Europeans on Hispaniola unleashed the fukú on the world, and we've all been in the shit ever since. . . .
>
> A couple weeks ago, while I was finishing this book, I posted the thread fukú on the DRI forum, just out of curiosity. These days I'm nerdy like that. The talkback blew the fuck up. You should see how many responses I've gotten. They just keep coming in. And not just from Domos. The Puertorocks want to talk about fufus, and the Haitians have some shit just like it . . .

I'm not entirely sure Oscar would have liked this designation. Fukú
story. He was hardcore sci-fi and fantasy man, believed that that was the
kind of story we were all living in. He'd ask: What more sci-fi than the Santo
Domingo? What more fantasy than the Antilles?

Rather than the consciousness of a typical immigrant Dominican kid, in *Oscar Wao* Díaz chooses to create a narrator whose consciousness and linguistic range and abilities are closer to his own. In this choice, he's told me that he learned from the example of fellow New Jerseyean Philip Roth and Roth's use of his fictional alter ego, Nathan Zuckerman. In his early Zuckerman novels, Roth focused on Zuckerman's life, particularly his trials and tribulations as an author and a Jewish son. But in novels such as *I Married a Communist*, *American Pastoral*, and *The Human Stain*, Zuckerman narrates the tale of other characters. This allows Roth to tell the story in a language that uses the full range and sensibilities of his skills as a novelist, a language where he never feels like he has to pull back or put on the stops because such language would seem unrealistic in the mouth of his narrator. At the same time, by using Zuckerman, Roth posits a narrator who, in various ways, has a personal stake in the story he is telling. This is the same choice Díaz makes for his narrator, Yunior, in *The Brief Wondrous Life of Oscar Wao*.

But the key to that book's narrative voice also lies in the audience Díaz chooses for Yunior's narration: That audience is made up of college-educated Dominicans from the same generation as Yunior (and Díaz), Dominicans who have immigrated to the United States early enough to speak English without an accent or much of an accent and who are thoroughly conversant both with American culture and street language and with Dominican culture and Spanish. Through his choice of this audience, Díaz is able to create in Yunior an immigrant voice that is brilliantly colloquial, intellectual, and both Dominican and American.

Just as importantly, with such an audience, the economy of explanation is clear, both for Díaz and for his narrator, Yunior. No Spanish need be translated; a familiarity with Dominican culture is assumed (though Yunior still must footnote an explanation of the reign and history of Trujillo); pop cultural references can be dropped without explanation or context. In contrast to *The White Tiger* and Balram's formal address to the premier of China, Yunior's voice is intimate and alludes to a shared experience.

For many readers of Díaz's generation, including those who are not Dominican, Yunior's voice resonates with and speaks to them. Thus, there are ways in which non-Dominican readers feel they are dropping in on an intimate conversation, and because the speaker and listener understand each other, the outside reader can intuit much of what is being said—including the Spanish—through context. (At the same time, my very assimilated Nisei mother found *The Brief Wondrous Life of Oscar Wao* impenetrable, whereas she loves Jhumpa Lahiri's work. As I've said earlier, each aesthetic choice provides both benefits and losses.)

In his aesthetic choices, Díaz refuses to place either Yunior or Oscar at the margins of his storytelling or of the culture. He also shows other authors from immigrant or marginalized communities how they might tell their tales without resorting to an economy of explanation where everything must be made clear to a white mainstream readership or some vague picture of a majority audience.

In this moment when we are becoming more and more aware of the increasing diversity of America, Díaz's Yunior points to an aesthetic answer that is different from Flaubert's godlike author and more like the immigrant Conrad's Marlow.

A final word on the question, Why is the narrator telling the tale?

This is a useful question to ask even if the tale is told in the third-person omniscient mode, where who the narrator is may never be concretely identified. Any storyteller tells a story for a reason, and if the author doesn't know that reason, asking this question can help focus and shape the narration.

With first-person narrators, the why of the telling is often clearer—and if it is not, perhaps it should be made so. Often, there's a sense that the story or the protagonist haunts the narrator, as Gatsby haunts Nick Carraway or Kurtz haunts Marlowe or Ahab Ishmael. Of course, there can be other reasons, such as Balram Halwai wanting to tell the premier of China the truth about Bangalore's economic boom.

In terms of time, Yunior tells his story of Oscar after a few years have passed since Oscar's death. As with Marlow and Kurtz, Yunior is still close enough to the story to remain haunted by it, because it is a *fukú*, or curse story. At the beginning of the novel, after a long disquisition on the nature of *fukú*, Yunior tells the reader:

> As I'm sure you've guessed by now, I have a fukú story too. I wish I could say it was the best of the lot—fukú number one—but I can't. Mine ain't the scariest, the clearest, the most painful, or the most beautiful.
>
> It just happens to be the one that's got its fingers around my throat.

Yunior is compelled to tell this story, in part because he was Oscar's friend and as such wonders if he could have done anything to save Oscar from his ill-fated destiny. At the same time, his telling of this story constitutes his own *zafa*, his own counterspell against the *fukú*. Yunior's affection for Oscar and his sister, whom Yunior briefly goes out with, is clear, and his telling is, in a way, a redemption of Oscar, a rescue from meaninglessness or absurdity. From the very beginning, we know why Yunior is telling his story, and that is part of what binds the novel's familial story together and keeps the reader engaged with the telling.

The question, Why is the narrator telling the story? is also crucial to the writing of memoir; indeed, fiction writers can learn from memoirists and how they answer this question (and vice versa). I'll explore all this in the next section and essay.

III

Narrative and Identity
in Memoir

The Four Questions of
the Narrator in Memoir

MARGUERITE DURAS'S *THE LOVER*
AND MARY KARR'S *THE LIARS' CLUB*

Contemporary memoir has borrowed many techniques and principles from fiction, particularly when the memoir employs a narrative structure. While many critics have noted this borrowing, it is less obvious how a study of memoir can benefit from a consideration of four questions regarding the narrator: Who is the narrator? Whom is the narrator telling the story to? When is the narrator telling the story? Why is the narrator telling the story?

With memoir, the answer to the question, Who is the narrator? seems obvious at first: The narrator is the person writing the memoir. In actuality, however, this question is more complicated than it appears. Memoirs recount events and experiences of a past self. Thus they re-create not just those events and experiences but also that past self, who exists in the text as someone different from the present narrating self.

In a way, then, the present narrating self approaches this past self as if the past self were a separate character, which in a way she is. What is not always clear is that the present narrating self is both a creation of the writer and a character in the memoir.

Most literary memoirs then invoke two selves: who you were then and who you are now telling the story of who you were then. These are two different selves and in a way two different characters. To grasp the implications of this difference, it might be helpful to consider fictional narratives where the narrator is different from the main character: The past self is Kurtz, Ahab, Gatsby, Oscar Wao; the present narrating self is Marlow, Ishmael, Nick, Yunior.

Many beginning memoirists fail to understand this dialectic, and their portrait of the present narrating self can often be vague or disembodied. Moreover, they fail to see how the present narrating self is the vehicle through which the writer addresses the four questions of the narrator, particularly the last question, Why is the narrator telling the story?

I've spoken here of the present narrating self as a somewhat stable entity, and as captured in the text, she is. But my former Stonecoast MFA student, Helen Peppe, author of the memoir *Pigs Can't Swim*, has reminded me that the process of establishing that present narrating self is a messy and complicated one, subject to the movement of time. As she observed in an e-mail to me, "I think one of the challenges of memoir writing is to tell the story in a way that takes into account how we change everyday, that the difference between then and now can be only a second. When I go to these presentations on narration, the presenter talks about the then narrator and the now narrator as spanning years, but we change in some way every day. If we didn't, we'd be dead."

Among other things, Peppe is alluding here to shifts in the ways she understood and configured her racial identity as a white person and the sexual abuse she endured as a child. It took time and struggle for her to explore and understand these aspects of her experience, which were fundamental to the creation of the present narrating self in her memoir and what that narrator focused on in telling the story of her past self. Thinking over the process of writing her memoir, Peppe implies that she herself and thus her present narrating self went through crucial shifts and re-formations of her identity and her relationship to her past self. All this took time. Sometimes these shifts also become part of what is recounted in the memoir.

In memoir then, a crucial and revealing question is: When is the story being told? How much time separates the present narrating self from the past self?

When I teach writing memoir to undergrads, a problem often arises. If they are writing about an event or experience when they were sixteen, there is often not enough difference between the present narrating nineteen-year-old self and the past sixteen-year-old self. The present narrating self doesn't possess sufficient distance or perspective, hasn't lived enough to be able to understand her experiences at sixteen in a new light. She isn't able to uncover aspects of that experience or ways of looking at it that might reveal something unknown or undiscovered, nor does she generally have enough distance or maturity to crack the denials and defenses of her sixteen-year-old self and regard that self as a separate person, a separate character. Thus she often cannot then see those around that sixteen-year-old self, particularly her parents, in a different light, as more three-dimensional human beings. I've found that this problem, which stems from a lack of temporal distance, can occur even with writers in their twenties.

By way of contrast, it's useful to look at Marguerite Duras's autobiographical novel, *The Lover*, which begins:

> One day, I was already old, in the entrance of a public place a man came up to me. He introduced himself and said, "I've known you for years. Everyone says you were beautiful when you were young, but I want to tell you I think you're more beautiful now than then. Rather than your face as a young woman, I prefer your face as it is now. Ravaged."

With that opening, the reader feels assured that enough time has passed for the narrating self to develop a considered perspective on the events of the past. The present self is not just much older and decades removed from the experience she will write about, but she is also past vanity. Note too how this opening remark characterizes the present narrating self as someone who is ready to welcome the truth, no matter how harsh it might be. Then there's the other change that time has brought to the circumstances of her writing: all the principals, that is, her family, are dead. She has no one anymore to protect: "I've written a good deal about the members of my family, but then they were still alive, my mother and my brothers. And I skirted around them, skirted around all these things without really tackling them."

In these circumstances of her old age, Duras returns to a period of her life that she's written about before. But she tells us that she is going to explore a different layer of that experience, aspects that have long been hidden—in her writing and perhaps in her memory, a silence she has been living with. To break this silence is the purpose of this autobiographical novel, which reads so like a memoir:

> The story of one small part of my youth I've already written, more or less—I mean, enough to give a glimpse of it. Of this part, I mean, the part about the crossing of the river. What I'm doing now is both different and the same. Before, I spoke of clear periods, those on which the light fell. Now I'm talking about the hidden stretches of that same youth, of certain facts, feelings, events that I buried. I started to write in surroundings that drove me to reticence. Writing, for those people, was still something moral. Nowadays it often seems writing is nothing at all. Sometimes I realize that if writing isn't, all things, all contraries confounded, a quest for vanity and void, it's nothing.

Nearing seventy, Duras's narrating self describes the past from the perspective of the present, from someone who knows what eventually happened to her teenage self, that is, someone who knows her fate. In this way, she can function as one of Berger's storytellers with a godlike perspective looking at her past self traveling through time: "Now I see that when I was very young, eighteen, fifteen, I already had a face that foretold the one I acquired through drink in middle age." In the pages that follow, the present narrating self will describe what her fifteen-year-old self knows about her beauty and her sexuality. Then she describes what her fifteen-year-old self does not know. This dialectic between the present narrating self and the past self provides a resonance and depth to the writing that would not otherwise be present if the knowledge and understanding of the present narrating self were not given voice to. In the distance between the past moment when, at fifteen and a half, this French colonial girl meets her first lover, a Chinese banker, while crossing the Mekong River, and the present moment of the telling, more than a half century later, time becomes a third and very palpable character.

One final advantage that Duras employs in writing *The Lover* also stems in part from age (well, age and talent). Her narrator knows whom she is telling this story to—to the readers of Duras. Throughout the narrator makes reference to previous works. Sometimes she does this to contrast with the present work. At other times it's a sly and knowing nod to her longtime readers. Describing the limousine of the Chinese bankers, she writes: "It's a Morris Leon-Bolle. The black Lancia at the French embassy in Calcutta hasn't yet made its entrance on the literary scene." Given the nature of her work and her career, Duras's narrating self knows whom she is addressing quite intimately, since they are intimate with her work. It's a nice position to be in.

On another level, though, her choice of audience here is not so different from the one Díaz makes with his narrator, Yunior: She is writing to the members of her tribe.

Now some "tribes" may contain more people or seem more powerful or prominent than others. But that doesn't mean a writer of memoir can't make an aesthetic choice and assume that her narrating self could be speaking to members of her tribe, whatever that tribe may be.

In the opening of *The Woman Warrior*, Maxine Hong Kingston makes an address to her imagined readers that focuses the economy of explanation of her text and acknowledges whom she is addressing her tales to: "Chinese-Americans, when you try to understand what things in you are Chinese, how do you separate what is peculiar to childhood, to poverty, insanities, one family, your mother who marked your growing with stories, from what is Chinese? What is Chinese tradition and what is the movies?"

Through these remarks, Kingston not only designates the immediate or prime audience for her tales but also the purpose of her memoir, why she is telling these tales—she wants to answer these questions. In the end, she never comes to final or definitive answers; in a certain sense, from the very beginning, she knows these questions are impossible to answer. Still, in another light, the asking is the answer.

But *The Woman Warrior* also posits a deeper reason for its narratives. In the opening chapter, "No Name Woman," Kingston tells the story of an aunt who back in China gave birth to a baby out of wedlock, how the aunt's adulterous affair ended in disaster for the family—the villagers attack and ransack their home—and in suicide on the part of the aunt. Like Díaz's Yunior in *The Brief Wondrous Life of Oscar Wao*, Kingston is haunted by a death that, in the light of Chinese customs and culture, can also be regarded as a curse: "My aunt haunts me—her ghost drawn to me because now, after fifty years of neglect, I alone devote pages of paper to her, though not origamied into houses and clothes. I do not think she always means me well. I am telling on her, and she was a spite suicide, drowning herself in the drinking water."

Kingston is telling the stories of her past then as antidote or counterspell, a *zafa* to ward off any curse from her aunt's ghost and her ancestors.

As I've watched student writers begin memoirs, I've witnessed how at first they labor hard just to get down the events of the past, working against gaps in memory, against their own denial or that of others in their family; this part of writing involves struggling to connect with and unearth the painful memories of the past, traumas, and secrets. In the midst of such difficulties, it's understandable that the question, Why am I telling this story? might be neglected. But at a certain point, the writer of memoir must ask herself this question.

When Díaz was working on *Oscar Wao*, he and I had a discussion one night about the motif of the curse. Eventually, he saw it as a way of binding together his tale of three generations of one family. It seems to me that many memoirs are, at their heart, a *zafa*—a counterspell to ward off or end a curse, to transform the past into something more than a burden or a sentence of doom. This is, I've suggested, part of the raison d'être for Maxine Hong Kingston's *The Woman Warrior*.

A similar purpose lies at the heart of Mary Karr's *The Liars' Club*. The memoir opens with a chaotic night when Karr is seven. The family doctor is questioning the young Karr, asking her, "Show me the marks," and assuring her that he won't hurt her. The sheriff is at the door, and the young girl thinks, "*I done something wrong and here's the sheriff.*" Further details are presented, almost randomly: A fireman moves through the room, there's an ambulance outside. Doors slam. She's being led away by the sheriff. Neither of her parents is present. Her dad's at work. Her mother has been hauled away "for being Nervous."

The implication here is that the mother has done something to Karr and her sister, has hurt them, but the exact nature of what has happened is unclear, at least in the mind of Karr at seven, as she is pictured. Instead, the young Karr is more concerned with where the sheriff will take her to stay. Despite the young Karr's worry that she and her sister don't go to the Smothergills' home, the voice of the narrating present self informs us, "I don't remember who we got farmed out to or how long." And then this narrating present self takes firm control over how she is going to present the story of Karr's childhood and her family:

> Because it took so long for me to paste together what happened, I will leave that part of the story missing for a while. It went long unformed for me, and I want to keep it that way here. I don't mean to be coy. When the truth would be unbearable the mind often just blanks it out. But some ghost of an event may stay in your head. Then, like the smudge of a bad word quickly wiped off a school blackboard, this ghost can call undue attention to itself by its very vagueness. You keep studying the dim shape of it, as if the original form will magically emerge. This blank spot in my past, then, spoke most loudly to me by being blank. It was a hole in my life that I both feared and kept coming back to because I couldn't quite fill it in.
>
> I did know from that night forward that things in my house were Not Right, this despite the fact that the events I have described so far had few outward results. No one ever mentioned the night again.

The events of this night become a tipping point, a turn toward the "Not Right" that make it a significant, if not *the* significant, event of Karr's childhood. Karr, or rather the present narrating self, states that she's not going to tell us at this point what exactly happened that night because that night lived on in her childhood, as she describes it, as a "blank spot . . . a hole in my life that I both feared and kept coming back to because I couldn't quite fill in."

The present narrating self wants the reader to experience that night and its memory the way her past self experienced it while growing up. At the same time, the present narrating self is aware that she's setting up a question in the reader's mind, one that the reader will want answered by the end of the book: What really happened that night? Thus, this question becomes part of the narrative drive of the book. Implicitly, the present narrating self is assuring us that, eventually, she will tell us what happened. Note that narrative drive can often stem from an announced and/or deliberate withholding of information. The reader continues on to obtain key revelations. (At other times, information—such as a warning or prediction or prophecy—can create narrative momentum.)

As the book proceeds through two designated time periods, Texas 1961 and Colorado 1963, the present narrating self recounts more events and experiences that further amplify the ways the family is "Not Right." There are hints at the existence of secrets that might explain why this is so, and why the family seems haunted not just by the ghost of this night but by other ghosts who occupy other blank spots in the family's memory, other zones of silence.

The key revelations in the book take place in the final section, "Texas Again, 1980," when Karr is twenty-five; her childhood is over; she has moved away from home but has returned. Her father's dying; he's had a stroke. Her father's old commander visits him and suggests to Karr that if she can find her father's army medical records confirming that he was wounded in World War II, perhaps she can get the army to see his present condition as a result of those wounds and thus pay for his medical care.

Searching in her parents' attic, Karr finds a box of photos, with labels, and this leads her to question her mother about her past. Before she does so, though, she calls her therapist, who tells her to write out her questions, and in this list, Karr reveals casually the nature of what happened on the night which opens the memoir, the night her mother was hauled away: "*Whose wedding rings were those? Who were the two kids Grandma Moore showed me school pictures of? After she died, why did you go nuts? What were you doing with the knife that night? Why did you tell Dr. Boudreaux you'd killed us? What happened to you in the hospital?*"

Eventually Karr gets her mother to talk about her past; they go to a bar where they both begin drinking and the mother tells her tale. She reveals she had been married several times before she married Karr's father. Moreover, one of those marriages resulted in two children, but her mother's husband and his mother took those children and disappeared. By the time Karr's mother finally found them, her children reacted to her as if she were a stranger, and she decided it would be best if they stayed with her father, since she felt he was far better equipped, both financially and because of his mother, to care for the children. Taking in this past and this revelation of her mother's pain, Karr asks her mother about "the night":

> These were my mother's demons, then, two small children, who she longed for and felt ashamed for having lost.
>
> And the night she'd stood in our bedroom door with a knife? She'd drunk herself to the bottom of that despair. "All the time I'd wasted, marrying fellows. And still I lost those kids. And you and Lecia couldn't change that. And I'd wound up just as miserable as I started at fifteen." Killing us had come to seem merciful. In fact, she'd hallucinated we'd been stabbed to death. "I saw blood all over you and everything else. Splashed across the walls."

After her mother's confession, Karr and her mother, both drunk, drive home from the bar:

> The sunset we drove into that day was luminous, glowing; we weren't.
>
> Though we should have glowed, for what Mother told absolved us both, in a way. All the black crimes we believed ourselves guilty of were myths, stories we'd cobbled together out of fear. We expected no good news interspersed with the bad. Only the dark aspect of any story sank in. I never knew despair could lie. So at the time, I only felt the car hurtling like some cold steel capsule I'd launched into onrushing dark.
>
> It's only looking back that I believe the clear light of truth should have filled us, like the legendary grace that carries a broken body past all manner of monsters. I'm thinking of the cool tunnel of white light the spirit might fly into at death, or so some have reported after coming back from various car wrecks and heart failures and drownings, courtesy of defib paddles and electricity, or after some kneeling samaritan's breath was blown into stalled lungs so they could gasp again. Maybe such reports are just death's neurological fireworks, the brain's last light show. If so, that's a lie I can live with.
>
> Still, the image pleases me enough: to slip from the body's tight container and into some luminous womb, gliding there without effort till the distant shapes grow brighter and more familiar, till all your beloveds hover before you, their lit arms held out in welcome.

The curse of the past has been lifted by Karr's insistence that she and her mother descend back into the past. But at the time this occurs, it doesn't quite feel that way to the twenty-five-year-old Karr.

It is only nearly fifteen years later, when the present narrative self is coming to the close of her memoir, that the present narrating self can see what happened on that drunken afternoon between the twenty-five-year-old Karr and her mother as the end of something, as the granting of some sort of grace and absolution. In this narrative framed and created by the forty-year-old Karr, she possesses a perspective on this moment that the twenty-five-year-old could not achieve. Thus, she ends this tale of her childhood, this tale that has served as her *zafa*, her counterspell to end her family's curse. And we the reader know finally why she has told us this tale.

In my work with writers of memoir, I've found that they often have not asked the question of why the narrator is telling the tale of the past self. Sometimes such a question seems superficially obvious to the writer, and the writer may believe at first that the themes or subject matter of the memoir answer this question. But by confronting this question as a direct part of the memoir's narrative and purpose, writers I've worked with have found that it forces them to think more deeply about their material, about the dialectic between the present narrating self and the past self; this, in turn, helps the writer to present the past in a more complex and investigatory way.

Often this question leads to a reconsideration of how the memoir structures or introduces its narrative of the past self. This doesn't necessarily mean that the memoir answers all the questions the narrating self poses about the past, but it does mean that those questions anchor and illuminate the narration of the past and the structure of the narrative. In the process, the writer draws readers into her memoir, helping them to understand why it's important that the narrator is telling the story she is telling.

At the same time, the questions that the present narrating self asks at the start of a memoir—that is, the reason why she is telling the tale—can imply or posit a goal for the present narrating self. In this way, as the present narrating self tells stories about the past self, the present narrating self is also setting out on a quest. This quest is for the truth or the deeper truths about the past, or for a fuller understanding of the past, or to answer particular questions about the past.

The process of the telling then becomes its own story, and thus the present narrating self can evoke or resemble certain figures—a detective, an investigative reporter, a historian, a therapist. That is, the present narrating self is trying to solve or discover a crime; to reveal a lie or the true facts and circumstances; to research and create a deeper understanding of the past; to reach a reconciliation with the past, find a way to heal the wounds of the past. Thus some memoirs often have two story lines, one involving the past self and one involving the present narrating self.

The Past and Present Self in Memoir

VIVIAN GORNICK'S *FIERCE ATTACHMENTS*
AND MAXINE HONG KINGSTON'S
THE WOMAN WARRIOR

If memoir tells the story of the past, it often starts with the premise that the past does not understand the past.

Within this dialectic, the writer, in the present, forges the voice of the memoir and a complexity of consciousness that the past self did not possess. The struggle is not simply to put down what happened or who one was; it is also to reveal or discover a fuller and more layered reading and understanding of the past and who that past self has become.

In this way, memoir is the expression or creation of a new identity or self and a new relationship to the past.

Though the description I have just given does not apply to all memoirs, I would assert that it applies more often to those memoirs that obtain the richness and complexity we seek in other forms of literature—namely, literary memoirs. In such memoirs, the voice of the narrator in the present looking back on the past is generally established very early on, often through the use of contrasting perspectives.

Here, for example, is the opening paragraph of Vivian Gornick's *Fierce Attachments*:

> I'm eight years old. My mother and I come out of our apartment onto the
> second-floor landing. Mrs. Drucker is standing in the open doorway of the
> apartment next door, smoking a cigarette. My mother locks the door and
> says to her, "What are you doing here?" Mrs. Drucker jerks her head back-
> ward toward her own apartment. "He wants to lay me. I told him he's gotta
> take a shower before he can touch me." I know that "he" is her husband.
> "He" is always the husband. "Why? He's so dirty?" my mother says. "He feels

dirty to *me*," Mrs. Drucker says. "Drucker, you're a whore," my mother says. Mrs. Drucker shrugs her shoulder. "I can't ride the subway," she says. In the Bronx "ride the subway" was a euphemism for going to work.

What does the eight-year-old Gornick understand of this conversation between her mother and Mrs. Drucker? "I knew that 'he' is her husband," Gornick writes. But however worldly this eight-year-old might have been, she surely did not understand all that the two adults holding this conversation understand. The reader can intuit this adult understanding without it having to be explained. So it would seem, at first glance, that the "show don't tell" aesthetic allows this little incident to proceed succinctly and vividly.

But examine the next paragraph:

> I lived in that tenement between the ages of six and twenty-one. There were twenty apartments, four to a floor, and all I remember is a building full of women. I hardly remember the men at all. They were everywhere, of course—husbands, fathers, brothers—but I remember only the women. And I remember them all crude like Mrs. Drucker or fierce like my mother. They never spoke as though they knew who they were, understood the bargain they had struck with life, but they often acted as though they knew. Shrewd, volatile, unlettered, they performed on a Dreiserian scale. There would be years of apparent calm, then suddenly an outbreak of panic and wildness: two or three lives scarred (perhaps ruined), and the turmoil would subside. Once again: sullen quiet, erotic torpor, the ordinariness of daily denial. And I—the girl growing in their midst, being made in their image—I absorbed them as I would chloroform on a cloth laid against my face. It has taken me thirty years to understand how much of them I understood.

The perspective of this paragraph is not that of the eight-year-old Gornick; it is that of the adult woman, thirty years later. This present self assigns the adjectives "crude" to Mrs. Drucker and "fierce" to her mother; it voices the wonderful line that "they performed on a Dreiserian scale" and portions out the stages of existence in her tenement as "sullen quiet, erotic torpor, the ordinariness of daily denial." This last phrase implies that the narrator self in the present will pierce through that denial of the past; as she makes clear in the next two sentences, that piercing cannot come from her younger self. Indeed, the women and the environment she grew up in instead induced or instructed in the younger Gornick a state of unconsciousness: "It has taken me thirty years to understand how much of them I understood." As a child, Gornick experienced this world of women and imbibed, without knowing, certain ways of acting in the world and perceiving other women and herself. But the child could not articulate that this process was occurring, much less how or why or what it entailed. Only the adult Gornick can do this.

Two voices are present then: that of the past self and that of the present narrating self.

As I mentioned in the preceding essay, at the beginning of *The Woman Warrior* Maxine Hong Kingston tells one of her mother's stories, about an aunt back in China who got pregnant while her husband was away in America. After she is reviled and attacked by her fellow villagers, the aunt gives birth to her child and then drowns herself and the child in the family well. The aunt's tale is a story about the breaking of taboos and what inevitably follows from such transgression; it is a story about extravagance and profligacy in a world of poverty and austerity, a story about silence and shame. Kingston's mother ends it with an admonition and a warning: "Don't let your father know what I told you. He denies her. Now that you have started to menstruate, what happened to her could happen to you. Don't humiliate us. . . . The villagers are watchful."

Kingston's memoir recounts the struggles between her and her Chinese-born mother and her mother's stories of the past, and it contrasts her mother's past with Kingston's childhood growing up in America as the daughter of immigrants. Throughout the book, the mother's interpretations of the past and the present weigh heavily on and inform Kingston's own sense of herself. In the process, Kingston attempts to understand her childhood in terms of both how she as a child experienced it and what it means to her now, in the present:

> Whenever she had to warn us about life, my mother told stories that ran like this one, a story to grow up on. She tested our strength to establish realities. Those in the emigrant generations who could not reassert brute survival died young and far from home. Those of us in the first American generations have had to figure out how the invisible world the emigrants built around our childhoods fits in solid America.

For some readers, it is the mother's stories, her past and her character, that dominate the book, but for other readers, especially the children of immigrants, just as crucial, and perhaps more essential, is Kingston's development of her own voice and her own perspective on the past. The mother knows she is Chinese and thus who she is. Kingston, on the other hand, is a Chinese American, and what that means is neither obvious nor clear to her. The book is a struggle for self-definition, a search for a language to describe who she is. When she starts the memoir, her identity is a question or, rather, a series of questions. Though in certain ways she never answers these questions with any finality, asking them and searching for answers propel the memoir forward.

Near the end of the memoir, the adolescent Kingston confronts her mother with an outburst of grievances, which ends with the following declaration:

> And I don't want to listen to any more of your stories; they have no logic. They scramble me up. You lie with stories. You won't tell me a story and then say, "This is a true story," or, "This is just a story." I can't tell the difference. I don't even know what your real names are. I can't tell what's real and what you make up. Ha! You can't stop me from talking.

In writing her memoir, Kingston acknowledges both the gift of her mother's stories and their mystery; they have helped form who she is as a person and as a writer. Her charge as her mother's daughter and as a writer is not an ultimate determination of the truth or falsehood of her mother's stories; no, it is to uncover their multiple meanings and interpretations. To understand this, the present narrating self must reexamine her own history and how she became the person she is. The daughter acknowledges that she had to leave home "in order to see the world logically" and that away from home, in college, she "learned to think that mysteries are for explanation." But that is only the viewpoint of one of her selves, the self who obtained a college education. This self became conversant with the America outside her parents' home, the place where they "shine floodlights into dark corners: no ghosts." But in her memoir, the ghosts are present and won't go away. The person who writes about them, in the present, is divided and haunted, is able to see her childhood both from the eyes of outsiders and from the eyes of her mother.

Kingston's memoir now serves as a model for memoirs by other immigrant children, asking the same questions concerning the story and meaning of their hyphenated selves.

Story and Narrative Structure
in Memoir

I

We as human beings almost always know the truth about ourselves and our relationship to the world—to those around us, to our past, to what we have done, to what we have experienced. Sometimes that knowledge is hovering there just at or below the surface. But sometimes that knowledge is deeply buried in our psyches and resides in the unconscious, that is, clouded over by a variety of factors, by fear, denial, and resistance. In those instances, we must work to look deep into the abyss of ourselves, see ourselves for who we are, and recognize the truths of our past.

The memoirist's investigation into the past, then, is often difficult and can run into numerous blocks. For instance, in cases of trauma, what allowed the younger self to survive that trauma is psychological repression or denial. Without such repression, the terror and constant reminder of that trauma, the child's knowledge that she does not have control of what is happening to her, would have been too much for the child to endure. As Mary Karr writes in *The Liars' Club*: "When the truth would be unbearable the mind often just blanks it out."

Thus it is only as an adult that the author possesses the resources, maturity, strength, and freedom to access the truth of the past and survive. Obviously, this search for the truth entails a struggle within the narrator's present self; this struggle occurs between the part of her that resists and fears the truth of the past and the part of her that seeks to tell the whole of her tale, to understand and express as fully as possible the reality of the past. Often this telling is spurred on in various ways by the current life of the present narrating self—a series of failures, breakdowns, psychological problems. To put it in the terms of Campbell's mythic hero, her kingdom is fallow, is not flourishing.

In confronting the past, the present voice of the memoir's narrator is engaged in a search for language. Here it's useful to recall my previous definition of creative writing: *Creative writing is the search for and creation of a language that will express what the writer unconsciously knows but does not yet have a language to express.* The voice of the present self struggles to journey from denial to the truth, from incomprehension or repression to expression and understanding.

Thus the majority of literary memoirs relate the story of the past and at the same time reflect on that story. In such cases, it is often essential for the reader to be given a portrait of who the past self has become, an image of the self who is telling the story now. To understand the story of the past self, the reader needs to know the fate of that past self, which can only come from a portrait of the present self. To understand why this is so, consider the following example: Say the memoirist is writing about being caught up in the juvenile justice system at age sixteen; it makes a difference whether the present narrating self is telling her tale from a prison or as a teacher or public defender. Who the present self is tells the reader the fate of the past self (whether that fate is revealed at the start of the memoir or in the middle or at the end is a question of a narrative strategy).

At times, though, the portrait of the present self may not come easily at first. Often, as the writer starts a memoir, the voice remains a bit too anchored in the earlier consciousness, the earlier self. The writer has not quite developed a voice that delineates things the earlier self does not see or understand, particularly the lies the earlier self is telling himself, the gaps in his consciousness.

At the start of the writing, then, the firmness of the present self is often far less established than that of the younger self. It is in the writing of the memoir that the author finds the voice of the present narrating self.

II

The raw materials of memoir are the events and experiences of the past self. Many successful memoirs take these events and experiences and shape them into a story.

If both fiction and memoirs tell stories, the difference between the two is that *in fiction, the writer creates the story; in memoir, the writer discovers the story.*

To discover how to shape the events of the past into a story, it is useful for the memoirist to understand the temporal perspective that the writer of memoir shares with all storytellers. As I've said earlier, a storyteller knows what happened and what the outcome of the story is. That is why the storyteller can see what happened as a narrative with a narrative structure—a beginning, a middle, and an end. The storyteller apprehends or discovers this structure and understands it in a way the characters in the story cannot. This is true even when the story is autobiographical, since in that case the writer is looking at himself as a character from the point of view of the timeless, of one who knows what happened and the fate of the protagonist or main character.

Generally, the ending of a story occurs when the protagonist either succeeds or fails in the pursuit of his goal. Thus, the present older narrator self knows—if he is clear about the goal the younger self was striving toward—whether the younger self succeeded in his goal and how he accomplished it (that is, the means by which he accomplished it). He also knows which were the crucial turning points, which were the false leads and dead ends. He knows when the younger self failed and why, and he can articulate that in a way that the younger self could not. He knows too how even those failures shaped the younger self and taught him about himself and his world, and therefore, in a dialectic—thesis, antithesis, synthesis—helped forge his journey forward.

In memoir, it is most often the writer's past self who serves as the first and most obvious protagonist. In constructing the story of her past as a narrative, the memoirist must confront the first rule of story: A protagonist must have a goal or a desire. If there is no goal or desire, there is no story.

If readers do not know what the goal or desire of the protagonist is, they will have difficulty understanding what the story is about—and thus they will not perceive the structure of the story.

In order to write about her past as a story, the memoirist often must discover the smaller day-to-day goals of her past self. On a larger level, the writer must discover the overall goal of her past self for the time the memoir covers.

Once the memoirist discovers the goal(s) of her past self, the pursuit of the goal(s) can be structured as a story.

In order to do this, it is useful to remember how the discovery and pursuit of a goal in story can be broken down into three acts.

Act 1 involves the eruption or intrusion of the goal or desire (or mission or journey) in the protagonist's everyday life. Act 1 ends when the protagonist takes up or realizes the goal or desire.

In act 2 the protagonist struggles to achieve that goal or desire (struggle and doubt, as Mamet puts it).

Act 3 is the final battle in the protagonist's struggle to achieve that goal or desire.

What then are the crucial events in act 1? In terms of story structure, they are the eruptions or intrusions of the goal or desire. Joseph Campbell says that in myths there are often two calls for the hero's journey.

In many instances, there may be a change in outward circumstances that seems to bring about this acceptance of the second call. In classic detective stories, the detective often refuses the call to the case and then his partner or friend takes the case and is killed. In the first *Star Wars* movie, Luke has been obligated to his uncle and aunt and so cannot leave his home planet. But then he returns from discovering Obi-wan Kenobi and finds his aunt and uncle have been killed.

I think it's useful to understand that these external events can be read as metaphors for what is happening in the psyche of the protagonist. This is true both with the specific protagonist of the story and with the universal hero's journey of which the protagonist is a particular manifestation. In other words, the events of the story are literally the events of the story. But the events of the story are also metaphors for the journey of the psyche.

The call and initial refusal of the goal by the protagonist often illustrates another basic principle of story: conflicting desires.

In the detective case, the detective has some reason for not wanting to take the case—he's got other cases, it doesn't pay enough, he doesn't take this sort of case, he doesn't like the client, and so on. Whatever the client is offering—for example, money, emotional appeal, sexual allure—is not enough to set up an irreconcilable desire. The detective can refuse easily.

But as so often happens in detective films, once the detective's friend or colleague has been killed, the ante has been raised; the reasons for taking the case are greater—love or affection or admiration of the friend, duty, revenge, and such. Thus the way that the protagonist looks at the positives and negatives of the choice—that is, the conflicting desires—has shifted. The equation of conflicting desires has become more irreconcilable; the protagonist is under more tension. And as a result of that pressure—of the new incentives or desires—the protagonist takes up the case.

It is when the protagonist takes up the quest that she makes the transition from the old world into the new world. This is the end of the first act and the beginning of the second act.

In the mythic journey, there is obviously a physical correlative to this transition. In *Star Wars* Luke enters the bar with all the strange and dangerous aliens. He then leaves the planet where he has been stranded.

But all this again can also be seen as a metaphor. Luke is now willing to enter strange new dangerous places because his psyche has entered a new place.

In working with students trying to structure their memoir as a story, I've found that often the goal or quest itself has not been clearly stated.

To resolve this problem, the writer of memoir needs to understand some aspects of the goal—or what David Mamet calls, quoting Hitchcock, the MacGuffin. In *Three Uses of the Knife*, which analyzes the three-act play structure, Mamet writes: "That which the hero requires is the play. In the perfect play we find nothing extraneous to his or her single desire. Every incident either impedes or aids the hero/heroine in the quest for the single goal."

Mamet goes on to discuss ways the goal is defined in politics and classic cinema and plays. He finds that the goal often has two qualities: (1) the goal is often left conceptually vague, which allows more of the audience to identify with it; (2) the goal is often concrete and generic. The concreteness allows the person to take actions toward achieving the goal. One can take specific actions to search for the Maltese Falcon or letters of transit, as in the classic Humphrey Bogart films. The generic nature of the goal again allows more of the audience to identify with it:

> Peace with Honor, Communists in the State Department, Supply Side Economics, Recapture the Dream, Bring Back the Pride—these are the stuff of pageant. They are not social goals; they are, as Alfred Hitchcock told us, *The MacGuffin*. This was, of course, Hitchcock's term for "that which the hero wants," and his devotion to the concept explains much of his success as a film director.
>
> He understood that the dramatic goal is *generic*. It need not be more specific than: the Maltese Falcon, the Letters of Transit, the Secret Documents. It is sufficient for the protagonist-author to know the worth of the MacGuffin. The less specific the qualities of the MacGuffin are, the more interested the audience will be. Why? Because a loose abstraction allows audience members to project their own desires onto an essentially featureless goal. Just as they do onto the terms Americanism, or A Better Life, or Tomorrow.

It is easy to identify with the quest for a secret document, somewhat
harder to do so with a heroine whose goal is identifying and understanding
the element radium. Which is why in dramatic biography writers and direc-
tors end up reverting to fiction. To be effective, the dramatic elements must
and finally will take precedence over any "real" biographical facts.

Here Mamet runs us right into the tension or problem of memoir. In drama
you can alter or create the goal to create a quest and a situation that can be em-
bodied in actions and dramatic events. You can alter or create a goal that the majority of the audience can identify with.

You do not have this liberty to fictionalize in a memoir—as opposed to a Hollywood "bio pic." The events of the story have occurred. You cannot make them
up.

But Mamet is speaking of the dramatic needs of a screenplay or a play. A
memoir can certainly possess narrative and dramatic elements even if the story
it tells is not as vividly and concretely dramatic as a Hollywood film. If a memoir
is not a screenplay, that doesn't mean the writer must simply give up and say,
"Well, then, there's no need to try to find a narrative." The choice is not between
a Hollywood narrative or none at all.

Moreover, it's interesting what Mamet says subsequent to the remarks above:

We viewers don't care—if we wanted to know about the element radium,
we'd read a book on the element radium. When we go to the movies to see
The Story of Marie Curie we want to find out how her little dog Skipper died.

In a drama, as in any dream, the fact that something is "true" is irrelevant—we care only if that something is germane to the hero-quest (the quest
for a MacGuffin) as it has been stated to us.

The power of the dramatist, and of the political flack therefore, resides in
the ability to state the problem.

I would submit that the power of the memoirist also resides in the ability to
state the problem, to articulate the quest.

So at some point in the writing process, if the memoir is to be structured as a
story (and granted not all memoirs are), the writer must answer certain basic
questions:

1. What is it that the protagonist wants? What is her goal?

2. What actions does the protagonist take to pursue her goal?

3. In taking actions to pursue her goal, does she face irreconcilable conflicts?

4. How does she resolve these irreconcilable conflicts? Has she convinced herself that she has resolved an irreconcilable conflict by lying to herself about the irreconcilability of that conflict?

5. What are the lies the protagonist tells herself? Does she lie to herself about the irreconcilability of two conflicting desires? How do those lies eventually lead to further difficulties, complications, or even punishment?

The writer of the memoir must ask these basic questions to understand how the story in her memoir is to be structured. Again, I cannot emphasize enough that finding the answers to these questions requires thinking, a deeper understanding of the material.

Beginning writers, both of memoir and of fiction, often do not do this thinking; they do not attempt to reach a deeper understanding of the narrative structure of the material, partly because they don't know which questions to ask. They don't know the structures of narrative or understand how they function.

But I believe this resistance sometimes occurs because the beginning writer doesn't conceive such work as part of writing. Writing for many is the working on a particular passage, on a sentence or a description or a piece of dialogue. It becomes defined as work with a micro perspective. The macro perspective, the questions of such things as overall story structure and basic premises and problems with story, are not defined as essential. Or the writer doesn't feel that they are part of the real work of writing.

But I would submit that they *are* essential, to fiction and to memoir.

At a certain point, in trying to gather the draft or drafts of a memoir, the writer will be faced with the question, Do I put the events in temporal order—as in a standard story—or do I use some principle other than temporal order to organize the material?

One advantage of setting the events in temporal order is that the story as a journey toward the goal becomes clearer. One disadvantage is that it becomes harder then to organize the material thematically.

An example of a memoir that sets its events in temporal order would be Tobias Wolfe's *This Boy's Life*. An example of organizing the material thematically would be Maxine Hong Kingston's *The Woman Warrior*. In the latter, there's a certain semblance of temporal progression to the sequence of pieces and within the individual pieces, but in the end, the book seems more organized by theme.

A temporal order tends to make the memoir read more like a novel and thus possesses the attractions of the novel for general readers. A thematic organization is obviously less like a plot-driven novel and, in successful memoirs of this kind, makes up for that lack with depth of perception and analysis.

If the events of the author's life are recognizably dramatic, the temporal organization will generally be a more effective means to highlight such dramatics because it makes the story of the dramatics more accessible and clearer. By dramatics, I don't necessarily mean only events such as say escaping from a country at war or serving as a child soldier or winning the Olympics. Dramatics can also occur in a clear struggle between the protagonist and an antagonist. In *This Boy's Life*, much of the drama involves the struggle between the young Toby and his stepfather, Dwight. Moreover, young Toby is constantly getting into trouble and lying to both his mother and Dwight. In *The Woman Warrior*, there is certainly tension between Kingston and her mother, but it's not a clear protagonist-antagonist relationship; in the end, the events surrounding Kingston's life as a child are not particularly dramatic, though those of her mother's past life are.

In my first memoir, *Turning Japanese*, I used a temporal narrative structure like that in *This Boy's Life*. In my second memoir, *Where the Body Meets Memory*, I used a more thematic structure, though that book has a certain temporal order too.

Temporal Narrative and Identity in My Memoirs

My first memoir, Turning Japanese: Memoirs of a Sansei, recounts a year I lived in Japan and is set in a temporal order. I chose this narrative structure partly because the setting and meeting of various Japanese people helped make the events singular and, at times, dramatic. The one-year time frame also made it easy to set things in temporal order. It's the narrative structure of the work that caused one critic to remark that the memoir "reads like a novel" and even caused some readers to mistakenly think it is a novel.

In setting up the overall structure of Turning Japanese, I used Jon Franklin's Writing for Story: Craft Secrets of Dramatic Nonfiction as a guide. Specifically, I used Franklin's outline of starting each chapter with a complication for the protagonist; three attempts or actions to resolve the complication then follow, and before the chapter concludes, a new complication is introduced that will be addressed in the next chapter.

Franklin's structure is a version of the basic idea of story: the protagonist has a goal and takes actions to reach the goal. In each chapter or section of Turning Japanese, my past self confronts a particular complication/goal; that complication/goal was something I had to uncover and then structure the chapter around. In one chapter, the goal was to find a vehicle to enter and study Japanese culture; that entailed making contact with a Japanese magazine editor, attending a shamisen lesson, which didn't work out, then attending a class by a master artist of Butoh, a contemporary Japanese dance form that I was able to study (note that this chapter follows the classic three attempts to reach a goal, since any determining pattern can be revealed in three attempts—success, failure, success—or failure, failure, success; failure, failure/success, failure). In another chapter, the goal was getting to and surviving a Japanese political demonstration and avoid being arrested, since non-Japanese were not allowed to attend such demonstrations.

I should note that it was only in my fourth or fifth draft that I finally worked out a chapter-by-chapter outline; only then did I have a firm enough sense of what the book was about and what its general contents should be to do this. My first versions of the book were separate essays, more on the postmodern nature of contemporary Japan than anything about myself. But from the start, my writing group kept constantly advising me, "More narrative, more you."

Like many writers, though, I initially resisted their advice; then, gradually, I entertained it, and finally, I acted on it. It took four drafts, though, before I was able to craft the opening chapter that anchors the whole book within the context of my identity as a Sansei, a third-generation Japanese American. In a way, I had been consciously avoiding such an investigation into my own ethnic and racial identity, yet at the same time, I had been unconsciously searching for a language to do so. Only after I found such a language did my writing group confirm that I had found the voice—the present narrating self—to tell the story (and yet, even after I sold the book, my editor asked for "more narrative, more you"). It's hard to underestimate how much resistance I had to overcome, how much work I had to do—including overcoming my own internalized racism— to get to these opening simple sentences:

> I am a *Sansei*, a third-generation Japanese American. In 1984, through luck and through some skills as a poet, I traveled to Japan. My reasons for going were not very clear. . . .
>
> I had applied for a U.S./Japan Creative Artist Exchange Fellowship mainly because I wanted time to write.
>
> Japan? That was where my grandparents came from, it didn't have much to do with my present life.
>
> But then Japan had never seemed that important to me, even in childhood. On holidays when we would get together with relatives, I didn't notice that the faces around me looked different than most of the faces at school. I didn't notice that my grandfathers were in Japan, my grandmothers dead. No one spoke about them, just as no one spoke about Japan. We were American. It was the Fourth of July, Labor Day, Christmas. All I noticed was that the food we ate—*futomaki, mazegohan, teriyaki, komaboku*—was different from what I liked best—McDonald's, pizza, hot dogs, tuna fish salad.

Later, after I finished *Turning Japanese*, when I read Joseph Campbell's *The Hero of a Thousand Faces* I realized that the structure of the book resembled that of classic myths—a hero is called to leave the old kingdom and travel to a new one, seeking an elixir or gift, in this case, the book itself, to bring back home to renew the old kingdom. Since the classic structure of the three-act play stems from and corresponds to the journey of Campbell's hero, *Turning Japanese* also possesses a three-act structure. This structure includes the protagonist's initial refusal to take up the call to the hero's journey—that is, part of me was reluctant to travel to Japan, to learn about Japanese culture, or to engage the issues of identity that Japan ultimately raised for me.* The book's third act involves my parents coming to Japan and my trip to my grandparents' hometown, a final act of returning to my family's roots.

Turning Japanese also makes use of the A-line, B-line, C-line structure delineated earlier in my analysis of Junot Díaz's "Fiesta." While the A line of my memoir depicts the events of the year I spent in Japan, a B line explores and recounts smaller narratives of my earlier years, particularly concerning my problematic relationship with my parents. The book also includes C material that deals with imagining moments in the life of my parents and my relatives, particularly in connection with the internment of Japanese Americans during World War II.

My other memoir, *Where the Body Meets Memory*, is an exploration of my search to understand my identity as a Japanese American in America and how my past and my family's past helped forge that identity. Unlike *Turning Japanese*, this memoir is organized more thematically, though there's a loose temporal order to the sections. I sometimes wonder if it might have been a better book if I could have organized it into more of a story. But in the end I was more involved with the thematic concerns of that book, the questions of race, sexuality, and identity. In certain ways, I was using my life more as an example, the closest at hand, rather than because of its inherently dramatic story.

For me, one model for this type of memoir was James Baldwin's essay, "Equal in Paris," where he tells of his being arrested in Paris. There the narrative sections are also secondary to the essay sections. The account is interesting, but the conclusions that Baldwin draws about race in America through that experience are really the heart of the essay. In the end, he decides that, despite all he hated about American racism, he was safer and more comfortable living with a racism and racists he understood as opposed to the French, whose racism and racists he could not understand.†

---

* The middle of the second act, the act of struggle and doubt, is my flirtation with a German woman and how that set off a crisis in my marriage. The third act or final battle involves looking directly at my identity through the lens of my family—the visit of my parents, with whom I've had several disagreements, and my visit to my grandparents' hometown, a trip that I kept putting off.

† In *Turning Japanese*, I reached a similar conclusion. Though as the title implies, I first found myself in love with Japan, its people and culture, I gradually began to realize in Japan that, in very essen-

Where the Body Meets Memory is subtitled *An Odyssey on Race, Sexuality and Identity*, and a major focus is on my racial identity. Narratively, *Where the Body Meets Memory* follows my life from childhood through adolescence into adulthood, and it parallels that progress with sections of my mother's life—her childhood in the internment camps—my father's life—his adolescence and early adulthood after the camps—and my grandfather's marriage. In this way, the memoir became not just my story but a family saga of three different generations of Japanese Americans.

As I wrote both memoirs, it became clear that without a three-generation perspective, I could not understand the ways culture/ethnicity and race affected my grandparents, parents, and thus me. For example, the internment of Japanese nationals and Japanese Americans during World War II was a clear act of racism, as President Reagan and the government finally admitted in its apology in 1988. Yet the differences in the ways my grandparents and parents reacted to the internment were, in part, a result of their cultural differences; my grandparents were raised in Japan, while my parents were Japanese American and their identities were a mix of their parents' Japanese cultural values and the American values and outlook that came from growing up in America.

As for myself, I had been raised with almost no knowledge of Japanese culture; my parents did not speak Japanese in our home, and I took this to stem from the fact that they were born in America. What I later came to realize was that their shedding of most remnants of Japanese culture from their childhoods and their fervid attempts to assimilate into white middle-class American life had been influenced by their experience of being imprisoned in the internment camps when my mother was eleven and my father fifteen. Since my parents never conducted acts of espionage, their crime was, implicitly, their ethnicity and race (indeed, *no* Japanese American was ever convicted of espionage). To explain how this experience affected them, I use the following analogy: If you are convicted of shoplifting, after prison, to show you're reformed, you do not shoplift anymore. But what do you do if your crime is your race and ethnicity? That was the dilemma my parents faced.

Since I was a product of this familial history of generations, I could not in-

tial ways, I was not at all Japanese but American (I could not, for example, abide the hierarchical and position/title dominated nature of Japanese society, and I much prefer the more democratic—with a small *d*—American societal structure). At the same time, because *Turning Japanese* explores a year I spent in Japan, it focuses more on the cultural/ethnic roots of my identity as a Japanese American and less on my racial identity than *Where the Body Meets Memory*.

vestigate or understand my own identity and story without the lenses of both culture/ethnicity and race.

I suspect that this dual perspective and the exploration of multiple generations may more and more become part of memoirs where white writers investigate their racial identity. For as Baldwin has pointed out in his introduction to *The Price of the Ticket*, acquiring a white identity has entailed in part losing ethnic identity and forgetting the past:

> To do your first works over means to reexamine everything. Go back to where you started, or as far back as you can, examine all of it, travel your road again and tell the truth about it. Sing or shout or testify or keep it to yourself: but *know whence you came.*
>
> This is precisely what the generality of white Americans cannot afford to do. They do not know how to do it—: as I must suppose. They come through Ellis Island, where *Giorgio* becomes *Joe*, *Pappavasiliu* becomes *Palmer*, *Evangelos* becomes *Evans*, *Goldsmith* becomes *Smith* or *Gold*, and *Avakian* becomes *King*. So, with a painless change of name, and in the twinkling of an eye, one becomes a white American.
>
> Later, in the midnight hour, the missing identity aches. One can neither assess nor overcome the storm of the middle passage. One is mysteriously shipwrecked forever, in the Great New World.

Baldwin argues here that the actual identity of white Americans is far more complex historically and generationally than the official white identity allows. For that official white identity is based on a false premise, and in order to maintain the premise, it constantly tries to picture a present without a past or minimizes the effects of the past on the present (e.g., racism is a thing of the past). Ironically, in certain ways, southern white writers have tended to understand this better. Despite his caveats urging those in the civil rights movement to go slow, Faulkner obviously contemplated the sin of slavery and its continued effects on the life of the South. "The past isn't dead," he once remarked. "It's not even past." Such an understanding is one that fuels most memoirs.

I would add here a word of caution: ethnicity should not be viewed simply as an added flavor or spice or a sentimental familial legacy. White writers who investigate their ethnic identity without contextualizing that identity within the history of whiteness will produce an inadequate portrait of both the present and the past. Similarly, Faulkner's portraits of whites and blacks, despite their complexity, were also flawed and never overcame the white supremacy he grew up with and imbibed and never adequately interrogated and challenged. In many ways, we as a culture are still waiting for white writers to engage in the difficult and hard work of dismantling white ideology; such work is absolutely integral to keeping us from repeating the past dressed up in new disguises—or given the recent 2016 election, fearfully donning the robes of the past in order to preserve the powers embedded there through systemic racial injustice.

The Use of the
Reflective Voice in Memoir

JAMES BALDWIN AND HILTON ALS

Particularly in those cases where the events of the past don't offer a riveting dramatic story, the reflective voice, the voice of the present interpreting and contextualizing the past, can be a crucial element in memoir. I'm probably more of this school than some writers are. Perhaps it's a matter of temperament. Dostoyevsky, Proust, Woolf—a lot of interior investigation. Hemingway, Cormac McCarthy—very little.

Then too there may be other social or political or historical factors in the material the writer is working with that require reflection and analysis. For instance, the Japanese American writer Garrett Hongo has remarked to me that the "show don't tell" aesthetic is a "white man's game." In saying this, Hongo points to the fact that through our educational system, through the culture and the society all Americans live in, the literate American reader has been taught how to view and interpret the world through the white heterosexual male lens. In contrast, if the writer is a Cuban American bisexual or a Pakistani Parsi American, she cannot count on the reader to possess the tools to contextualize and understand her experience. Even more importantly, she herself may not possess the tools to contextualize and understand her experience—very little in the culture or society around her or in her education would be useful in such a task. Indeed, this gap, this absence may be what has prompted her to write a memoir.

Certainly, this was the case for me. In *Where the Body Meets Memory*, the given I started with was what happened during my childhood, the ways my parents and I interacted. That was what was known. What was unknown and unconscious was the question of who my parents were—in particular, how they were shaped both by their Japanese-born parents and by their experience of being interned with other Japanese Americans during World War II. This familial and collective history was not something I understood or even knew about as a child.

Thus in certain places in my memoirs, as I present the past, I'm portraying how I understood that past as a child; at the same time, I'm delineating how, in the present, I was coming to understand that past in a greater cultural, historical, and political context through the writing.

What exactly do I mean by this? I knew, for example, that my father freaked out at my long hair and adoption of the counterculture during the late sixties and early seventies. That sort of father-son interaction was happening all over America at that time, and that historical context provides an explanation of who we both were—a Depression-era father and his baby-boomer son at the advent of the social changes wrought by the sixties.

But my father was also a Nisei, a second-generation Japanese American who had been interned because of his race; his defense of white middle-class culture/ norms arose out of a different historical and political past than a typical white middle-class father of his generation. Thus in my memoir, I examine the factors of race and history and their conjunction in order to arrive at an understanding of my father's psychology. I try to provide a picture of him coming out of the camps and reentering American society after the war ended, and I cite this as a way of depicting the formation of his psychology. That depiction is in part based on the premise that I could not understand who I had been and who I needed to become without understanding who my father was and how he became who he was.

In writing my memoirs, I came to realize that my parents' imprisonment during World War II had a profound effect on their psyches. Both consciously and unconsciously, they believed they had to show they were not Japanese and to do that, they had to be "not 100 percent American, but 200 percent American," as my father's white teacher in the camps told him. To them, that meant assimilating; it meant losing their attachment to Japanese culture and, in a way, to their parents, and instead converting to Christianity; it meant trying to become like white middle-class Americans, which meant accepting a white-based racial hierarchy. And that was the way they had raised me. My own internalized racism therefore had an intricate history that started before I was born, and which I discovered only through the process of creating *Turning Japanese* and *Where the Body Meets Memory*.

One prime task of the reflective voice, then, is the interpretation of experience. Sometimes this interpretation comes with time, maturity, perspective. Sometimes it derives from knowing what happened afterward. At other times, the author acquires tools of analysis and interpretation that he didn't possess previously—therapy, issues of identity, medical models, political theories, historical perspectives, critical theory, cultural and gender studies, and various other ideas and methods of contextualization.

In certain instances, this interpretation is an essential part of the story—or even the story. For example, once a person discovers that he's gay or transgendered, the past means something entirely different from what it meant when he was in denial about his identity or didn't even know such an identity was possible. A similar process may be involved with an investigation into the writer's ethnic or racial identity.

In *The Devil Finds Work*, Baldwin opens with an account of his family situation; his father obviously dislikes, even hates him, and calls him ugly,* and it's clear to the young Baldwin that his mother, like Baldwin himself, is also considered particularly ugly. Amid these difficult family dynamics, Baldwin recounts how a white teacher helped introduce him to works of literature and the cinema. The kindness and openness of this white teacher bewilder the young Baldwin, since they cut against the grain of his previous experiences with white people:

> Bill Miller was not at all like the cops who had already beaten me up, she was not like the landlords who called me nigger, she was not like the storekeepers who laughed at me. I had found white people to be unutterably menacing, terrifying, mysterious—wicked: and they were mysterious, in fact, to the extent that they were wicked: the unfathomable question being, precisely, this one: what, under heaven, or beneath the sea, or in the catacombs of hell, could cause any people to act as white people acted? From Miss Miller, therefore, I began to suspect that white people did not act as they did because they were white, but for some other reason, and I began to try to locate and understand the reason.

As Baldwin's present narrating self looks back on his past self as a child, he contrasts what the younger self understood about his world and what he did not; the latter clearly involved the question of his racial identity: "I knew that I was poor, and knew that I was black, but *did not yet know what being black really meant* [italics mine], what it meant, that is, in the history of my country, and in my own history."

In the writing that follows this cinematic initiation by his white teacher, Baldwin explores his experience with various works of the America cinema. He uses those works to analyze how blacks perceive themselves, and just as signifi-

---

* As a child Baldwin did not know that the man he referred to as his father was not his biological father.

cantly, how whites perceive not just themselves but blacks, and the racial realities and history of America (an example of Du Bois's double consciousness). In the process, Baldwin provides an implied investigation of what his being black means "in the history of [his] own country, and in [his] own history."

The rest of *The Devil Finds Work* thus becomes an expansive gloss on the autobiographical opening. Many of the films Baldwin discusses—and skewers—are liberal films on race from the fifties and sixties, including *In the Heat of the Night*, *Guess Who's Coming to Dinner*, and *The Defiant Ones*. The latter involves two escaped convicts, played by Tony Curtis and Sidney Poitier, who are handcuffed together, and it attempts to show how a bond develops between the two men, despite their racial differences. As is often the case with Baldwin, he investigates the psychology of race in ways that white society still has not processed:

> It is impossible to accept the premise of the story, a premise based on the profound American misunderstanding of the nature of the hatred between black and white. There is a hatred—certainly: though I am now using this word with great caution, and only in the light of the effects, or the results, of hatred. But the hatred is not equal on both sides, for it does not have the same roots. . . . Black men do not have the same reason to hate white men as white men have to hate blacks. The root of the white man's hatred is terror, a bottomless and nameless terror, which focuses on the black, surfacing, and concentrating on this dread figure, an entity which lives only in his mind. But the root of the black man's hatred is rage, and he does not so much hate white men as simply want them out of his way, and, more than that, out of his children's way. . . .
>
> Liberal white audiences applauded when Sidney, at the end of the film, jumped off the train in order not to abandon his white buddy. The Harlem audience was outraged, and yelled, *Get back on the train, you fool!*

The whole film is based on a premise of an equal and similarly motivated racial hatred, a premise that is part of the myth of white innocence; this myth, Baldwin implies, is what white audiences are applauding. The film never investigates, much less acknowledges, the nature of this white projection—either the belief in white innocence or the white terror of blacks—nor does the film recognize the fact that blacks have long understood the falseness of that projection. That is what makes Poitier's action ridiculously absurd to the Harlem audience.

Throughout his *Collected Essays*, Baldwin lays out fundamental differences between the ways whites and blacks conceive of their identities and interpret their experiences, their social reality, and their mutual history. Whether on public housing or the black ghetto or the police or personal relationships or religion or cultural productions like film, the divergence between black and white viewpoints is not simply a difference in politics but a deep and complexly divided account of what the American experience has been and continues to be.

The implications of this for artists is a questioning of both aesthetic practice and quality. As in his critique of the absurdities in *The Defiant Ones*, Baldwin implicitly argues that realism in art depends on an agreement about the nature of reality, but over and over, he finds that there is no such agreement between whites and blacks; even when there is agreement about the facts—and there rarely is—there is a fundamental difference in hermeneutics, in the interpretation of those facts. This difference is always present, even when white writers or artists present their sense of reality or personal stories without any reference to the questions of race.* My argument in this book is, in part, a lesson from Baldwin: white identity in general can no longer remain a hidden or settled issue; it needs to be investigated, questioned, challenged.

Baldwin insists that we cannot make sense of the American experience without understanding that whites and blacks are intimately and inextricably connected, that neither can be properly understood without the other. As he writes at the end of his essay "Stranger in the Village,"

> The time has come to realize that the interracial drama acted out on the American continent has not only created a new black man, it has created a new white man, too. No road whatever will lead Americans back to the simplicity of this European village where white men still have the luxury of looking on me as a stranger. I am not, really, a stranger any longer for any American alive. One of the things that distinguishes Americans from other people is that no other people has ever been so deeply involved in the lives of black men, and vice versa. . . . This world is white no longer, and it will never be white again.

The innocence that white Americans cling to is based on a rejection of their connection to black people; this rejection in turn stems from their refusal to see blacks as equal and as who they actually are—and not the image that whites have created of blacks or their reality or their interpretation of reality; that, in

---

* In contrast to Baldwin's understanding that his identity as a black man required an examination of the psyche of whites, Hemingway felt he didn't have to interpret his experience for himself or for others, nor did he need to consider how blacks viewed him; his place in society and his identity were seemingly self-evident—he was a white heterosexual male. That was obviously not the case for Baldwin, who was both black and homosexual. The "show don't tell" aesthetic could not work for him.

turn, stems from the white refusal to see how America's racial history has created its racial present. The result is a moral and spiritual crisis that continues into the present. As Baldwin observes, "People who shut their eyes to reality simply invite their own destruction, and anyone who insists on remaining in a state of innocence long after that innocence is dead turns himself into a monster."

Though Baldwin continues to speak to current racial conflicts and thus is often viewed in a political context, his true focus is moral and spiritual, and it is through the moral and spiritual that he arrives at the psychological, rather than through a focus on the familial or the "facts" of autobiography. Lies, moral evasions, and oppression beget a sickness of the soul, and when the soul is sick, professions of political goodwill will avail nothing. Before political change regarding race can occur, a true spiritual reckoning must take place. And as Baldwin frequently explains, one cannot face in others what one has not faced in oneself; he applies this lesson both to whites and to blacks and, as a writer must, to himself.

Thus Baldwin will not separate the personal from the political or the private from the public, and he interprets them through the moral and the spiritual; they are all inextricably interconnected, and when it comes to issues of race, he argues that we cannot make sense of our society, of what we experience and who we are without seeing all these as a whole. In the opening of his famed autobiographical essay, "Notes of a Native Son," the public and the private, the political and the personal are woven together in a mode of expression that stems from Baldwin's biblical roots and the allegorical ways blacks have interpreted Christianity and made it their own; this allegorical approach runs throughout Baldwin's essays, particularly early on, when he eschews reportage or the mode of social realism, and it is part of the reason why these essays possess a timeless, classical quality:

> A few hours after my father's funeral, while he lay in state in the undertaker's chapel, a race riot broke out in Harlem. On the morning of the 3nd of August, we drove my father to the graveyard through a wilderness of smashed plate glass.
>
> The day of my father's funeral had also been my nineteenth birthday. As we drove him to the graveyard, the spoils of injustice, anarchy, discontent, and hatred were all around us. It seemed to me that God himself had devised, to mark my father's end, the most sustained and brutally dissonant of codas. And it seemed to me, too, that the violence which rose all about

us as my father left the world had been devised as a corrective for the pride of his eldest son. I had declined to believe in that apocalypse which had been central to my father's vision; very well, life seemed to be saying, here is something that will certainly pass for an apocalypse until the real thing comes along. I had inclined to be contemptuous of my father for the conditions of his life, for the conditions of our lives. When his life had ended, I began to wonder about that life and also, in a new way, to be apprehensive about my own. . . .

He had lived and died in an intolerable bitterness of spirit and it frightened me, as we drove him to the graveyard through those unquiet, ruined streets, to see how powerful and overflowing this bitterness could be and to realize that this bitterness was now mine.

Baldwin's father is, yes, his personal father, but in this account, his father also becomes a prophet like Jeremiah as well as a Job-like figure, inseparable from the events that surround his funeral or the ways his son is struggling to understand how he himself will come to terms with the violence and hatred at the heart of American racism, the racism that broke down his father into bitterness and rage. Baldwin understands that his father's life and the Harlem riots are intimately related, and that they present a spiritual question both for America as a country and for Baldwin as an individual soul. That Baldwin is able to yoke seamlessly all these disparate elements in a few paragraphs is part of his essential genius.

In many ways, we have still not yet come to terms with Baldwin's vision and the greatness of his work or how his approach to the personal and autobiographical demonstrates a very different path into the issues of race and of memoir.

In memoirs where story or narrative is less prominent or present, the voice of the present narrating self often dominates or plays a more central role. The presentation of the past self in such works is perhaps less dramatically rendered, and the present narrating self focuses on questions about the past self and how that past self became the present narrating self.

In such memoirs, it is often crucial to include a more complete portrait of the present self than I sometimes see with my students' work. At the same time, the success of this type of memoir depends less on the narrative drive of the text and more on the depth of its analysis and understanding of the past and the present and of the identities of the past and the present self and the dialectic between the two. The movement is toward greater honesty, clarity, analysis, understanding, a more complicated and/or a truer picture of both selves.

Now, in many ways, everyone who writes does so to explore the issues of his or her identity, but writers of color and indigenous writers write to access and explore the complex history, realities, and consciousness of people of color—all of which are, in various ways, denied and devalued by the dominant culture. The same can also be true for GBLT writers. At times, then, writers write against an enforced silence that they are aware of; at other times, they write against an enforced silence in themselves that they might not be aware of.

Thus perhaps the most difficult aspect of writing about their identities is exploring those areas where they as individuals participate in their own silencing, where they are afraid to explore or investigate, where there are truths that they don't want to express because of the pain such truths uncover and the shame they recall and the wounds these writers don't want to remember and confront.

In many memoirs by writers of color, one can see the writers struggling to unlock or free themselves from the dominant culture and let their true individual voices speak. For writers of color, the greatest struggles are sometimes not so much directly against the dominant (white) culture as against the dominant (white) culture in the writers themselves or against the ways their own communities have silenced them. But to engage in this struggle, writers must sometimes trace back to the point where the silencing began, and their struggle involves moving toward and into the origins of that wounding, that silencing. Oftentimes, the origins of this wounding or silencing are in the family. But they can also involve the society around the writer, and not just the obvious voices of forces of repression; sometimes writers must confront the ways the ostensible categories of their ethnic or racial identities can erase or flatten who they actually are.

If Ta-Nehisi Coates, author of *Between the World and Me*, is currently viewed as the heir to Baldwin, to my mind, a perhaps more original heir is Hilton Als, whose writings interrogate his identity as a gay black man whose mother was from Barbados. In a long memoir-like essay, "Tristes Tropiques," that opens his collection *White Girls*, Als explores his extremely close friendship with a black man he dubs "Sir or Lady." Although the two are never lovers, and SL sleeps with a number of white women, SL and Als are viewed not just as a couple but almost as twins in the cultural and fashion world of New York in which they work and socialize.

As he recounts the history of their friendship, Als explores the two men's complicated relationships both with actual "white girls" and with cultural representations of "white girls": "By the time we met we were anxious to share our black American maleness with another person who knew how flat and not descriptive those words were since they did not include how it had more than its share of Daisy Buchanan and Jordan Baker in it, women who passed their 'white girlhood' together."

Als traces the influences of "white girls" on himself, moving from Daisy and Jordan to second-wave feminists like Shulamith Firestone to, in a later piece, his seeing Vivian Leigh for the first time in *Gone with the Wind*: "I would have made her forget that I was colored and that she could lynch me if she wanted because I knew I could make her love me." Such a statement contains a clear-eyed acknowledgment of how complexly people's identities are both influenced and configured by the culture around them, for the younger Als's feelings about Leigh stem not just from the racial hierarchy and oppression she represents but also from his nascent feelings about his gender and orientation and the ways his identification with Leigh allows a path beyond the rigid gender or racial categories the society has offered him.

As Als makes clear, trying to describe himself, SL, and their relationship requires a new language, one not provided even in the black culture that they've inherited and live within:

> No narrative preceded us. We were not "menchildren" in a promised land, as Claude Brown would have it. We did not consider ourselves as having "no name in the street," as James Baldwin did himself. We did not suffer the existential crisis that afflicts some male Negro intellectuals, as Harold Cruse presumed. We did not have "hot" souls that needed to be put on ice, as Eldridge Cleaver might have said. We were not escapees from Langston Hughes's "Simple" stories. We were nothing like Richard Wright's *Bigger Thomas*, nor did we wear white masks, as Frantz Fanon might have deduced, incorrectly. We saw no point of reference in *The Life and Loves of Mr. Jiveass Nigger*, by Cecil Brown. . . . In short, we were not your standard Negro story, or usual Negro story. . . . We were not interested in the sentimental tale that's attached itself to the Negro male body by now: the embodiment of isolation. We had each other, another kind of story worth telling.

In a better world, I shouldn't have to comment on certain aspects of this passage: First, it is addressed to an audience familiar with these literary references and what they signify in the history of black culture. Second, if the reader is not familiar with these authors or history, the reader will not fully appreciate the impact of what Als is saying here or how it might be perceived by different black readers, given its witty, ironic tone. Third, Als refuses to simplify or ignore the intersections that make up his identity, whether of race, gender, orientation, or, later in the book, ethnicity and the West Indian influences of his mother's background.

For example, in the essay "Philosopher or Dog," Als critiques how *The Autobiography of Malcolm X* erases Malcolm's Grenadian mother, whose existence posits an alternative narrative and identity that Malcolm never acknowledged. Als argues that that absent narrative permanently alters his view of Malcolm and constitutes a fundamental flaw in *The Autobiography*. Among other things, Als believes that Malcolm makes much more of his white grandfather's importance in his mother's family than would have occurred in matriarchal Caribbean culture. Als implicitly uses this cultural investigation of Malcolm to challenge and complicate Als's portrait of his mother in his own writings; in doing this, he calls out the ways certain black writers create a one-dimensional portrait of the mother as defined solely by her suffering (one of those ready-made chains of signifying blackness that Morrison alludes to critically in *Playing in the Dark*):

> Writers of a color who find their expression—so called—in their "otherness" and "difference" do so in a manner comfortable to the legions who buy their work not to read it, oh no, but because these writers confirm the nonideas stupid people assume about otherness and difference—two words that define privilege in the epoch of some.
>
> If pressed by the thumb of thought, where does the idea of this otherness and differences come from? It is an acquired habit really. One learns it in infancy, sitting on the knee of someone—perhaps Mom—who may not be unlike oneself in a respect: her appearance. Appearances speak not of themselves but of preceding generations and the haunting of each subsequent one with: Because I appear not unlike you, we are each other. What folly! The belief that the dimensions of some mother's mask, say, fitting—becoming— one's physiognomy is oneself. What manipulation! To appropriate her mask of a different sex—if you are a boy—a different generation—if you are a child—so experientially different—if you are a person—because experience is an awful thing. Truly, who "loves" it? In order not to have it—experience— we do a number of things, chief among them speaking to stupid people who cannot possibly understand us. . . .

> The cowardly experience described previously—applying that mother's
> mask, say, to protect oneself. How easily this is done!

Let me make clear: Als's critique here of "otherness and difference" is not the
same as the writing instructor who tells students of color to avoid writing about
race or being "political." Instead, Als is trying to get at the "difference" in any
particular individual of color's experience, the specifics of what makes that person and that writer an individual and not simply a member of a race or a group.
He is talking about the ways writers of color can sometimes avoid the pain and
hard work of discovering and exploring the singularity of who they are and what
they have experienced. The choice is not between being a member of a group
and being an individual; instead one must understand how one is both, how
contradictions and complexities arise from and within this dialectic.

Als is the Pulitzer Prize–winning theater critic for *The New Yorker*, and in his
reviews of black theater artists, he demonstrates an informed and empathetic
understanding of their worldview and experiences; yet he also critiques those
instances where they drift toward stereotype or generalization or fall short of
three dimensionality or full complexity. That he brings the same critical eye to
his own work is part of what makes him such a provocative and insightful essay-
ist and memoirist.

Memoir is a reenvisioning the past self and thus coming to terms with the limitations of one's past self.

A person's blind spots can stem from personal psychological blocks, but
they can also result from larger historical, cultural, or societal limitations. T. S.
Eliot argued that a writer should be aware that people of other times and other
places have thought and felt and acted differently than those around her. The
more the writer is able to do this, the more sophisticated she is—and thus the
writer will be more aware of the alternative ways of viewing both herself and the
world.

Sexism; ethnocentricism; class, racial, or orientation bias; or simply in-
sularity—these are some of the charges that arise when a writer or narrator is
not aware of viewpoints other than her own. This blindness may have a psychological component, but it also involves culture, education, politics, and life
experience.

One implication of all this for the memoirist is that the truth is not simply
what happened. It is how what happened is interpreted, how it is contextualized, how it is evaluated and analyzed.

The Reliability of the
Narrator in Memoir

In a work of fiction, even autobiographical fiction, the sophisticated reader will assume the writer is different from the first-person narrator. The first-person narrator is a creation, however closely he or she might resemble the writer.

People don't necessarily assume this with memoir. Instead, they assume that the first-person narrator is commensurate with the writer; the view of the first-person narrator and the actual living writer concerning what is on the page is one and the same.

A key issue lurking here is the question of the reliable narrator.

As I explained in the previous essay, the reflective voice separates the present narrator from the memoir's account of and picture of the self in the past. This establishes a distance between the present narrating self and the past self, a distance that enables judgment, interpretation, contextualization.

Without the reflective voice, that is, without a critical present narrator, the reader may be uncertain about how to assess or judge the narrator's younger self. As a result, the reader may more readily assume that the way the younger self views herself and her experiences is commensurate with the writer's evaluation of the younger self and experiences. The reader would then be more likely to think that the writer may be slanting the tale in some way and may not be a reliable narrator of the events of the past.

If the reader of a memoir thinks that the narrator is unreliable, that is clearly a problem aesthetically. In such a case, the reader may make judgments of the younger self that the younger self does not make of herself. At the same time, the reader will not assume that the writer is aware that the reader can interpret the information in the text in a way other than how the younger self understands that information.

Say, for instance, the past—and younger—self possesses a view of an ex-lover that appears to most readers to be one-sided or blind to the past self's own flaws or part in a breakup. Without the voice of the present narrating self somehow indicating a different view, how is the reader to know that the past self's view of the situation is not also the view of the writer in the present?

In other words, if the reader concludes that the narrator is unreliable, the reader thinks that the clues or evidence through which he makes this conclusion are inadvertent on the writer's part. They occur because the writer is unaware of the implications of what she has written.

In fiction, the situation is different. In fiction, if the narrator is unreliable, the reader will assume that that unreliability is something the writer is aware of and is creating; that is, the writer is leaving clues through which the reader can detect that narrator's unreliability. As a result, the reader will judge and contextualize what the narrator says and the story she relates accordingly.

In contrast, in memoir, the reader is not inclined to separate the writer from the narrator, and that is a crucial difference between the two genres.

How does a narrator establish reliability and a sense of trust with the reader? Is the achievement of that reliability for a nonfiction writer the same as for a fiction writer?

One way the narrator establishes reliability is by acknowledging two things: First, there are other viewpoints; she may not be able to articulate or know all those other viewpoints, but she is aware they exist and she makes the reader aware that she is aware. She may try to speculate what those viewpoints might be. But if those speculations seem slanted or unfair, then her reliability falters in the reader's eyes.

The narrator's ability to speculate fairly or accurately about others depends in part on the narrator's ability to read other people. This is a skill. Some people are better at it than others.

But there is also a conceptual and psychological side to the question of reliability, which leads to my second point: to be reliable, the narrator must possess and make clear her awareness of her own subjectivity. This involves first an understanding of her own motives and inclinations. Is the narrator aware that she, in the past or the present, might have unconscious motives? Is she willing to investigate them? Is she aware she may have blind spots? Is she willing to investigate the nature of those blind spots and their causes? Is she willing to be at least as critical of her past self as, if not more than, she is of the other people she writes about?

In my memoirs, in order to establish the reliability of my account, it was important for me to do two things. First, I needed to give adequate voice to the ways my parents viewed the past and the present and how their interpretation of the past differed from mine. In doing this, I had to consider both my parents and my past self in a way similar to the ways a fiction writer might view the characters in a novel. The views of my past self and my present narrating self were not omniscient.

Thus, in both memoirs, I viewed my past and the history of my family from the viewpoint of a Sansei, a third-generation Japanese American. My parents' viewpoint was that of the Nisei, the second generation. On an absolute level, I could not be certain that my view was any truer than theirs. What I could be certain of was that the truth did include both my view and theirs.

This brings me to my second point about the establishment of the narrator's reliability in memoir, one that may at first seem counterintuitive. Rather than assuming an objectivity I did not possess, I made it clear that I was approaching my past from my own subjective viewpoint. I needed to be open and up front about the limits of my own personality and character; I could not hide my faults or misdeeds.

But my subjectivity involved more than my own particular personality and psychology or the particular events of my past. That subjectivity also involved an examination of my racial and ethnic identity and an acknowledgment of how that formed a lens through which I viewed my experiences. It involved seeing myself not just through the lens of individuality but also through that of my membership in a group—Japanese Americans, particularly third-generation Japanese Americans.*

Such a view goes against a dominant strain in American thought and culture: the emphasis on the individual (as in that familiar white bromide, "I don't see race"). To understand the limits of this particularly American slant, consider the British novelist Doris Lessing, who was born in Iran and spent her childhood in Zimbabwe. Lessing's consciousness of her identity as a woman and gender

---

* The history of the Issei (first generation), the Nisei, and the Sansei is distinct from that of other immigrant groups. Like other Asians, the Issei were forbidden from becoming citizens or owning property, but immigration from Japan, and Asia in general, was halted by the racist Asian Exclusion Act of 1924, and unlike other Asian governments, such as China, Japan strictly enforced this ban from its side. It was mainly the Issei and the Nisei on the mainland who were imprisoned by the U.S. government during World War II, while my generation, the Sansei, did not experience the internment whose existence in many mainland Japanese American families was kept a zone of silence. It is impossible, then, to tell the story of Japanese Americans or my family without referencing race and racial politics.

roles is well known. What's perhaps less recognized is how she grew up in a racial environment where she was highly aware that she lived within the context of a group: she was a white colonist living among African colonials. Thus, in her book of essays *Prisons We Choose to Live Inside*, she writes:

> The fact is that we all live our lives in groups—the family, work groups, social, religious and political groups. Very few people indeed are happy as solitaries, and they tend to be seen by their neighbors as peculiar or self-ish or worse. Most people cannot stand being alone for long. They are always seeking groups to belong to, and if one group dissolves, they look for another. We are group animals still, and there is nothing wrong with that. But what is dangerous is not belonging to a group, or groups, but not understanding the social laws that govern groups and govern us.
>
> When we're in a group, we tend to think as that group does: we may even have joined the group to find "like-minded" people. But we also find our thinking changing because we belong to a group. It is the hardest thing in the world to maintain an individual dissident opinion, as a member of a group.

Sometimes, when I work with students writing memoir, they have difficulty seeing themselves as a member of a group. This membership can involve any number of elements—sex, sexual orientation, ethnicity, race, religion, class, generation, culture, history, region, and so on (note: the inability or refusal of white writers to acknowledge their racial identity can also be viewed as marking them as part of a group). In this way, investigating the limitations and subjectivity of one's viewpoint leads to a new articulation of one's identity, a search for a language to describe and contextualize one's membership in a group. Often, when a beginning memoirist cannot articulate a portrait of the present narrating self or even refuses to, her membership in a particular group may be involved in this resistance.

As I was writing *Turning Japanese*, when I looked at how certain white American males tended to write about Japan, what often bothered me was their assumption that their viewpoint was objective and without bias. They generally never investigated or questioned their own identity and so never investigated or questioned how their own identity might shape the ways they viewed the Japanese or interpreted various aspects of Japanese culture.

For example, one commentator argued that the Japanese were particularly insular, and as evidence of this, he used an anecdote about a white *gaijin* (foreigner) who spoke fluent Japanese and was looked at with amazement or disapprobation by the Japanese people he encountered. This white male writer never considered the fact that I've experienced such reactions when I speak English— even though I grew up here in America, and my family has been here for three generations and over a century. In other words, this author wrote seemingly unaware of the insular way that native-born white Americans often view people of color or immigrants; as a result, at least for me as a reader, his lack of awareness of his own subjectivity/bias made his assessment of the Japanese unreliable.

In *Turning Japanese,* my view of Japan came out of my position and experience as a Japanese American; in delineating this lens, I was acknowledging my subjective position. I was not presuming an objectivity that I did not possess.

Narrative Drama in
Mary Karr's *Cherry* and
Garrett Hongo's *Volcano*

In looking back on one's earlier self, the writer of memoir might also ask a version of the type of questions actors ask: What was my motivation? What did I want? How were my actions designed to get me what I want? These questions of course are similar to the basis of story: What is the protagonist's goal? What does the protagonist want? What does the protagonist do to get what she wants?

In considering these questions, I often tell my students to think about acting: If you are an actor, you cannot act a situation. Nor can you act a general desire, such as a desire for love. Such a general desire can only be acted on if there is a more specific goal—for instance, to walk across the bar and talk to a particular woman; to arrange for two dates a week on Match.com.

In any given scene in a memoir or in any section of narrative, then, it is helpful to ask: What was the goal of my past self in this scene or in this particular time period? What actions did I take to achieve this goal?

If the writer isn't clear about the motives of the younger self, her goals and desires, then she can't tell a story about the younger self.

Inevitably, in the pursuit of a goal, a character faces both external and internal hurdles or barriers. Recall, for instance, when Macbeth ultimately decides to murder Duncan. Macbeth struggles between two opposing desires: one is to be loyal to his king; the other is Macbeth's desire to replace his king.

Now there are times when a character reaches a level of lucidity and admits this irreconcilability, yet understands that he must choose one direction. By the end of *Macbeth*, Macbeth achieves a certain stature because he finally admits the path he has chosen, and he takes it to its conclusion, despite the consequences. But *Macbeth* is a tragedy, and in his persistence Macbeth becomes a tragic hero. In real life, most of us continue to try to lie about our irreconcilable desires. Or else events and consequences force us to confront our lie.

Thus in analyzing the story of her past, the writer can start by looking for the lies she sees the younger self telling herself.

In order to understand how these principles work, let us look at the following scene from Mary Karr's memoir, *Cherry*:

> What I wanted formed in my head for a good instant before I said it: "I want titties, goddamn it, Daddy. Not some bra."
>
> His eyes widened slow at what I'd dared to say. "You want titties?" He threw back his head and hooted with laughter, howling up at the dusty light fixture.
>
> I hurled a handful of pecan husks into the bowl and stood up. Mother came in wearing a nightgown and rubbing lotion into her hands. "What is it?" she said. Her head was wrapped in a towel like a swami.
>
> I tore into my room and power-slammed the door into its molding. The window glass shivered. I hurled myself down on the lavender-flowered spread. Part of me knew I'd crossed the border into some country where he didn't—or wouldn't—tread.
>
> I instinctively knew the rules laid down for girls' comportment, but I wasn't yet resigned to them, for to place my head into that yoke was to part with too much freedom. One day I sat on my porch sucking the long ears of my Bugs Bunny popsicle into a syrupless white dunce cap when a herd of boys my age on bikes pedaled into view. They were shirtless, sailing down the street in careless whooshing speed.
>
> One blond boy named Corey was somebody's cousin down from Houston for the summer. He was slim and brown and expressionless in a way that let me manufacture complex thoughts for him. (Was it Chekhov or Tolstoy who complained about what deep personalities we can manufacture behind "some little scrap of face"?) His surfer cut hung in a bright wing across his forehead. He stood stock still in his pedals for the entire strip of road past my house like the figurehead on a ship's prow, and his thoughtless beauty dragged from me the faint tug of something like desire. His body was thin-muscled as a grey-hound's. Maybe his hurtling motion made enough wind to cool him off, but he didn't look to suffer from the heat I felt so squandered in.
>
> This wasn't desire as it would become. Not yet. The cool fire circled more in my abdomen than between my legs, and it was vague and smoke gray. I pictured no boy yet—not even John Cleary—gathering me into his arms.

Despite what Nabokov's Humbert wanted to think, I've never met a girl as young as I was then who craved a bona fide boning. But glowing nonspecifically from my solar plexus was this forceful light. I wanted John Cleary or Corey or some other boy to see that light, to admire it, not to feed off it for his own hungers. When I closed my eyes at night, I did not manufacture naked bodies entwined. Mostly I didn't even venture into kissing. Rather my fantasies at that time were all in the courtly mode. I pictured John Cleary/ Corey taking my hand for the couples' skate at the rink, how we'd cut a slow circle together in a spotlight, with his gaze inventing me in the stares of those we passed.

But the boys' bicycle pack also sent a stab of envy through me. If I couldn't yet capture John Cleary with my feminine wiles, then surely I deserved to enjoy the physical abandon he got, liberties I instinctively knew were vanishing. (I know, I know. Psychoanalytic theory would label this pecker envy and seek to smack me on the nose for it. To that I'd say, o please. Of actual johnsons I had little awareness. What I coveted was privilege.)

In this passage, Karr's younger self tries to lie about an irreconcilable dilemma. On the one hand, she is aware that the rules of comportment are different for girls than boys and that breaking these rules may bring various negative consequences. On the other hand, she wants the freedom to act like a boy. As people often do, she tries to ignore or evade the terms of this dilemma. (Whether, as a girl, she should have to confront this dilemma is clearly a different question.)

As this scene unfolds, Karr's younger self attempts to take and achieve the same freedom, the same privileges that the boys have. Thus, she takes an action to achieve her goal.

That's how right before sixth grade I came to peel off my T-shirt, mount my pink-striped Schwinn, and set off down the oyster shell of Taylor Avenue wearing only red shorts.

By the time I reached the first porch where a line of ladies in their rockers were sipping iced tea, it was clear I'd made a terrible mistake. Their eyes widened, and their heads turned rigidly to one another and back at me as if on poles. After I rounded the corner, I felt their stares slide off my back. A different kid would have gone hauling butt back to her garage. She would have stayed inside till some car wreck or church supper had drawn the local talk from her escapade. But I was not bred to reversals. I only had to make it one loop around the block to finish.

Karr's younger self persists in that action—she continues to ride around the block—even when it's clear her action has led to results she neither expected nor desired. The assessment of her character and her action comes from the older present narrating self looking back on her younger self.

In the end, Karr's younger self suffers embarrassment for taking this action. This is a clear case of that other principle I often invoke: When we take a specific action, we intend and believe that this action will achieve a certain result. In normal, everyday routines, our expectations about our actions are generally met. But in story or in trying to achieve something we struggle for, the results or consequences of our actions are often not as we expected. Other people—and often we ourselves—react in ways we did not predict or foresee. And this is indeed what happens to the young Mary Karr.

All of this is a way of saying that in these few short pages, Karr tells a story. Her protagonist takes up a desire, a goal. In confronting this desire, she faces an irreconcilable dilemma. Being the age that she is and given her character, she denies this irreconcilable dilemma. She believes she can act like a boy, and she does so. After she acts, the world reacts in ways that tell her she cannot act like a boy; the world humiliates her. She fails to achieve her goal—and yet she clearly sets herself on a course of independence that will serve her in the future. And the story ends.

Garrett Hongo's *Volcano* contains a section that I often use to demonstrate the construction of a narrative structure in memoir.

Hongo's narrative starts with the section "Terrible Angel," which opens with a description of his MFA workshop and his visiting instructor, C. K. Williams. Teachers often function as the threshold guardians who appear in myth; they are there to test the protagonist and see if the protagonist is worthy of moving on in his hero's journey. In Hongo's description, Williams is viewed as a formidable presence and a harsh taskmaster. He comes "swaddled in prestige" from his acclaimed work; he's won a Guggenheim. He requires the students to write a poem a week ("Outside of class, everyone grumbled. How was decent poetry to be written on demand?").* Beyond this, he holds the students to the highest standards: "Our tall instructor would have at us, bashing, castigating, lectur-

---

* The students here who object to writing a poem a week do not understand the nature of the creative process. Feeling inspired does not necessarily lead to a good poem, nor does feeling uninspired cause a lousy poem. As William Stafford has told us, the key to writer's block is to lower your standards. Just accept what comes. Creativity arises from a willingness to experiment and to fail, not from a pressure to succeed.

ing us on our mental laziness, on our lack of ambition." He reads to them from Rilke, Tadeusz Rozewicz. The class holds him in awe.

Hongo's younger self deemed not only the work of his fellow students but also his own as meriting Williams's severe critiques:

> Class was a torture. People had a hard time speaking up. When they did, they praised shit, so far as I could tell. They *wrote* shit.
>
> I wrote shit too. I didn't trust anybody. *Poetry?*—I said to myself. *Not with these people.* Looking across the seminar room to a scowling man with dark curly hair tight against his head, I felt afraid and intimidated.

Here a perceptive reader will sense that this assessment of the younger past self and his motivations is voiced not by the younger self but the present narrating self. This becomes even clearer as the section moves on, as the present narrating self articulates the vulnerabilities that the younger self was afraid to confront:

> I defended. Against him, against the workshop, against *whites*, against my own inspiration. I brought in poem after poem—my poem per week—dramatic monologues impossible to critique. . . . I wrote *lousy*. I wrote to be *lousy*. I was afraid to let the workshop and this Turk of a teacher know what it was I cared about, what it was I worried I could not bring myself to be dedicated to.
>
> What I cared about was the inner city, about my teenage life brooding on the social complexities of my integrated high school—unusual in that it was a third white, and a third black, and a third Japanese American.

The protagonist's goal here is clear: he must succeed in the eyes of his very critical teacher. At the same time, he lies to himself about his irreconcilable conflict: his instructor is demanding more from him than is reasonable. What that is the younger Hongo doesn't quite know, but some part of him knows he is lying to himself and holding back in his poetry. He knows poetry requires vulnerable honesty, but he can't bring himself to be vulnerable before this imposing white teacher and the mostly white workshop participants. Note how the younger Hongo uses his awareness of his racial Otherness to excuse himself from what is required to achieve his goal; of course, he is racially isolated in the workshop, but that's not the ultimate reason he's holding back. Instead, he wants to keep his own past, its pain and complexity at a distance. (Note: this is an instance where the past self uses his racial identity to avoid rather than reveal the truth.)

A little later, the section wanders from the workshop into a flashback from Hongo's teenage years; ultimately, this leads to a section that contextualizes Hongo's experience in high school in terms of class, ethnicity, and race. In the next section, "Fraternity," he tells the story of an ill-fated romance between Hongo's teenage self and his classmate Regina, who's Portuguese American.

Both Hongo and Regina sense that their relationship challenges the existing racial, ethnic, and cultural norms of their high school. They can't go to the Japanese American dances, and they can't go to the white dances. Instead, they go to the Chicano dances, where the young Hongo and Regina dress the part, helped by Hongo's Chicano friend: "Pacheco . . . advised me to grow a mustache and let my black hair go long in the back, to slick it down with pomade and to fluff it up front, then seal it all in hair spray. I bought brown Pendletons and blue navy-surplus bell-bottoms. I bought hard, steel-toed shoes."

For a few months, Hongo and Regina are able to pass through their racially demarcated high school without incident. Then Regina is accosted by a white football player, who grabs her arm so violently, it breaks. It's not quite clear whether this action is racially motivated, but it is implied by what happens next. After a Japanese American boy taunts Hongo with the news of what has happened to Regina, Hongo rushes to her house. But on the way, he is set upon by a troop of Japanese American boys who beat him up for dating outside his group. Here the present narrating self provides an intricate historical, political, and psychological reading of this incident that the younger past self did not yet understand. To make sense of his story, Hongo must resort to the reflexive voice:

> A kid from Hawai'i, I'd undergone no real initiation in shame or social victimization yet and maintained an arrogant season out of bounds, imagining I was exempt. It was humiliating to have been sent to Camp. The Japanese American community understood their public disgrace and lived modestly, with deep prohibitions. I was acting outside of this history. I could cross boundaries, I thought. But I was not yet initiated into the knowledge that we Japanese were *not* like anyone else, that we lived in a community of violent shame. I paid for my naïveté with a bashing I still feel today, with cuts that healed with scars I can still run my fingers along.

Afterward, these two incidents of violence create a space between the younger Hongo and Regina that cannot be mended or breached.

In the next section, "The Legend," Hongo turns back to his MFA workshop, and his younger self's struggle with poetry and with his instructor Williams. In this section, the narration moves quickly through the term: "For seven weeks, I'd brought in my defenses against my own needs. I'd composed well-wrought studies in the rhetoric of cool, in the sophistry of jive." The writing then goes over in detail two poems Hongo submits to the workshop, one a monologue of William Holden's character as the floating corpse at the end of *Sunset Boulevard*, and one a monologue based on Kurosawa's interpretation of *Macbeth*, *Throne of Blood*. C. K. Williams reacts to both poems with cutting dismissive remarks ("What next? *Two Gentleman of Osaka*?").

The following week is difficult because the younger self senses he has run "out of fakes and verbal juking, exhausted [his] repertoire of rhetorical feints and darts." At this point, all the younger Hongo feels he can resort to is his own "experience." He writes and submits a poem that's quite different from the ones he's been producing, a poem about an encounter between a young white woman weeping on a Los Angeles city bus and a young black man who tries to comfort her.

Narrative structures often make use of three attempts. If the protagonist fails after three attempts, the reader assumes that the protagonist will continue to fail. Hongo the writer sets up this third poetic attempt as the final battle, partly by describing the feelings of the younger self this way: "I was filled with anticipation and resolve. I told myself that if Williams trashed this one, if he messed with me this time, why, I'd kill him." Clearly, we are in the third act, the decisive struggle.

But note: The younger self has been handing in poems to the workshop for weeks. It is through focusing on these last three attempts that Hongo the writer shapes this section as a narrative, as the third act of the younger self's experience with Williams and the workshop.

When the poem is presented to the workshop, Hongo the writer slows the narrative down so it takes place moment by moment (the final battle, because it's crucial, often requires a more precise and detailed temporal focus). Classmates dismiss the poem. "Ohhhh, this is so sentimental," says one. Another observes, "I can't believe this . . . A black guy and a white girl? Where did you come up with this story—*The Naked City*?" "*The Twilight Zone*," someone else adds. There's a paragraph-long description of the class's awkward postures and their nervous anticipation of how Williams will react.

When Williams says, "You're all wrong," the class is of course surprised, and the writing draws the moment out, slows the pace of the narrative (this also forces the reader to wait in anticipation for Williams's reaction; delay can be used to increase narrative tension): "He pointed to my pages and tapped at them with a fore-finger. Things were so silent, we could hear the pad of his digit against the barely flapping stack of Xerox bond."

Against the class's comments and expectations, Williams pronounces that the poem is "*the real thing*," and he wonders why the younger Hongo has been wasting his time with "*all that other shit*." In that moment, Williams as the threshold guardian transforms from a negative, harsh figure to, almost comically, someone who gazes at the younger Hongo with "large lemur-like eyes . . . the kindest eyes [he'd] ever seen."

The poem is, of course, a metaphor for the younger Hongo's relationship with Regina and the racial barriers they faced, and we read Hongo's experience in the workshop in light of the tragic ending of their relationship. At the same time, what happened to the younger Hongo, the savage beating by members of his own tribe, while indirectly a result of his actions, came about not *directly* because of his actions but more from his ignorance of the unspoken rules of the ethnic community that he was both a part of and a newcomer to—that is, he did not know the severity of the taboo he was breaking or the racial and historical origins of that taboo. The narrative about the workshop provides an arena where the younger Hongo takes definite actions to determine his fate, where he acts more like a protagonist. That is, I think, one of the reasons Hongo employs the framework of his workshop experience and its narrative in his presentation of this teenage interracial relationship.

In my classes, I present this section of *Volcano* to teach how, in memoir, narrative structure can be discovered and constructed. But I also use it to demonstrate how the technical blocks in a person's writing can stem from, or cover over, a psychological block. The older present narrating self here knows what happened to the younger Hongo—he became a poet (the poem from the workshop is in his first book); he succeeded in his quest—so that the older present self looks back at the younger self knowing his fate and how he reached that fate. In the process, he's able to articulate a principle of his own artistry and the artistry Williams was trying to teach him; this is a principle that the younger Hongo only embraced when he finally became honest with himself and began to own his particular experiences in the racially charged environment of Los Angeles:

> A long and difficult way, years long, had suddenly ended with that moment; with those words, Williams had fixed and inscribed a *standard* to my ambition, giving me a charge that, from that point on, became the center of my resolve. He'd recognized the poetry within me, telling me what *my* poetry

> was. . . . He would accept none of the false words I had been typing and handing in each week. From me, he held out for a truth—that there is a world of feeling and specificities among the vast and monolithic Other of race in America. When I gave it, he gave back. It was a blessing.

Note here Hongo's emphasis on "feeling and specificities," a phrase Hilton Als would probably approve of. Racism and racial hierarchies generalize, and one danger for writers of color is to assert and write only in oppositional generalities. In contrast, "feeling" is experiential and particular—both to an individual and to a particular time and place. History is not solely events of significance, nor does it involve only the political. Hongo's writings are acutely attentive to a history of "feeling," which is perhaps rightly more the provenance of poets and creative writers than of historians.

On the Line between Memoir
and Fiction

In *A Poetics of Women's Autobiography*, Sidonie Smith writes of the impossibility of the autobiographer ever recapturing the entirety of her subjectivity or her experience. She argues that the "I" of the narrative "becomes a fictive persona": "Involved in a kind of masquerade, the autobiographer creates an iconic representation of continuous identity that stands for, or rather before, her subjectivity as she tells of this 'I' rather than of that 'I.' She may even create several, sometimes competing, stories or versions of herself as her subjectivity is displaced by one or multiple textual representations."

To understand Smith's point, imagine the following scenario: At thirty, a writer writes a memoir of her childhood. Then, at sixty, she writes another memoir of her childhood. Which memoir is true or truer? And is truth—that is, the literal truth—the most pressing question for a reader of either memoir?

At the same time, if one admits the "fictive" nature of autobiography, the question remains about how the autobiographer or memoirist on a practical level addresses the problem of this form. I'm talking here about the sorts of strategies and questions that might anchor a discussion in a writers' workshop or in the mind of the writer, as opposed to an academic analysis. For in actual practice, the line between fiction and nonfiction in literary memoir is often less rigid and more ambiguous than people on both sides of this question sometimes acknowledge.

In my memoir *Turning Japanese*, as I've noted, I used various narrative structures to recount my experiences living in Japan for a year. In the process, I had to address certain basic questions: How much was I willing to fictionalize in order to achieve narrative structure? Could I alter events? Could I rearrange the sequence of events? Could I alter the cast and persona of the characters I encountered in

Japan? Could I alter the picture I was creating of myself? My wife? What were the ethical and aesthetic issues involved in answering these questions?

Just as importantly, since the work was to be nonfiction, what was accuracy? Sometimes I was working from notes written almost immediately after the events, but with other events, I had no notes. In some instances, I was dealing with events from my childhood or even from my parents' and grandparents' lives that occurred before I was born. What did it mean to be faithful to my memories or present accurate accounts of events I had not even witnessed? Or for that matter, to events I had witnessed? Think, for instance, of a memoirist like Frank McCourt, who in *Angela's Ashes* renders dialogue that occurred when he was a young child. Clearly, McCourt is not providing an exact transcription of what was said.

Over the course of writing my first memoir, I constructed my own answers to these questions. For example, with dialogue, I wrote what I felt was accurate according to my memory or my sense of the people I knew. Or at least I started the dialogues in such a fashion. When the conversations relied on notes, I generally kept to them. Yet I also let the dialogues move in ways that didn't absolutely reflect my memory or in ways that I had not planned if somehow the scene demanded this. My sense of these demands sometimes involved practical questions, such as transition, logic, and progression of the conversation or placement of the people, but I also allowed for heightening or slight exaggerations to create tension and dramatic interest or to sharpen some ideological or intellectual difference.

In this way, I was following a principle I had learned from writing poetry: If the aesthetic truth of the writing seems to ask for fictionalizing, I would do so. Yet I was writing a memoir, not a novel or a poem. So where did the line between the two exist for me?

Eventually, I came up with a set of rules for the memoir that allowed a certain amount of what might be called fictionalizing but still, in my eyes, kept the writing within the realm of memoir.

In terms of the overall narrative, I decided I could not alter major events. This proved particularly tricky when dealing with my encounter with Gisela (not her real name), a German woman with whom I had a brief flirtation. Though nothing overtly sexual occurred—there was no physical contact between us— the fact that I did not immediately inform her that I was married constituted a breach of marital trust, and I wanted to make this clear to the reader. I realized that the whole question of betrayal would have been more dramatic and, at the same time more easily rendered, if I were writing fiction. There the obvious solution would have been for the protagonist to have sex with the woman or at least for them to physically touch. To choose the more accurate rendering required a subtlety and complications that were more difficult to convey.

I did decide that I could alter less important events, and perhaps even more significantly, I could rearrange the sequence of events to heighten the narrative flow. For example, take the fire festival that ends the first half of the book and comes immediately after the argument between my wife and me over my flirtation with Gisela. In actuality, the fire festival did not take place at this time, nor did I go there alone, as I do in the book, but instead I went with my wife. But placing me in isolation at the fire festival increased the uncertainty and consequences of the argument and my actions. In a similar fashion, my trip to my grandparents' hometown did not come at the end of my stay in Japan, as it does in the book. But I wanted to use the trip as an ultimate goal, which keeps being deferred and which could act as a culmination of my time there.*

In the end, I felt comfortable changing the sequence of events in my trip to Japan, and I accepted that as a legitimate aesthetic device. A knottier problem was how to portray myself and those around me. Obviously, the portrayal and analysis of oneself and others involve subjective judgments. But beyond this, as I started to rearrange and construct a narrative through line, as I began to dramatize rather than describe or analyze, the nature of the book and its characters began to change.

In dialogues, as I set various characters in opposition to me, it became apparent that if I exaggerated slightly certain personality traits or tendencies of mine, I could create more tension and interest. Again, I gave myself permission to avail myself of these fictional techniques, pushed on by the writing process.

Then too I developed my own sense of how I would portray my relationship with my wife and our marriage. I wanted to be as open about our conflicts and tensions as I could. After some discussion, my wife and I reached an agreement about this issue (the question of how the writing of memoir interacts with one's

* Another instance where I altered actual events occurs later in the book when I take a trip to Osore-san (Mount Osore), where I engage in a séance with one of the famous blind women shamans there. In real life I took this trip with friends who do not appear in the book. But I felt that introducing a whole new set of friends near the end of the book would have bogged down the narrative momentum and also would have been confusing and weakened the narrative, providing the reader with too many characters to digest. My solution was to have friends who had already been introduced accompany me on the trip; in writing about the trip, I used dialogue reconstructed from actual conversations we had had at other times and in other places.

personal relationships is a whole other essay). But I also felt that because I was the one telling the tale, if anyone was going to look worse in the relationship, it would be me. This decision to tilt things against myself as the book's protagonist was also reinforced by my sense that it made the book more interesting and highlighted certain issues in ways that were more dialectical.

Self-assessment is, of course, difficult, as is assessing one's own writing. But I believe that the person portrayed in *Turning Japanese*, the past self, is a bit more naive, a bit more self-righteous, a bit more irritable and opinionated, a bit more insecure, and a bit more self-centered than I was in real life. For instance, one alteration of my own person I constructed occurs at the very start of *Turning Japanese*. There, in part to contrast with my wife's eagerness to visit Japan, I deliberately exaggerated my own reticence about going to Japan and learning about Japanese culture and deliberately heightened my Francophile leanings and my general fear of travel. Such exaggeration provided the protagonist with a much further distance to travel, as he acclimated himself to Japan and learned to love the culture there. It also provided opportunities for humor and drama that wouldn't otherwise be available.

Of course, fiction writers have used such techniques over and over again, and the uncertainties such exaggerations bring up have plagued writers of autobiographical fiction. In considering these issues, I have in part been influenced by Philip Roth's fictional practices rather than his autobiography, *The Facts*. As Roth frequently notes, readers often mistake Roth the author for his fictional protagonists. In actuality, Roth has maintained that he is constantly distorting and changing real life to accord with the demands of fiction; autobiography and fiction, he insists, are not the same. In an interview with the *Paris Review*, Roth was asked whether his character's rage at Milton Appel, a critic who accuses Zuckerman of being a self-hating, anti-Semitic Jew, reflects "the expression of a kind of guilt on [Roth's] part?" Here is Roth's answer:

> Guilt? Not at all. As a matter of fact, in an earlier draft of the book, Zuckerman and his young girlfriend Diana took exactly opposite positions in their argument about Appel. She, with all her feisty inexperience, said to Zuckerman, "Why do you let him push you around, why do you take this shit sitting down?" and Zuckerman, the older man, said to her, "Don't be ridiculous, Dear, calm down, he doesn't matter." There was the real autobiographical scene, and it had no life at all. I had to absorb the rage into the main character even if my own rage on this topic had long since subsided. By being

true to life I was actually ducking the issue. So I reversed their positions, and
had the twenty-year-old college girl telling Zuckerman to grow up, and gave
Zuckerman the tantrum. Much more fun. I wasn't going to get anywhere with
a Zuckerman as eminently reasonable as myself.

One way of stating this point is that issues of accuracy in fiction are not as
important as issues of aesthetic interest. But unlike Roth, I believe that maintaining such a tension is also important in memoir, although to a lesser extent.
For example, there were vast stretches of time in Japan when my wife and I got
along amicably, when we sat spooning together in bed reading or watching tele-
vision. I myself get bored with the idea of writing about such occasions, and I
wasn't going to inflict them on the reader. No, the more revealing and energiz-
ing incidents during our stay in Japan were our arguments. But by highlighting
these and even at times exaggerating them slightly, I did not give a literally accurate portrayal of our marriage.

A question then arises: How do such alterations and exaggerations of the
protagonist affect our readings of autobiography or memoir? When Clark Blaise
and Bharati Mukherjee wrote *Days and Nights in Calcutta*, a memoir about their
travels together in India, they decided that the book would be improved if they
exaggerated slightly Blaise's character and position as a white male. Through
such highlighting, not only was the book made more dramatic, but certain other
truths were revealed. Would a more satisfactory way of reading such a work be
to take the portrayal of their relationship as a version of the truth, rather than
the whole truth? But isn't this what we do with autobiographical fiction?

At the same time, there are clearly limits to this: If readers found out I wasn't
Japanese American or that my parents hadn't been in the internment camps,
neither of my memoirs could be considered a legitimate memoir or a work of
nonfiction.*

---

* Once we stray from these larger areas, though, things become fuzzier. For instance, in the eyes of
many readers, Bruce Chatwin has written two travelogues, *In Patagonia* and *Songlines*, the second
a book about his investigation into the ways Aborigines in Australia map the landscape through
songs. After I finished *Songlines*, by chance I read an interview with Chatwin in which he pronounced the book a work of fiction. However, there's nothing to indicate this on the book cover
and, in fact, the narrator of the book calls himself Bruce Chatwin. Chatwin declared *Songlines* a
work of fiction in part because he made up a major character, the Russian émigré who serves as
his intermediary with the Aborigines. In the interview, Chatwin was asked about the division between fiction and nonfiction. He responded: "I don't think there is one. There definitely should
be, but I don't know where it is. I've always written very close to the line. I've tried applying fiction
techniques to actual bits of travel. I once made the experiment of counting up the lies in the book
I wrote about Patagonia. It wasn't, in fact, too bad: there weren't too many. But with *Songlines*,
if I had to tote up the inventions, there would be no question in my mind that the whole thing

Beyond the facts and events of a writer's own life, if his memoir involves his relationship with his parents, it's often the case that his imagination must inevitably enter the writing. How else can he picture the lives of his parents before he was born, or who they might have been beyond their interactions with him as a child? And what about his grandparents or even his great-grandparents?

In Japan, for instance, I realized that as my knowledge of Japanese culture and history grew, I could create a more complete picture of who my grandparents were. This in turn affected my understanding of my parents; I realized that until I visited Japan, I had known only the side of my parents that reflected American culture. I could not picture what it was like for them to go from the household of their Japanese immigrant parents to the streets of America because I had not known much about Japan or Japanese culture.

So, as I proceeded in the drafts of *Turning Japanese*, I began to imagine moments in the lives of my grandparents and parents, as well as in the life of my uncle. But even though I now knew something about Japan and Japanese culture, I was faced with another void: neither of my parents had talked to me much about their parents or about their lives as children, just as they had not said anything to me about the internment camps. For them the past was better kept in the past, silent, forgotten.

In writing *China Men*, which focuses on the men in her family, Maxine Hong Kingston encountered a similar dilemma. While her mother was quite voluble about her past, Kingston's father was not; she was faced then with the problem of how she would write his story. In *China Men*, Kingston finally says to her father, "I'll tell what I suppose from your silences and few words, and you can tell me that I'm mistaken. You'll just have to speak up with the real stories if I've got you wrong."

With Kingston's words in my head, I decided I would simply re-create the past of my parents and other relatives as best I could. Early on in my writing of *Turning Japanese*, this appeared to represent a different task from writing about my own life. But at one point, looking at an early draft, my editor remarked that some of my writing about my father was more vivid than anything else in the book. I thought about this and realized that when I was dealing with my own life I was only putting down what I could remember. If I could not remember

---

added up to a fictional work." Similarly, Hilton Als has said that in his essay collection *White Girls*, "Tristes Tropiques" contains fictional elements, and "It Will Be Home Soon," ostensibly based on an interview with Richard Pryor's sister, is entirely fictional, though nothing in the book or on its cover indicates this.

what a person was wearing or what the weather was like that day, I wouldn't place these elements in the scene. When I was writing about my father's life, all of it was imaginative re-creation; I entered the freedom one enjoys in fiction to provide all the details and to use whatever details my imagination came up with.

In a way, this marked a crucial turning point in my writing of the memoir. I realized then that I should avail myself of the same freedom when I was writing about my own memories. As a result, the scenes involving my life became in a way more fictional and, at the same time, more vivid, more compelling, as writing. For me, this seemed more important than any rigid distinctions between genres. The line between memoir and fiction still did not seem clear. But the line between dull and interesting writing? That was a line I wanted to cross.*

---

* In my opinion, there is a difference between the autobiography of a public figure and a memoir written by a private figure. When a president writes an autobiography, everything in the book must be factual and accurate; no dialogue can be altered from what was actually said (unless there's an indication that the dialogue is a loose re-creation). Most literary memoirs are not read for their historical accuracy and are not intended as literal history. No one actually believes, for instance, that throughout his childhood, Frank McCourt took notes or tape recorded all the dialogues that appear in *Angela's Ashes*. At the same time, if readers discovered that McCourt's father was not an alcoholic, that would alter our opinion of the work (e.g., the case of James Frey's *A Million Little Pieces*). My point is that literary memoir is practiced in a gray area between the historical accuracy of a public figure's autobiography, and the exaggerations, distortions, and invention of autobiographical fiction.

IV

The Writer's Story

V. S. Naipaul

THE KNOWN AND THE UNKNOWN

There is the Paris of Catherine de Medicis at the Tuileries, as Hugo wrote;
of Henry I at the Hotel-de-Ville, of Louis XIV at Invalides; Louis XVI at the
Pantheon, and Napoleon I at the place Vendome, but there is also the Paris of
those who did not rule, the poets and vagabonds, and it was the Paris of Henry
Miller we were in . . . this Paris where you woke bruised after tremendous
nights, indelible nights, your pockets empty, the last bills scattered on the floor,
the memories scattered too. We went upstairs with three girls apiece and the
club officer napped in the car.

—James Salter, *Burning the Days*

I'll tell you a little story. . . . There's an elegant lady in England . . . getting on
now. She wrote a novel about a lady with a lover; the lady had a moral crisis—
"Would I condemn others when I'm immoral . . . ," you know that kind of
thing, all very delicate and beautiful. And this novel came out a few days before
the pound took its enormous dive—it seemed it was going to touch one dollar
fifty. And I thought, the dive of the pound—the extended event—has destroyed
the value of this novel, which implies that this world is of value, that values are
steady and are going to go on. But when your pound crashes, you cannot make
those assumptions anymore.

—V. S. Naipaul in an interview

To forge or discover one's identity as a writer is almost never an easy task. Some
beginning writers are tempted to focus on models who appear more central and
celebrated, who represent a known direction and destination.

But what if you're a writer who feels that there's something marginal in your
identity? The path forward may be particularly obscure, indeed may seem not to
exist at all. But then the truly new is almost always strange, and the truly strange
is almost always new.

In short, some look for precedents and predecessors and find many. Some look and find few or seemingly none.

We live in a time when the centers of culture and literature are being complicated and decentered by the new and unprecedented, by difference. This is a reflection both of an increasingly globalized culture and an increasingly varied population in many countries. The causes of this diversity are myriad: race, ethnicity, questions of sexual identity and orientation, migrations and immigrations, exiles, globalized travel, the expression of difference allowed by the Internet, where new, particularized, or marginalized audiences, groups, and communities are constantly being formed.

For young or beginning writers engaged in the task of discovering who they are as a writer and what their subject and vantage point might be, I present here two starkly different approaches to identity, culture, and the literary canon. In part, I argue that one of these writers, whose origins were particularly obscure, has come to be representative in ways he never imagined as a young writer, and certainly no one around him surmised when he started out.

Implicitly, this essay is also about my own development as a writer and my perpetual exploration of my own "minority" status, the seeming obscurity of my origins and position in the culture in which I live and write. I came here by many "crooked and indirect paths," and I surmise that many writers coming after me will find this to be the case for them.

James Salter, V. S. Naipaul—two writers whom I first encountered in my early thirties, two writers whom I love, each representing for me a literary path, a way of writing.

The first, Salter, is a Jew who grew up in New York and who changed his name in order to . . . well, it isn't quite clear. To remove his ethnic and religious heritage? To take on the image of a WASP writer? In interviews, Salter refused to discuss the matter. The question of his personal ethnic/religious identity was one he wished to avoid, or perhaps, one he did not think essential to his task—though, of course, such a stance is, on another level, a statement of identity.

Salter is, as they say, a writer's writer. As with Nabokov, you read Salter for the sentences, though Salter's language is less ornate and piquant, and its precision and elegance more straightforward. Nabokov's writing was that of an émigré, of an eccentric and idiosyncratic genius. Salter's style is that of a native-born American and bears a strong relationship to Hemingway's example—the writing presumes certain givens, certain knowns, certain values and systems of judgments that, if not universal, are assumed to be widely recognized.

Salter opens his memoir, *Burning the Days*, with this vignette:

> The true chronicler of my life, a tall, soft-looking man with watery eyes, came
> up to me at the gathering and said, as if he had been waiting a long time to
> tell me, that he knew everything. I had never seen him before.
>
> I was in my fifties. He was not much older but somehow seemed an
> ancient figure. He remembered me when I was an infant, riding in a horse-
> drawn carriage on Hope Avenue in Passaic. He named my birthday, "June
> tenth, 1925, am I right? Your picture was in *The New York Times* when you were
> a captain in Korea and had just shot down three planes. You married a girl
> from Washington, D.C. You have four children."
>
> He went on and on. He knew intimate detsails, some a bit mixed up,
> like a man whose pockets are filled with scraps of paper. . . . As if it were an
> attempt to try to be of some importance. "You went to Horace Mann," he
> said. "The football coach was Tillinghast."

To Salter, this anecdote says, "There is your life as you know it and also as others
know it, perhaps incorrectly, but to which some importance must be attached."
But what strikes *me* about this opening is the assumption that the life and world
Salter is speaking about are known by others—and implicitly, by the reader. Of
course, the reader who opens Salter's memoir doesn't know the particulars of
Salter's past. But the context of that life, its setting? That is known; that is assumed. Salter doesn't have to explain his references here to a literate American
reader—Passaic, the *New York Times*, the war in Korea, even Horace Mann (where
Jack Kerouac went to high school). Salter's background, his place in the world,
is neither an enigma nor a mystery to him or this apparent stranger at a party—
or implicitly, to us. When Salter writes about where he grew up, he describes it
as a place we all know: "There is the immortal city—Grant's Tomb domed and
distant in the early days, the great apartment buildings with their polished lob-
bies, the doormen and green awnings reaching out to the curb." (One understands implicitly that Bed Stuy or the Queensbridge Houses aren't part of this
immortality, though millions know their significance in our cultural history.)

In the memoir that ensues, through the brilliance and beauty of the writing,
the moments and days Salter chooses to recall take on luminescence and depth,
the quality of being etched in stone: his time as a fighter pilot in Korea; his time
in Paris as an aspiring writer, meeting such literary "kings" as Irwin Shaw; his
time in the film business, encountering beautiful Italian actresses and working with Robert Redford. The writing floats on the glamour of certain names,
speaks of the "worlds above," worships the famous and the immortal: "In the

past I have written about gods and have sometimes done that here. . . . Frailty, human though it may be, interests me less. So I have written about certain things, the essential, in my view. . . . The rest is banal." To write this way requires a certainty of belief and values, a sense of knowing not only that the gods exist but that *we all agree on who they are.* There is a center, a glittering capital of the world. Stars. Luminaries. Kings. Immortals. Things history cannot destroy.

As a young writer, I fell in love with Salter's writings. And though feminist critiques mitigated some aspects of my appreciation for his literary antecedent, Hemingway, I still read both of these authors with pleasure and admiration, still appreciate their luminous, vividly etched prose. At the same time, I'm also aware that my pleasure and admiration accompany a sense of ressentiment and bafflement at the romantic and seemingly universalized aspects of the worlds these authors describe, since their worlds are not the world I occupy or ever will. Both have a drive to aestheticize, glamorize, mythologize, and centralize their own experience, the people they encounter, and the worlds they have lived in. In truth, I suppose I envy such strategies because, rightly or wrongly, I don't feel them appropriate or suited to who I am and my position in the world, to the subject matter that occupies most of my writing as a third-generation Japanese American.

Instead, I've found in the writings of a very different writer, V. S. Naipaul, a more useful mirror to the world in general and my particular portion of it. I say this, despite mixed feelings about his work and persona, misgivings echoed in any number of critiques of his work and his life. He has been denounced by many for racism and sexism both in his writings and his remarks, and I agree with many of these critiques.

Beyond all this, while I find a ready sense of pleasure in reading Salter or Hemingway, I don't quite feel the same reading Naipaul. Indeed, I probably prize Naipaul for offering just the opposite of pleasure. I read him for the hard truths he uncovers, for his relentless, unstinting, and inquisitive intellect, and perhaps, most of all, for the discomfort he causes in his readers, for the unsettling and unpleasant aspects that he focuses on in the worlds he has traveled through. If there is an antiromantic, Naipaul is it. He refuses to aestheticize, glamorize, mythologize, or centralize. But his ability to write like this is not a skill that came easily to him. He had to fight for such ability, such clearsightedness, and in many ways, his first opponent in this battle was himself.

In this battle, Naipaul faced questions similar to those Salter faced, questions both writers of color and white writers continue to face today: What is my identity as a person and as a writer? How do I place myself and create my work within the tradition of the writers who have come before me? But for Naipaul, his own particular answers to these questions led him to challenge certain received notions of what the tradition could include.

Rather than one of the capitals of the world, V. S. Naipaul grew up in Port of Spain, Trinidad, amid the Indian population there—that is, as part of a tiny ethnic/racial-minority population on a small island in the Caribbean archipelago. Like Walcott, Rushdie, and Achebe, Naipaul came to England as what I call the "scholarship boys," writers from the colonies or former colonies; Naipaul bore with him the legacy of his colonial Anglocentric education. Such students grew up under the aegis and legacy of empire; they were taught that there was indeed a center, a capital of the world. Thus, as Naipaul indicates in the autobiographical novel, *The Enigma of Arrival*, when he left Trinidad he had visions of himself writing like Somerset Maugham or Evelyn Waugh, producing novels about English country houses. As for the life Naipaul and his family lived in Trinidad, the young Naipaul deemed that unsuitable for literature. Many younger writers from marginalized backgrounds may feel a similar sentiment and even be encouraged by misguided instructors to assent to such a view; given the power of the majority, of dominance, of whiteness and cultural prestige, what do I have in my background, such a younger writer may think, to compete with this?

Only later did Naipaul realize that this provincial, colonial, ethnically bound island life would be his first subject. Gradually, he learned the history of his small island and how its cultural and racial mixture came into being; he came to understand that this history included not only that of his own island but that of the whole Caribbean archipelago.

At the same time, he ended up living the rest of his life in England, and that too shaped his viewpoint of his past; he experienced the English not in books but in actuality. Given where he grew up and his racial and ethnic identity, his struggle to make a place for himself in English letters was a task of almost insurmountable difficulty. Considering the marginality of the place and the people he came from and the enormity of transforming that place and people into literature, we should not be surprised that Naipaul speaks often in his writing and interviews of his sense of isolation, of a "rawness" in his nerves.

How does a writer from the margins, from a position like Naipaul's, confront the limitations of that position? In part because he came from such an isolated place and community, because he came from the periphery and not the center, Naipaul felt he had to travel to make up for his lack of sophistication.

His wide experience of the world would help compensate for the fact that he could not assume a universal acceptance of the significance of his background and experience in the way, say, either of the Amises automatically could. He understood that he needed to learn, as Eliot instructed in his definition of wit, that there were other cultures and ways of living, both in the present and in the past, than the one he grew up with.

Over and over in his writings, Naipaul asks, What is the world? For him, this question involves who is viewing that world and from what perspective, and his critical eye toward European culture and the center of the literary world has perhaps been less noticed than his critiques of the so-called Third World.

For example, at one point in *A Writer's People* he remarks, "It is amazing to me . . . how often I was baffled by famous novels of the time. I didn't understand Graham Greene's *The Quiet American*, which was a hit in 1955. It was set in Indo-China and was about the war to come. . . . I didn't understand the book partly because I didn't read the newspapers, or read them in a selective way." The younger Naipaul's befuddlement might ostensibly be attributed to the fact that, growing up in Trinidad, he would have had little exposure to the geopolitics of postwar America. But for Naipaul his ignorance possessed deeper roots:

> As soon as I begin to examine the matter I see that this ignorance of mine (there is no other word for it), this limited view, was an aspect of our history and culture. Historically, the peasantry of the Gangetic plain were a powerless people. We were ruled by tyrants, often far off, who came and went and whose names we very often didn't know. It didn't make sense in that setting to take an interest in public affairs, if such a thing could be said to exist. What was politically true of the Gangetic plain was also true of pre-war colonial Trinidad; in this respect at any rate the people who had made the long journey by steamship from India found nothing to jolt them.

The younger Naipaul, though, didn't let his bafflement before Greene's work become a stopping point. Eventually, he had to ascertain what his younger self lacked and then "read and write himself out of it."

But in this essay, Naipaul is not finished. He further complicates this picture of his younger self's ignorance with a critique of Greene. Naipaul argues that Greene, in his own way, also suffered from a blind spot or a lack of sophistication; this blind spot came from the seemingly privileged and central vantage point from which Greene writes:

If in 1955 I didn't know what *The Quiet American* was about, and had to leave the book two-thirds of the way, it was because Graham Greene hadn't made his subject clear. He had assumed that his world was the only one that mattered. He was like Flaubert in *Sentimental Education*, assuming that the complicated, clotted history of mid-nineteenth-century France was all-important and known.

Naipaul's point rests on a crucial dialectic: If you come from the margins, you know you are not central; you cannot assume that others will be familiar with the portion of world that fostered you, much less assume its importance. You are aware there are other ways of looking at yourself and your portion of the world than that of those you grew up with. The bafflement of the younger Naipaul before Greene's novel carried seeds of humiliation—a familiar Naipaulian emotion—and thus, for Naipaul, a spur to address gaps in his knowledge.

But if, like Greene, you reside in the dazzling center or, to use Czesław Miłosz's phrase, "the glittering capital of the world," you can easily believe that the center is all there is or all that is worthwhile. You do not have to pay attention to the worldview of those at the periphery; they must understand you, not the other way around. Thus Naipaul implies that for Greene, celebrated as he was— indeed because he was so celebrated—no such reversal of ignorance took place, despite the Third World settings of his fiction: "And it seemed, in a strange way, that at the end, when the dust settled, the people who wrote as though they were at the centre of things might be revealed as provincials."

Those who charge Naipaul with Eurocentrism—for which a case can be made—often overlook the ways he turns his cold, critical eye on the culture and society he once worshipped as a scholarship boy.

In Naipaul's writings, the most illuminating example of the learning process he underwent is explored in *The Enigma of Arrival*. Much of this novel is spent scanning the landscape, his neighbors, and the rhythms of the English countryside surrounding a cottage where a writer from Trinidad of Indian descent takes up residence. The writing is bucolic, leisurely, and on the surface, makes little of the intrusion of this dark-skinned colonial Trinidadian among the white rural British. And then, after just a little over a hundred pages of local color, Naipaul launches into a description of the journey that took the narrator of the novel from Trinidad—"just off the northern coast of Venezuela"—to England.

It is impossible to read this portion of the novel without viewing it as a portrait of Naipaul's younger self. I'm crossing a certain line here, but I'm going to write about this section of the novel as if it does reflect Naipaul's own experiences because I believe doing so clarifies certain issues crucial to his development as a writer.

As the fictional doppelgänger for Naipaul describes his journey and then his subsequent first years in England, he repeatedly distinguishes between what his younger self experienced and what his younger self deemed worthy of writing about. Given his colonial education and the English literature he had read, the young Trinidadian of Indian ethnicity aspired to glamour and sophistication, to "a particular kind of writing personality. . . . Somerset Maugham, aloof everywhere, unsurprised, immensely knowing; Aldous Huxley, so full of all kinds of knowledge and also so sexually knowing; Evelyn Waugh, so elegant so naturally." With such a mind-set, the younger writer, scribbling notes on the plane ride to New York, did not write of the gathering of relatives who saw him off at the airport back in Trinidad:

> I did not note down that occasion in my writer's diary with the indelible pencil sharpened by the elegant Pan American World Airways stewardess in the little airplane. And one reason was that the occasion was too separate from the setting in which I wrote, the setting of magic and wonder. Another was that the occasion, that ceremonial farewell with stiff little groups of people hanging about the wooden building at the edge of the runway, did not fit into my idea of a writer's diary or the writer's experience I was preparing myself for. . . .
>
> Though personal adventure was my theme, I was in no position to write about something more important, the change in my personality that travel and solitude had already begun to bring about.

The older narrator looks back at his younger self and provides a context for that self that his younger self could not have provided. He delineates what the younger self knows and what he thought he knew and then what the younger self truly did not know. He often uses variations on the word *ignorance* in reference to his younger self:

> He knew little about his community in Trinidad; he thought that because he belonged to it he understood it; he thought that the life of the community was like an extension of the life of his family. And he knew nothing of other communities. He had only the prejudices of his time, in that colonial, racially mixed setting. He was profoundly ignorant. He hadn't been to a restaurant, hated the idea of eating food from foreign hands. Yet at the same time he had dreamed of fulfillment in a foreign country.

He looked for adventure. On this first day he found it. But he also came face to face with his ignorance. This ignorance undermined, mocked the writer, or the ambition of the writer, made nonsense of the personality the writer wished to assume—elegant, knowing, unsurprised.

On the ride from the airport to his hotel in New York, the young writer is bullied and cheated by the cab driver, stripping him of "the few remaining dollars" he had on him. Though the young man has some money hidden in his suitcase, that money is unavailable when he reaches the hotel, and he is again humiliated by not being able to tip someone at the hotel. In his room, the young man takes out a roasted chicken that his family has sent with him, a result of the "Indian, Hindu, fear about [his] food, about pollution." But he has no eating utensils or plate, and he doesn't know if he might get them from the hotel.

What ensues is a classic Naipaul scene of humiliation, a revealing illumination of the gap between who his younger self imagined himself to be and who he truly was:

> I ate over the wastepaper basket, aware as I did so of the smell, the oil, the excess at the end of a long day. In my diary I had written of the biggest things, the things that befitted a writer. But the writer of the diary was ending his day like a peasant, like a man reverting to his origins, eating secretively in a dark room, and then wondering how to hide the high-smelling evidence of his meal. I dumped it all in the wastepaper basket.

Thus began the younger Naipaul's education into his place in the world. Almost from the moment he left Trinidad, he felt a gap beginning to develop between the man he was and the writer he thought himself to be. Into that gap came doubt, doubt about the abstractness of his education and reading, about his knowledge of the world derived almost solely from books. From this came doubt about his background and position in the world, a sense of his vulnerability and isolation. At the time, this doubt was too much for him to bear, too much to admit, the humiliation too great; he could not quite allow it into his consciousness. To do so would have been too devastating, too shameful.

It was only later, through great struggle, through travel and study and writing, that Naipaul began to overcome the gap between the writer and the man.

In *The Enigma of Arrival*, Naipaul is open about how much of this gap between the man and the writer stemmed not just from his position as a colonial but also from race. After he has arrived in England, the young Indian Trinidadian writes a story, "Gala Night," about a dance after dinner on the ship he had taken from

New York. Again, the older narrator notes the experiences he had left out of the story; one of these experiences involves his younger self's quarters on the ship, a narrative that starts with an odd, seemingly unexplainable occurrence: "Only now, laying aside the material of 'Gala Night,' I remember having to stand about for some hours while they decided where to put me."

After this wait, the younger writer is given a cabin "absolutely to [him]self in a higher class." He is pleased by this arrangement because he has felt anxious about having to share quarters and thinks of this as "traveler's luck." Later, there is a commotion, voices outside his cabin, and the lights come on, and the young Indian Trinidadian assumes someone is going to be lodged with him:

> But there was trouble. The man who had been brought in was making trouble. He was rejecting the cabin. His voice was rising. He said, "It's because I'm colored you're putting me here with him."
>
> Colored! So he was a Negro. So this was a little ghetto privilege I had been given. But I didn't want the Negro or anybody else to be with me. Especially I didn't want the Negro to be with me, for the very reasons the Negro had given. . . .
>
> I was . . . ashamed that they had brought the Negro to my cabin.

Reflecting on the feelings of his younger self, the older narrator sees a desperate refusal to acknowledge what he had shared with this black fellow traveler. For the younger self to acknowledge how the white world viewed that black traveler would have forced an acknowledgment of what that same world would have made of his possibilities of becoming a writer.

Eventually the narrator—and by implication, Naipaul himself—would have to come to terms with the ways race affected his own experiences and not just those of blacks:

> In Puerto Rico there had been the Trinidad Negro in a tight jacket on his way to Harlem. Here was a man from Harlem [the man complaining on the ship] or black America on his way to Germany. In each there were aspects of myself. But, with my Asiatic background, I resisted the comparison. . . . It was too frightening to accept the other thing, to face the other thing; it was to be diminished as man and writer. Racial diminution formed no part of the material of the kind of writer I was setting out to be. Thinking of myself as a writer, I was hiding my experience from myself; hiding myself from my experience. And even when I became a writer I was without the means, for many years, to cope with that disturbance.

Reading this passage, I cannot help but think of certain young Asian American writers I've encountered who seem determined to avoid any connection with the issues of race or their racial identity and who profess a desire to write about the "universal" without questioning where they have derived their notions of the universal. The worship of whiteness, of a center, of an elite world they so wish to enter has captivated them in ways they do not understand and are unable to acknowledge. It has divorced them from their own experience. And generally, little in their education has provided them with the tools to bridge this gap between the assumed universal and their particular experiences.

Six years later, when the Naipaulian author in *The Enigma of Arrival* returns to Trinidad, having made his start as a writer, his perspective has changed: "I was no longer interested in English people purely as English people, looking for confirmation of what I had read in books and what in 1950 I would have considered metropolitan material." Eventually he begins to research historical documents from the history of Trinidad and to see how the Port of Spain street on which he had grown up connects with that history and with the Spanish Empire and the Haitian revolution and the greater history of the Caribbean. He starts to write a book that would "arrive . . . at a synthesis of the worlds and cultures that had made [him]":

> The idea behind the book, the narrative line, was to attach the island, the little place in the mouth of the Orinoco River, to great names and great events: Columbus; the search for El Dorado; Sir Walter Raleigh. Two hundred years after that, the growth of the slave plantations. And then the revolutions: the American Revolution; the French Revolution and its Caribbean byproduct, the black Haitian revolution; the South American revolution, and the great names of that revolution, Francisco Miranda, Bolivar.

Through this investigation and writing about the historical context of his own life and community in Trinidad, the Naipaulian author's own larger past comes alive to him: "I found I could easily think myself back into that Port of Spain street of two hundred years before. I could see the people, hear the speech and accents."

And yet, as Naipaul so often makes clear, what never leaves him is his sense of isolation and alienation, the rawness of nerves and constant struggle to assert his voice, the memories of his own ignorance and humiliation that make up, in an ironical dialectic, the core experiences of his life. These discomfiting feelings and the experiences that engendered them constitute hard-won truths whose origins *The Enigma of Arrival* delineates. What results from these truths can be seen in both his nonfiction and his fiction. Certainly, one can detect these truths in his meticulous and brilliant—in some ways loving and in others satirical—portrait of his father in A House for Mr. Biswas, or in that memorable opening of his novel about Africa, A Bend in the River: "The world is what it is; men who are nothing, who allow themselves to become nothing, have no place in it."

During my career as a teacher, I have found that my students have increasingly come from places and circumstances resembling those of Naipaul, as do more and more of my colleagues. It's not just that these writers possess backgrounds from all over the globe or even from smaller nations like Sri Lanka, Grenada, Lebanon, or Vietnam; it's that they often have something very singular in their specific history: A young woman who grew up in North Carolina with a black American mother and a Nigerian father whom she did not live with and has not seen since she was thirteen. A mixed-race lesbian from Trinidad whose mother immigrated there from Ghana. A first-generation Muslim Indian American whose family emigrated from Tanzania, where they had lived for two generations, and who returned to Gujarat to explore his family's roots at the exact time of the anti-Muslim riots there. A forty-year-old woman who lives in Hong Kong, whose mother was Hispanic Cuban and whose father was Chinese West African, and who is writing a novel about a young woman of color with a similar background who forms a relationship with a white supremacist in California.*

The specific and idiosyncratic histories and cultural and ethnic backgrounds of my students do not always provide them clear identification with a specific ethnic or racial group; their difficulties with writing from and out of their own specificity is one reason that I often point them to Naipaul, who faced similar issues and problems. I would argue that this is part of what makes him emblematic, a writer who points to where both American and world literature are now headed. Certainly, his example is instructive in a wide-ranging number of ways. There is little glamour in it, despite the later accolades and prizes he has

* Such backgrounds are not very different from that of a president named Barack Hussein Obama, who was born in Honolulu of a white mother from Kansas and a Muslim Kenyan father. Later, after divorcing Barack's father, his mother married an Indonesian Muslim, and Barack lived in Indonesia, where he attended Indonesian-language schools, the first Muslim, the second Catholic. When he returned to Honolulu, with its majority Asian population, he had to learn about what it meant to be a black American outside his family from the few blacks on Oahu and also from readings, particularly The Autobiography of Malcolm X. Yet many tend to view Obama simply as our first black president as opposed to considering his more eccentric actual parentage, familial history, and childhood. In contrast, in Obama's initial memoir, Dreams from My Father, he explores more of the complexities of his identity—including his own feelings of racial rage. But then that book was written before he became a politician.

received, recognition that belies his earlier obscurity and struggles in the literary world. There is instead a courage without comfort—unless that comfort is simply the reward in the struggle to confront the hard truths about oneself and one's place in the world, the complexities and contradictions of that world, which "is what it is."

The Writer and
the Hero's Journey

In working on a book, we almost always come to a moment of crisis and doubt: This is the point where we wonder if we are ever going to complete the work we have started. We fear that the work is no good or that we lack the ability to finish the task. We're uncertain about where to go next or how to fix a crucial problem. We meet various forms of rejection or criticism—both from others and from within. We may even stop writing and feel that the well has run dry.

When writers come to me at such moments, I try to remind them of certain fundamental truths about the journeys we take with our writing. I repeat a simple premise: *We start writing a book to become the person who can finish the book.*

The person who starts the book is not the same person who completes it. We must grow and transform ourselves into that person. The process of writing is part of that growth and transformation. We don't get to determine beforehand the length or difficulty of the process. This is such a crucial point I'll repeat it: *As writers, we don't get to determine the length or difficulty of the process. We can only refuse or assent to it.*

If the project is a worthy one, we will inevitably arrive at a moment where we must face the specter of failure. Otherwise the project is too easy; no discovery or growth is involved. Discovery and growth can come only through struggle, from facing squarely our own limitations and failings and working through them and thus changing who we are.

In dealing with the task of writing, then, I've found that it's useful to contemplate the figure of the hero as it plays itself out in myths and the three-act play. Thus the process of completing a book can be understood as a mythic journey.

In the first act, the hero is surrounded by the familiar and may be expressing some doubts about staying with the familiar. She senses its limitations, its imperfections, and perhaps has become bored or dissatisfied with her existence there. In various ways, her kingdom is not flourishing.

Then comes a message and/or messenger calling her to another task, another land. As I've noted earlier, the hero will often balk at or refuse this call: "Find someone else, I'm not the right person" or "I can't take this on at this time." She may even find herself saying, contrary to her previous grumblings, "I'm fine where I am, nothing needs to change." But then something happens: a change of circumstances, a new form of the call, and she accepts.

The psychic upsurge that accommodates this acceptance is the energies of hope and optimism, the enthusiasm that stems from prospects of leaving the old and encountering the new. This is often accompanied by a sense of the justice or nobility, of the righteousness of the call.

So the hero leaves the familiar and enters a new country. To help save or reinvigorate her kingdom, she must bring about a new vision, defeat a great foe, bring back the magic elixir. Events often progress favorably at this point, with perhaps early successes and discoveries of newfound abilities. The moribund ways of the old kingdom have been left behind for new opportunities for growth and discovery.

But then the tide begins to turn. Or seems to. Difficulties start to crop up, setbacks. As failure and defeat seem increasingly a very real possibility, the hero finds herself mired in the crisis of faith that is the second act. As David Mamet has observed, this is the crucial point of the journey, the turning point of the play: The hero may have started out, armed at the beginning with energy and a vision, determined to complete a tremendous journey, to accomplish a great act (in our case, to write a book). But in the second act, the real nature of the task asserts itself and unexpected roadblocks appear.

At this point the hero says, "I'm sorry, but I'm giving up. I know I set out with this great goal, I know I said I would answer the call, but I could not have possibly foreseen how difficult the task would be. No one could have foreseen this. You tell me I should persist, but you don't understand and appreciate the difficulties I am up against. You don't see how few resources I possess and how many resources they, my enemies, my naysayers, the forces arrayed against me, possess. There is simply no way I can win. No one is supporting me, I have no allies, I'm all alone."

Here the hero may also say, "I know I said I would be up to this, that I would succeed. But here I find that my talents and resources are not enough. Perhaps I'm not the person for this job; indeed I doubt anybody might be, but it's certainly not me. I don't have the energy or enthusiasm I started out with. I don't have the will to go on."

But of course, in order to succeed, the hero doesn't quit. Instead, she says, like the character in Beckett's *The Unnamable*, "I can't go on. I'll go on."

One way of characterizing this crisis of the second act is that the hero misreads what is happening. She believes this crisis of faith, this apparent point of failure, is all there is. In her eyes, the crisis she faces marks the beginning of a third act or final battle in which the protagonist fails, and the forces arrayed against her will triumph.

Instead, this crisis contains a message, both from her psyche and from the world: To reach her goal in the future, the hero must change her view and understanding of the present; she must alter the way she approaches the present. This requires both imagination and a new plan of action. In part, the hero must discover possibilities and potentials in herself and the task that did not seem there just a short while ago in the great moment of crisis.

This may sound easier than such work actually is. It is difficult to turn away from the old solutions or approaches, from the familiar strengths and paths, from what has worked for us before. It takes courage to admit evidence of failure, courage to admit mistakes or wrong turns (e.g., to throw away pages or poems or stories or even whole drafts).

So how does this turn happen? First, the hero must see that she is capable of transformation. She must discover strengths inside herself, attributes or qualities that she has not perceived before, aspects of her psyche she has neglected. She must then work to develop those strengths.

In this process, she starts to open herself to seeing the world around her in a new way. She begins engaging the shadow work that will be one of the final tasks on her way to reaching the third act. She begins to see that where she has perceived only enemies there may actually be potential allies.

In his studies of mythology, Joseph Campbell talks about threshold guardians, forces that seem to bar entrance to the next place the hero needs to go. He explains that in Buddhist temples in Japan, the entryway is often guarded by a figure with a fierce face, the face of a demon. Yet if one takes in the whole figure, one sees that the hand of the terrifying figure is held out slightly with the palm up, with an implied beckoning motion.

In seeing the threshold guardians in a new light and understanding that they might not necessarily be enemies, the hero may be able to turn them into allies or to avail herself of their qualities.

This altered vision of the world helps the hero reassess the enemy or blocking forces and, in doing so, reassess herself. Part of this stems from a realization that the enemy or blocking forces are not as all-powerful as she has previously perceived. In her previous sense of the situation, she has found the enemy to be engaged in triumph after triumph, each triumph making the enemy stronger and more impossible to defeat. But now, in her altered vision, she may see that in each of those triumphs lies the seed for the enemy's downfall: The enemy possesses a hidden underbelly, a previously overlooked weakness, or the enemy's strength is built on a house of cards—the structure is real, but it is nowhere as indestructible as it has seemed, and indeed the higher and mightier it towers, the more vulnerable it is.

But how does the hero reach such a vision? In part, she must stop viewing the enemy from the outside; she must stop regarding the enemy as merely a mask of evil and all-powerful. She must apprehend and understand the enemy. But in order to do so, she may also be forced to see that those qualities that, up until now, have, in her mind, made the enemy the enemy, also reside in her. In other words, she has to give up the notion of her own pure innocence, her absolute distinction from her enemy.

Where before she has seen the enemy as the embodiment of evil, she must now see the enemy within herself and know it as a portion of her own psyche.

But writing, you may say, is an internal task, not a journey. It involves internal demons rather than exterior enemies. There's no villain to defeat; there's only you and the blank page.

As I've said earlier, the hero's journey is a metaphor. Just because a writer faces mainly internal conflicts does not mean that the allegory of the hero's journey cannot apply to the task of writing. The metaphor of the journey helps us illuminate the various transformations of the psyche.

If we look back, we can see that the call to writing in general as well as the call to write a specific book often comes from somewhere outside us—from a book or an incident, a conversation or a class, a friend or a teacher. We may have, at first, even rejected that call and waited for a second or even a third call, before we took up the task.

At a certain point, early on in the project, we might have been filled with energy and enthusiasm, a belief that our writing is moving toward success and publication. We found ourselves excited by new discoveries and connections, new sources for material, initial breakthroughs where a whole new dimension to the project was revealed.

But then the crisis occurs. Sometimes it comes from outside—a critique by a fellow writer or fellow writing-group members, a rejection by an agent or a publisher. Sometimes it comes from inside—we lose faith in the book or our abilities; we stop writing or find ourselves letting other activities interfere with the writing; we stop sending the book out or trying to get feedback and lock it in a drawer.

The particulars of these crises are unique to the writer and her project. Conversely, there is no one magic solution. And yes, sometimes books are not finished or do not find a publisher. But before we abandon the book and give up our journey, we might try to see if there is a way to continue, to discover a way of proceeding that we did not consider before or did not see.

Particularly in memoir or works of autobiographical fiction, the writer is often working against psychological repression. As I've said earlier, when a child experiences severe trauma or abuse, repression can often act as a survival mechanism; it allows the child to continue on after the trauma or abuse without constantly reconnecting to the fear, pain, grief, and rage engendered by such negative experiences. In many instances, it helps keep the child from going insane. The child thereafter constructs a narrative of her life that often puts those experiences at a remove or even erases them.

At a certain point in adulthood, however, that repression begins to break down in two major ways: First, the adult is conducting her life in ways that are guided and shaped by a narrative that is incomplete and fractured, that doesn't include key experiences and emotions; such a narrative gives the adult a false picture of who that person is and what her life has been. Second, the adult is expending more and more energy to repress those experiences and emotions. A common result of such repression is depression and other psychiatric symptoms. Just as importantly, the repression is connected to various beliefs and behaviors that somehow emulate or reenact those negative experiences; these then result in breakdowns and failures in various aspects of the adult's life, particularly in her closest relationships or her career. All of this represents *the return of the repressed*.

What is needed is a new narrative that is created in part through reconnecting to the past in a new way, through breaking through repression and recovering and recontextualizing the child she was and the negative experiences that she has denied for so many years. This is a formidable task, and for many people it may require professional help. But writing too can be instrumental in this process. The return of the repressed often occurs in the writing through indirect means—that is, through gaps in the text or through metaphors or through a sentence or paragraph here and there. Though the writer may at first ignore such signs of the repressed, they often continue to recur. This recurrence—that is, the reappearance of the repressed in the text—is a signal. It tells the writer that she is ready—and strong enough—to reenter the past, to form a new narrative. But for this to happen, the writer must be willing to assent to this call.

Breaking through repression can also involve trauma that stems from racism, sexism, homophobia, classism, and other ways individuals from marginalized groups can be wounded and silenced. This can occur to such an extent that the writer may, in her writing, deny not only having experienced such trauma but also even being a member of such a group. In a way, I myself had to break through such repression involving my ethnic and racial identity to write my first memoir; some form of this struggle also took place in my second memoir.

The process of revision, then, can often only be achieved by letting go, a decision not to cling to one's former image of oneself and one's writing. Only through this letting go can growth take place. Doing things in the same old way will not get it done.

For the writer, certain internal changes often involve shadow work, attempts to connect with areas of the psyche that the writer has avoided or neglected. Only by investigating these areas can the writer begin drawing out their powers.

This widening and deepening of the psyche helps the writer achieve the complexity and energy needed to move on with the writing or to revise the writing in a radical new way. In short, the writer may be facing a technical problem, but for her to address that problem fully, a psychological transformation must take place.

For example, the writer can't plunge into the depths of a character if she is hiding from such depths within her own psyche. If the writer is protecting a protagonist with whom she identifies or is holding back because she fears familial restrictions or is afraid of breaking through a psychic restriction, those tendencies must be challenged. Similarly, facing her own fear of losing control can help provide a writer with the freedom to unravel and loosen the narrative, to let the unexpected or untoward or upsetting enter the story, to allow for the happy accident that can lead to a new direction, to create a new more expansive, energetic, and taboo-breaking voice.

There may also be an external component to this crisis of faith. Sometimes at this point, we must look for and call on others for help, for both encouragement and criticism. We may face our version of an irreconcilable conflict: By nature some of us are used to going it alone; we came to writing in part because of our solitary natures. Seek help from others? That would be personal blasphemy. But blasphemy may be exactly what is needed.

In this process, the writer may also be called to change his relationship with those he sees as thwarting forces. For instance, what if he looks at those who have criticized his work or who have refused it as threshold guardians? Like the warrior guardians of Japanese temples, they may, if he looks or listens more closely, be offering him a key to the next door or passage, a password that will help him cross the border.

In Campbell's description of threshold guardians, as in the earlier example of C. K. Williams from Garrett Hongo's *Volcano*, it's obvious that teachers often function as such figures: We may at first see them as fiercely opposing, as criticizing our work and ambitions, only to realize later that they were trying to prepare us for the difficulties ahead, for the real nature of the journey. Those who were thwarted or scared off by these threshold guardians were never meant to complete the journey; those who persisted and learned from the teacher eventually moved on.

Sometimes we must learn from a teacher we may not particularly like, or we may need to acquire a new technique. Picasso could draw easily at twelve; it took Cézanne till he was forty to consciously learn what came to Picasso naturally. But then Cézanne's talent took off.

What is required then is openness, flexibility, a willingness to entertain something new. For writers, the crisis of the second act means we must be willing to revise both ourselves and our writing, and perhaps even our relationship with the outside world. The crisis doesn't mean that we can't complete the journey; it instead is a signal telling us what the journey requires. We can only listen to what it is telling us or refuse to listen.

It is helpful to know that others have experienced what you are experiencing, that even the greatest of writers must suffer and persist through their doubts. It comes with the territory and the task; there's no getting around it. All you can do is plow your way through.

One mistake lies in thinking you must know exactly where you are going or exactly what the final destination is. The trick is to keep moving, as much inside yourself, as outside. Here's the way the Sufi poet Rumi put it, recognizing that the greatest and most difficult distances we travel are generally internal:

Keep walking though there's no place to get to.
Don't try to see through the distances.
That's not for human beings. Move within,
but don't move the way fear makes you move.
                                        (trans. Coleman Barks)

But of course, faith is not always easy, especially when disaster seems all about you and defeat impending, when your mistakes echo in your ear along with a loud sense of your own limitations.

It is at that point that perhaps it's useful to remember: This is where your journey has led you; you could be nowhere else but here. This is what you signed up for.

No hero's journey, no great feat, can be accomplished without the crisis of the second act, without facing what seems at first utter failure or the seeming end. But eventually, the hero discovers that despite dwelling in a dark hour, this is not the time to give up. Yes, you may have made mistakes, but now you can learn from them. Yes, you may have misjudged the situation, but now you can reassess. Yes, you may feel alone, but now is the time when the people who can help you are at hand if you are able to readjust your vision, if you decide to reach out. Yes, you may be tired or depressed, but perhaps that fatigue or depression is what you need to spur a search for a new vision. It is preparation for the work to come.

As Rumi instructs: Don't let fear stop or guide you. All you can do is continue to have faith, continue to change yourself. Ask yourself what the next step is and make that step. Keep walking. Keep writing.*

---

* As with a single book, a writer's career is also a journey. As one progresses as a writer, the books often don't come any easier. Early success, like the first stages of the hero's journey, can give way to thorny difficulties and the specter of failure, the crises of midcareer and middle age. Each book may present its own three-act play, but one's career can also unfold in three acts.

Here the writer must struggle against a vision of the journey that entails a series of mounting successes as the true and natural progression—something that is rarely, if ever, the case. The transformations one undergoes in a lifetime of writing inevitably involve many highs and lows, moments of faith and doubt, successes, yes, perhaps, but also seeming failures and genuine failures.

It's important, then, to look at one's immediate circumstances in terms of the long run and the strange vicissitudes of the psyche's growth. This change in the temporal perspective is crucial here. Things look different when you know you are not in the third act of the villain's or the enemy's triumph but instead in the middle of your own second act. The third act is yet to begin.

Of course, getting through the crisis of the second act is much more difficult than my brief descriptions above imply. It's easy to understand such things conceptually; it's much more difficult to live through them, to undergo real change. Real—not cosmetic or facile—change. Deep change.

Acknowledgments

These essays reflect my experiences teaching at VONA, the writers' conference for writers of color, and its diverse range of students, faculty, and staff to whom I will be eternally grateful: Junot Díaz, whose brilliant insights inform this book; Elmaz Abinader, who helped save me by bringing me to VONA; Diem Jones, generous leader extraordinaire; Chris Abani, Suheir Hammad, Willie Perdomo, ZZ Packer, Mat Johnson, Evelina Galang, Vanessa Martir, Kira Lynn Allen, Serena Lim, and Liz Huerta. I want to thank all my VONA students for the innumerable lessons they have taught me.

The essays also derive from my teaching at the low-residency Stonecoast MFA program; I'm grateful to former director Annie Finch who brought me to that program. At Stonecoast I taught students in poetry, fiction, and memoir through lengthy correspondences that forced me to articulate my practices in ways I might not have otherwise. I'd like to thank my students for pushing me toward various insights. I'm particularly grateful to Helen Peppe and Alexis Paige, who have since become colleagues and valuable readers.

I'd like to thank my co-teachers in the Stonecoast workshop, "Writing About Race": Richard Hoffman; Alexs Pate, whose brilliance I've drawn on in this book, my great friend and colleague for over twenty-five years; Tim Seibles, who has supported me and my work for the same length of time.

I'd like to thank the students of my Loft class for writers of color and indigenous writers and Loft staff members Britt Udesen, Jen Dodgson, Sherrie Fernandez-Williams, and especially Marion Gomez, for her dedication and hard work to the spirit of that class.

Thanks to those at University of Georgia Press: Jon Davies, Erin New, freelance copyeditor Barbara Wojhoski, and particularly my editor, Bethany Snead, whose belief in and work on this book has been a godsend. My thanks to the anonymous UGA Press readers who definitely helped me improve the manuscript. My gratitude to Paul Mairet, who assisted me in preparing the manuscript and has worked as my assistant.

Other writers and artists have helped me particularly in understanding the areas of race and literature: Frank Wilderson III, Ed Bok Lee, Sun Mee Chomet, Juliana Pegues, Bao Phi, Quincy Troupe, Rick Shiomi, Ananya Chatterjea, Patricia Smith, Randy Reyes, Martín Espada, and Sun Yung Shin.

Garrett Hongo, my BFAM, has been an invaluable source of support and literary insight for years.

Finally, I want to thank my family: my parents, Tom and Terry Mura; my wife, Susan Sencer, who has read this manuscript innumerable times and who has lovingly supported me; and my children, Samantha, Nikko, and Tomo, who continue to inspire and teach me about the diversity they've grown up with and live with each day.

Appendix ∽

Seven Basic Writing Assignments

Assignment 1:
Some Questions about Process

I do this assignment with my students to get them to think more concretely about their writing process and what blocks they may be encountering with their writing. This questionnaire serves as a self-diagnostic and leads the writer to approach issues of the writing process with a solution-oriented approach.

Write down your answers to the following questions:

1. What do you like about your writing?

2. What do you like about your writing process?

3. How does a lack of confidence hinder your writing process?

4. How does that lack of confidence reflect some way you identify or characterize yourself?

5. How can you change that?

6. What do you want to change about your writing?

7. What do you want to change about your writing process?

8. How do you define yourself as a writer?

9. How would you like to change your sense of yourself as a writer?

10. What do you see as holding you back as a writer?

11. How can you overcome those limits or blocks?

12. How could a change in the way you identify or think of yourself help you to overcome those limits or blocks?

13. How do you react to criticism of your work?

14. How could you employ criticism of your work in a more useful way?

15. How is your writing limited by the ways you say, "I can't do that" or "That's not me"?

16. What are your goals for this course (or after reading this book)?

17. What are your goals for the next few years as a writer?

18. What is your image of the writer you want to become?

19. What are the subjects and themes you want to explore next as a writer?

20. Where do you think writing about these things will lead you?

List the topics, areas, themes you want to explore with your writing in the coming months, years.

Assignment 2:
Exploring Your Identity

(BASED ON THE LAND OF LOOK BEHIND BY MICHELLE CLIFF)

In her introduction to her first book, *The Land of Look Behind*, Michelle Cliff writes about investigating and claiming her identity. Cliff was a light-skinned black lesbian Jamaican who had been taught by her family to pass as white, and after leaving Jamaica, she began an academic career and was working on her dissertation on "game-playing in the Italian Renaissance." When Cliff decided that she needed to begin investigating her own identity, she discovered that she wasn't very articulate; she couldn't create much flow to her language. Yes, she could easily write intellectual academic prose—she even dreamed in medieval Latin—but writing about herself? That was hard. Nearly impossible.

Cliff was also working a nine-to-five job, so she just allowed herself to write fragments, notes. She collected quotations. *The Land of Look Behind* is a series of pieces written as fragments—one or two paragraphs at a time—or notes. As Cliff explains, that was all she could do at the time:

> My dissertation was produced at the Warburg Institute, University of London, and was responsible for giving me an intellectual belief in myself that I had not had before, while at the same time distancing me from who I am, almost rendering me speechless about who I am. At least I believed in the young woman who wrote the dissertation—still, I wondered who she was and where she had come from.
>
> I could speak fluently, but I could not reveal. . . .
>
> When I began, finally, partly through participation in the feminist movement, to approach myself as a subject, my writing was jagged, nonlinear, almost shorthand. The "Notes on Speechlessness" were indeed notes, written in snatches on a nine-to-five job. I did not choose the noteform consciously; a combination of things drew me to it. An urgency for one thing.

> I also felt incompetent to construct an essay in which I would describe the
> intimacies, fears, and lies I wrote of in "Speechlessness." I felt my thoughts,
> things I had held within for a lifetime, traversed so wide a terrain, had so
> many stops and starts, apparent nonsequiturs, that an essay—with its cold-
> blooded dependence on logical construction, which I had mastered practi-
> cally against my will—could not work. My subject could not respond to that
> form, which would have contradicted the idea of speechlessness. This tender
> approach to myself within the confines and interruptions of a forty-hour-a-
> week job and against a history of forced fluency was the beginning of a jour-
> ney into speech.

Despite the seemingly unfinished form of the prose, this writing helped her
to discover who she was and thus who she was as a writer. It was absolutely integral to her artistic development and led her to write several novels and nonfiction works. To put it in terms I often use with students: Cliff gave herself permission to write "badly." To move forward with our writing into a new area or
an area that presents psychic difficulties, at certain times we should not expect
eloquence or a well-formed structure. We should simply try to get down or dig
up hidden thoughts, emotions, experiences, intuitions. (As William Stafford instructed, the antidote to writer's block is to lower your standards.)

At the same time, as Cliff argues in her introduction, the fragmentary nature
of the writing in The Land of Look Behind also reflects something of her experience
and that of her people:

> We are a fragmented people. My experience as a writer coming from a cul-
> ture of colonialism, a culture of Black people riven from each other, my
> struggle to get wholeness from fragmentation while working within frag-
> mentation, producing work which may find its strength in its depiction of
> fragmentation, through form as well as content, is similar to the experience
> of other writers whose origins are in countries defined by colonialism. . . .
>
>   I wanted . . . directness in my writing, as I came into closer contact with
> my rage, and a realization that rage could fuel and shape my work. As a light-
> skinned colonial girlchild, both in Jamaica and in the Jamaican milieu of my
> family abroad, rage was the last thing expected of me.

In other words, the purpose of writing is not always to write beautiful sentences
or show off how brilliant we are. Sometimes the writing most valuable to our
progress is exploratory, tentative, disjointed. In this mode, we must put down
our armor and let our unconscious speak; by doing this, we can begin to ar-

ticulate repressed emotions and experiences, begin to approach our deepest wounds or trauma. And often this material provides our richest and most complex writing. But we may be able to find this material only when we seek exploration not perfection, process not product.

A Notebook about Your Identity

Keep a notebook. A book about claiming your identity. A notebook asking, "Who am I?"

The subject of this notebook is "you." Your identity. Your racial and ethnic identity. And any other ways you choose to identify yourself—gender, sexuality, class, region, country, family, immigrant, and so on.

Keep it as a diary or journal. A dream book. A quotation book. A book of secrets. A book of truths. A book of who you are. A book of rage. A book of your history, your family's history. A book of what you love. A book of what you hate.

Allow yourself to write in fragments. To not be articulate.

Allow all the languages inside you into the book. Ways of speaking. Dialect. Your bilingual being. Your multilanguage being.

Put in quotations that strike you.

Don't hold back. Anger. Love. Grief. Shame.

Put in the things you might feel ashamed of. Secrets. (As Cliff observed, there's often a voice inside us saying, "Don't reveal our secrets to them. Don't make us seem foolish, or oppressed.")

Begin writing about experiences that are difficult for you to write about. Trauma. Abuse. Repressed memories. At first you may only name or label these subjects. But keep returning to them periodically, writing what you can. This will allow or prod your unconscious to work at articulation and recovery in between the times you actually write (and your unconscious is both creative and knows how to heal itself; see Thomas Moore's *The Care of the Soul*).

Keep asking the question: Who am I? Who are my people? What history led to and produced me? What is the history I never learned that I need to know in order to know who I am? What is my buried history? What is the buried history of my people? My family? My country?

Create a second self, a new self, a doppelgänger. Allow the shadow self, the self you have been afraid to develop, or the self-certain voice that family, society, community may have tried to silence. As the Jungians suggest, allow yourself to seek the voices of the many gods within you.

———

Additional Assignment: Write about the first time you became aware of or discovered your racial identity.

Do this assignment with other facets of your identity that are particularly relevant to your writing: gender, orientation, class, region, generation, and so on.

Assignment 3:
Rewriting a Scene

BY BREAKING THROUGH
PSYCHOLOGICAL RESISTANCE
AND ENGAGING TECHNIQUE

In a writer's first drafts, the writer is often trying to discover what the piece is about and where it's going. At a certain point, she goes back over the individual sections and looks for ways she can improve them. In my classes, I often make an assignment where students work on rewriting an individual scene, infusing it with more density of imagery, commentary, and emotion. This scene can be from either fiction or nonfiction or even from poetry.

Sometimes the scene is difficult to write because it involves subject matter that resists the student. This may stem from the nature of the events, such as violence or sexual content. Or the fictional scene may be related to a painful event that occurred in the author's life. Whether in fiction or memoir, writing that connects to a personal trauma or a series of traumas the author has experienced will almost always evoke various forms of psychological resistance. For one thing, it's easier to keep an experience at an emotional distance if one talks or writes about it generally or summarily. The more detailed the writer's description of the experience becomes, the more she may connect with the difficult emotions and memories tied to that experience.

At the same time, the fact that this experience has come up in the writing is a clue from the unconscious: The writer may be ready at this point in her life to reenter and recall that experience. As the psychologist Arabella Kurtz notes in *The Good Story: Exchanges on Truth, Fiction and Psychotherapy*, cowritten with the novelist J. M. Coetzee, repression can act as a protective device, especially in childhood. When one is a child, one has little or no control or power over trauma and other forms of abuse; thus, repression can help the child to move on or even to stay sane. But when one reaches a certain age, these repressed memories may resurface, as they sometimes do in writing; that resurfacing generally signals that there is more to be uncovered and understood, that there is a new narrative to be constructed, one that includes the repressed or hazy memories.

As I often tell my students, if you want to dig a hole ten feet deep, you can't start digging at ten feet deep. You must dig the first inch, then the second. So with material that presents acute psychological resistance, you should give yourself permission to write superficially or badly at first. Sometimes, to simply get at the material, you need to write freely about anything you can think of concerning the topic, that is, without worrying about eloquence or structure or even purpose.

Overall, in this rewriting of a scene, I ask students to concentrate solely on one aspect or way of writing the scene at a time. In general, when you are working on only a single aspect of a piece, without thinking about any other aspect of the piece, the task seems and is easier. You're better able to see ways you can improve it and come up with new details, imagery, content, or ways of phrasing things.

For this assignment, take one scene from your work, probably some scene of significant change or action. Now do the following at separate times:

First, just freely write about the scene, putting down whatever details or thoughts or feelings that come to mind. Part of the purpose of this writing is to unsettle the unconscious and bring up difficult elements (if fiction) or repressed memories (if autobiographical). Don't worry about sentence structure or word choice or coherence. Then allow some time to pass.

Second, freely write again about the scene, again putting down whatever details or thoughts or feelings that come up. Again, don't worry about sentence structure or word choice or coherence. Allow some more time to pass.

Third, write about the scene by breaking it into parts or types of writing; write each part or type of writing separately.

To begin with, write about imagery surrounding the people involved in your scene; this imagery should range as widely as possible. Perhaps you may want to think of how the scene would be shot in a film—different angles and focus, various scenes and places around the main scene, from a wide-angle helicopter shot to close-ups of minutiae. Also think of ways you might evoke the history of the landscape or the locale or even what might happen to this place in the coming years (e.g., range backward and forward in time).

Next write a description of each of the characters; this should range from various aspects of their physical appearance to their clothes and their personal possessions.

Next write about the personal histories of the characters, from significant events and relationships to their jobs and station in life.

Next write about the aspirations and desires of the characters.

Next write an interior monologue for the participants in the scene (i.e., the thoughts and emotions they are having as the scene progresses).

Next write the scene as a play or completely as dialogue or as a screenplay. Write the instructions you might give to an actor playing the part of one of the characters or the choices an actor might make playing one of the characters (these would include not just significant actions but the little gestures or facial expressions or shifts in tone of voice that particularize a talented actor's performance of a role).

Optional: Write a dream that each of the characters had last night. Write the scene from different emotional states (i.e., a version where they are sad, angry, silly, uncomfortable, and so on)

Think of other ways of writing a part of the scene.

Finally, after you do all this, begin combining and integrating what you have written into a new version of the scene.

Inevitably, after students do this exercise, the revised scene is much more detailed, imagined, and emotionally present than the original. I then tell the student that the revised scene must now become a benchmark, a level of quality she knows she can reach and so must demand in other sections of the piece.

Assignment 4:
Using a Timeline to Revise Narrative Structure

In short stories, novels, and narrative memoirs, there often comes a point where the writer is confused or stuck when trying to construct a narrative structure. Sometimes, especially in memoir, this occurs because certain crucial events are not part of the writing yet. At other times, certain narrative elements are missing, such as a definitive goal or truly irreconcilable conflicts. Or certain structural elements, such as a true third act or final battle may be missing.

When narrative problems occur with a student's work, I often tell the student to write down all the events in the work if it's a piece of fiction or all the important or crucial events of the time period of the memoir. I may even have the student do this two or three times.

Next I ask the student to put those events in chronological order. I tell him that the story or novel or memoir doesn't need to be told in chronological order; indeed, many works in fiction and memoir eschew chronology. However, such a timeline allows the writer to see the events as they occur in time; this helps them better understand how one event can lead to or cause another, or how certain events may be linked to form their own section, or how the timeline of the events can be broken down into sections or into the mythic journey or a three-act structure.

Once the writer has done this timeline, he should look at it for various structural and fictional elements.

The first element the writer might look at is a combination of the hero's journey and the three-act play.

In *The Hero of a Thousand Faces*, Joseph Campbell studied myths from across the world and discovered that they almost all contained elements of what he called the hero's journey. He broke down the complete hero's journey into a sequential narrative. In *The Writer's Journey*, Christopher Vogler used the hero's journey to break down the structure of screenplays. Here's the basic structure, to which I've added the three-act structure:

ACT I (The Call)

1. Heroes are introduced in the **ORDINARY WORLD**, where
2. they receive the **CALL TO ADVENTURE**
3. They are **RELUCTANT** at first or **REFUSE THE CALL**, but
4. are encouraged by a mentor to

ACT II (Struggle and Doubt)

5. **CROSS THE FIRST THRESHOLD** and enter the Special World, where
6. they encounter **TESTS, ALLIES, AND ENEMIES.**
7. They **APPROACH THE INMOST CAVE**, crossing a second threshold,
8. where they endure the **SUPREME ORDEAL.**
9. They take possession of their **REWARD** and
10. are pursued on **THE ROAD BACK** to the Ordinary World.

ACT III (The Final Battle)

11. They cross the third threshold, experience a **RESURRECTION**, and are transformed by the experience.
12. They **RETURN WITH THE ELIXIR**, a boon or treasure to benefit the Ordinary World.

Campbell makes the point that when we first see the hero in the ordinary world, often something is wrong, something is awry or amiss, in that world and/or in the hero's life. In certain myths or stories, the kingdom is not flourishing or is fallow; there's a pestilence, a plague, a drought, corruption, an evil dragon, repressive forces, or a repressive ruler. All this can also be seen as symbolic, as a metaphor for a psyche that is faltering and is being asked (by outside forces, by the unconscious) to change. Often, I find that what is missing in student work is a description of the fallow kingdom; that is, at the start of the piece, there's no statement of the problem or conflict or contradictions that the hero or protagonist is facing. Without the description of the fallow kingdom, the reader doesn't understand why the hero is undertaking the journey or goal, doesn't feel what is propelling the hero out of the ordinary world.

As indicated above, the structure of the mythic hero's journey has its correlative in the three-act play (or screenplay). In the first act, the hero is in the ordinary world or the fallow kingdom and is called to take a journey, to take up a goal, usually twice. When the hero takes up the call, the journey, the goal, that is the end of the first act.

In myth, when the hero leaves the ordinary world and crosses into the new or special world, the journey may be relatively easy at first. The hero may find new powers, abilities, opportunities. But gradually things become more difficult; there is struggle and doubt and often, the crisis of the second act, when things become particularly difficult and dark.

The third act is the final battle. Often, the end of a story or novel may not work because there isn't a clear final battle. Or the final battle is not significant enough or difficult enough. Or the hero reaches the goal—or fails to reach the goal—not because of the hero's own actions (i.e., the hero is too passive).

So, in the first part of this assignment, after writing down all the events in the work or all the crucial events of the time period, look at the timeline you have created and try to see if there are equivalents to Campbell's structure of the hero's journey.

Then see if you can break the timeline down into three acts.

(Note that scenes or sections can also be broken down into three acts.)

Next, find the key actions the protagonist takes to pursue her goals, whether in an individual section of the work or in the work overall.

Next, using the principles outlined in this book, find the irreconcilable conflicts or desires that the protagonist faces.

Next, find the lies that the protagonist tells (both active lies and lies of omission). Recall that these lies are often about the irreconcilable nature of the protagonist desires, that is, the protagonist lies to himself. The protagonist then tells lies to others in order to pursue those irreconcilable desires.

Next, find the places where the protagonist makes plans and takes an action; mark where the action results in reactions by others or by the world or within the protagonist that the protagonist did not foresee.

Next, find the places where the psyche or others or the world pressures the protagonist to tell the truth and expose the protagonist's lies.

Note all these elements on the timeline. If some of the elements are missing, think about how you might construct them if you are writing fiction. If you are writing a memoir, see whether there are missing elements, events, experiences that will embody the missing pieces. Or see if you can reorganize or rewrite the narrative so that those missing pieces are there.

One thing to remember here is the principle of metonymy—the part for the whole. If there is a series of arguments involving a couple, the writer doesn't need to show and dramatize each and every argument. One detailed argument can serve to illustrate all the other arguments, which can then be summarized more quickly.

Another principle to remember is the use of three trials or three attempts. If the protagonist succeeds in the first attempt, then fails at the second (or vice versa), the third is the tiebreaker. If the protagonist fails in the first, the second, and the third attempt, the narrative and the reader may conclude that this will continue.

After you complete this assignment to this point, go back to writing the narrative with the timeline in mind. Refer to the timeline and revise it as the process goes on.

When I've asked writers to do this assignment, they inevitably come out of it with a firmer understanding of the narrative structure of the work, or they see ways of revising the work for narrative structure. Moreover, when students do this for the first time, they reach a deeper understanding of narrative structure and technique.

I do understand that writers, like all artists, work through intuition, through feelings and hunches. This timeline assignment is more structured, more left-brain oriented, more technical. However, especially when the writer is learning the structures and techniques of narrative, this timeline assignment is a useful tool. Here's an instructive analogy: After a while, Shakespeare stopped counting syllables when he wrote iambic pentameter; he didn't have to think about individual feet and the ten-syllable line. But when he was learning to write iambic pentameter, he did have to consciously keep these critical factors in mind to learn and become accustomed to the form.

So it is with learning narrative structure and technique. Often, the writer must consciously and sometimes mechanically use these structures and techniques, and in this learning, he might be best off not worrying about the overall quality of the work and concentrate on learning. Once the writer absorbs these structures and techniques, their use will become intuitive, and he may come to use them without having to do a conscious timeline (though even then a timeline may help if difficulties or blocks arise).

Once a writer has learned to construct a basic scene and a basic story, he can apply those lessons to any piece of writing. And I guarantee that the writer will inevitably be writing better work. This will be true even if the writer chooses to abandon or eschew the structures of the basic scene and story in some later work (just as learning to write meter and form and going back to write in free verse will provide the poet with a deeper understanding of how free verse works and how sometimes the ghost of meter and form may inhabit free verse).

Assignment 5:
Using the Storyteller's Principles— a Basic Checklist

The following is a list of the basic principles of narrative construction that are explored in this book. Use the list to analyze and critique the story or narrative piece you're working on. If one of these elements is missing, work on ways of revising the narrative to make that element present. In other words, use this list as a series of prompts to further revision and writing.

1. Think of story as a series of actions: these actions are attempts by the character to reach a goal/solve a problem/overcome a conflict/complete a journey.

2. So ask the question: What does my protagonist want? (remember: no goal or desire = no story).

3. So ask the question: How can I create a situation where my protagonist must take actions? (as opposed to remaining passive).

4. These actions by the protagonist are often in ascending order

    of difficulty

    of importance

    of increased tension.

5. In classic drama this ascension leads to the three-act play:

    I. The initial call to or announcement of the goal

    II. Struggle and doubt

    III. The final battle

6. Tension is created when the protagonist appears to be losing or struggling in the pursuit of the goal.

7. Each action represents a choice; with each choice there is a loss and gain

    that is, each action/choice leads to a different path

    and the chosen path may or may not lead the protagonist to the goal

    (the protagonist doesn't get to go back in time and make a different choice).

8. Sometimes there is tension between a conscious desire and an unconscious desire. In the course of a story, this unconscious desire may increasingly assert itself and bubble up into the consciousness of the protagonist, that is, the protagonist's actions make this conflict visible to the protagonist.

9. It may occur that the conscious goal of the protagonist at the beginning of the story is replaced at the end by a goal that was originally unconscious and made its appearance in the course of the story.

10. Sometimes the protagonist's unconscious desires remain unconscious

    that is, the reader perceives them but the protagonist does not

    (Hemingway's iceberg—the nine-tenths beneath the surface versus the story's visible one-tenth).

11. Tension is created each time a protagonist acts to pursue his goal and something thwarts his progress toward his goal.

12. There is often a gap between the intentions of a protagonist's action and the results: He takes action, and the world reacts in ways he didn't foresee or predict. Sometimes the thwarting or complicating reaction to the action comes from within the protagonist (i.e., the unconscious desire making itself manifest).

13. Arguments are a source of tension because the protagonist desires one thing and the antagonist desires something else (i.e., two conflicting desires).

14. External conflicts with other characters often reflect internal conflicts within the protagonist.

15. Internal conflicts or irreconcilable conflicts (desires) occur when the protagonist's actions for and his pursuit of the original goal conflict with his actions for and pursuit of another goal that he also desires—

that is, the protagonist wants goal A, but he also wants goal B, which conflicts with goal A.

16. When faced with irreconcilable conflicts/desires, protagonists often lie to others and to themselves in order to deny the irreconcilability.

17. When protagonists lie—especially about the nature of their reality—that lie will generally come back and bite them in the ass (i.e., the gap between expectations and results). Work on ways—other characters, circumstances—to expose the protagonist's lies or to put pressure on the protagonist to reveal the truth. A helpful analogy is to think of other characters as police investigators or prosecuting attorneys trying to trip up the protagonist and catch the protagonist in a lie. David Mamet: "A play begins with a lie. When the lie is exposed, the play is over."

18. The choices a protagonist makes concerning irreconcilable conflicts, desires, reveals his or her character (i.e., it is under pressure that character is revealed).

19. No conflict/irreconcilable desires/ tension/thwarting/difficulty = no story. Often, especially when the writer identifies with the protagonist in some way, the writer doesn't make the pursuit of the goal difficult enough for the protagonist.

20. Your job as the writer is to create difficulties for your protagonist in pursuit of the goal. In doing this, two models are useful:

   A. The God who rains down calamity on Job, who completely disrupts Job's happy and stable life.

   B. The devil, who tempts the protagonist, often with other desires and things the protagonist wants. The devil is probably the more useful model for creating irreconcilable conflicts/desires.

21. Out of the goals and conflicts of the protagonist come the themes of the story.

22. In the struggle toward and pursuit of the goal, the protagonist creates her own fate and reveals her character.

Assignment 6:
Write about the Problem

When you encounter a problem in your writing, don't wait until you think you've found the solution to resume writing. Instead, *write about the problem*. Describe it, what it entails; describe why it exists; describe how you feel about it; describe possible solutions or ways to address the problem.

Sometimes writers get stuck because they don't quite understand that writing is a process, a way of investigating the world and accessing our unconscious creativity and knowledge of the world. These writers don't use writing as a tool to explore problems that the writer faces, both in the writing and in the writer's life.

One instance of such a problem is when the writer thinks she should be someone or something else or have these specific qualifications before she can proceed. For instance, when a writer feels she needs a certain knowledge in order to proceed, what does she do if that knowledge is unavailable or is not 100 percent verifiable? If the writer describes this situation, that writing may make it clear that there is no other way to proceed, but without that knowledge or with partial knowledge, that this state of unknowing is the truth of her experience (this situation is reflected in the quotation from Maxine Hong Kingston's *China Men* in "On the Line between Fiction and Memoir," where she tells her father his silence about his past has forced her to make up his past).

Recently, I was talking to a writer friend who kept bemoaning the fact that the standard show-don't-tell style of fiction didn't suit him. I told him to open a story with that same complaint, describing what he thinks he's supposed to do as a fiction writer; then, I said, he should describe how he wants to tell the story—which in his case, would entail a more discursive, more telling than showing mode—and then see what happens.

If you are having difficulties writing about your past or about your family, describe those difficulties, examine what issues they involve. Then describe possible ways of proceeding, the options you find before you. Sometimes just writing the problem down can be the solution. At other times, writing about the problem can lead to the process through which you find the solution. In either case, this assignment will get you further in the process than if you simply sit around and complain about it to your friends.

Assignment 7:
Finishing the Book and
the Hero's Journey

What are the ways you need to change yourself—or your life—in order to finish the book you are writing?

The answer to this question might involve learning new skills as a writer. Or it may involve writing yourself—sometimes writing badly—into a different place: a new mode, a new approach to the material; past repressions or denials and into painful or traumatic experiences or parts of your life; into difficult emotions or hidden parts of yourself.

But the answer may also involve Rilke's famous line: "You must change your life." What are the concrete steps you need to take to do this?

Bibliography

Achebe, Chinua. *Hopes and Impediments: Selected Essays*. New York: Doubleday, 1988.
———. *Things Fall Apart*. London: Heinemann, 1958.
Adiga, Aravind. *The White Tiger*. New York: Free Press, 2008.
Alexander, Michelle. *The New Jim Crow: Mass Incarceration in the Age of Colorblindness*. New York: New Press, 2012.
Alexie, Sherman. *The Toughest Indian in the World*. New York: Grove Press, 2000.
Als, Hilton. *White Girls*. San Francisco: McSweeney's, 2014.
Bakhtin, M. M. *The Dialogic Imagination: Four Essays*. Edited by Michael Holquist. Austin: University of Texas Press, 1981.
Baldwin, James. *The Devil Finds Work*. New York: Dial, 1976.
———. *James Baldwin: The Legacy*. Edited by Quincy Troupe. New York: Simon and Schuster, 1989.
———. *Nobody Knows My Name: More Notes of a Native Son*. New York: Dell, 1961.
———. *Notes of a Native Son*. Boston: Beacon Press, 1955.
———. *The Price of the Ticket: Collected Nonfiction, 1948–1985*. New York: St. Martin's/Marek, 1985.
Berger, John. *And Our Faces, My Heart, Brief as Photos*. New York: Pantheon Books, 1984.
———. *Portraits*. London/New York: Verso, 2015.
Blaise, Clark, and Bharati Mukherjee. *Days and Nights in Calcutta*. St. Paul: Hungry Mind Press, 1995.
Brecht, Bertolt. *Brecht on Theatre*. Translated by John Willet. New York: Hill and Wang, 1964.
Césaire, Aimé. *Cahier d'un retour au pays natal*. Paris: Volontés, 1939. Translated and edited by James A. Arnold and Clayton Eshleman as *The Original 1939 Notebook of a Return to the Native Land* (Middletown, Conn.: Wesleyan University, 2013).
Chang, Jeff. *Who We Be: The Colorization of America*. New York: St. Martin's Press, 2014.
Chatwin, Bruce. *In Patagonia*. New York: Penguin Books, 1977.
———. *Songlines*. New York: Penguin Books, 1987.

Chotiner, Isaac. "Jonathan Franzen on Fame, Fascism, and Why He Won't Write a Book about Race: An Exclusive Conversation with the Novelist." *Slate*, July 31, 2016. http://www.slate.com/articles/arts/interrogation/2016/07/a_conversation_with_novelist_jonathan_franzen.html.

Cliff, Michelle. *The Land of Look Behind*. Ithaca, N.Y.: Firebrand Books, 1985.

Coetzee, J. M., and Arabella Kurtz. *The Good Story: Exchanges on Truth, Fiction and Psychotherapy*. New York: Penguin, 2015.

Conrad, Joseph. *Heart of Darkness, and The Secret Sharer*. New York: New American Library, 1950.

Díaz, Junot. *The Brief Wondrous Life of Oscar Wao*. New York: Riverhead Books, 2007

———. *Drown*. New York: Riverhead Books, 1996.

———. Introduction to *Dismantle: An Anthology of Writing from the VONA/Voices Writing Workshop*. Edited by Marissa Johnson-Valenzuela and Andrea Walls. Philadelphia: Thread Makes Blanket Press, 2014.

Du Bois, W. E. B. *The Souls of Black Folk*. New York: Dover, 1994.

Duras, Marguerite. *The Lover*. New York: Random House, 1985.

Eagleton, Terry. *Marxism and Literary Criticism*. Berkeley: University of California Press, 1976.

Eliot, T. S. *Selected Essays*. New York: Harcourt, Brace and World, 1960.

Espada, Martin. *Zapata's Disciple: Essays*. New ed. Evanston, Ill.: Curbstone Books/ Northwestern University Press.

Fanon, Frantz. *Black Skin, White Masks*. New York: Grove Press, 1952.

Foucault, Michel. *The Foucault Reader*. Edited by Paul Rabinow. New York: Pantheon Books, 1984.

Franklin, Jon. *Writing for Story: Craft Secrets of Dramatic Nonfiction by a Two-Time Pulitzer Prize Winner*. New York: Plume, 1986.

Franzen, Jonathan. *Freedom*. New York: Farrar, Straus and Giroux, 2010.

Freire, Paulo. *Pedagogy of the Oppressed*. Translated by Myra Bergman Ramos. New York: Herder and Herder, 1970.

Gates, Henry Louis, Jr. *Signifying Monkey: A Theory of Afro-American Literary Criticism*. New York: Oxford University Press, 1988.

Gornick, Vivian. *Fierce Attachments*. New York: Farrar, Straus and Giroux, 1987.

Gramsci, Antonio. *The Prison Notebooks: Selections*. Translated and edited by Quintin Hoare and Geoffrey Nowell Smith. New York: International, 1971.

Hongo, Garrett. *Volcano: A Memoir of Hawai'i*. New York: Vintage Books, 1995.

Joyce, James. *Dubliners*. New York: Penguin Classics, 1993.

Karr, Mary. *Cherry*. New York: Penguin Books, 2000.

———. *The Liars' Club*. New York: Penguin Books, 1995.

Kingston, Maxine Hong. *China Men*. New York: Vintage International, 1989.

———. *The Woman Warrior: Memoirs of a Girlhood among Ghosts*. New York: Vintage International, 1975.

Lahiri, Jhumpa. *Unaccustomed Earth*. New York: Alfred A. Knopf, 2008.

Lessing, Doris. *Prisons We Choose to Live Inside*. New York: Harper and Row, 1987.

Mamet, David. *Three Uses of the Knife*. New York: Columbia University Press, 1998.

McCourt, Frank. *Angela's Ashes*. New York: Scribner, 1996.

Moore, Thomas. *The Care of the Soul: A Guide for Cultivating Depth and Sacredness in Everyday Life*. New York: HarperCollins, 1992.

Morrison, Toni. *Playing in the Dark: Whiteness and the Literary Imagination*. Cambridge, Mass.: Harvard University Press, 1992.

Mura, David. *Turning Japanese: Memoirs of a Sansei*. New York: Anchor Books, Doubleday, 1991.

————. *Where the Body Meets Memory: An Odyssey of Race, Sexuality and Identity*. New York: Anchor Books, Doubleday, 1996.

Naipaul, V. S. *Conversations with V. S. Naipaul*. Edited by Feroza Jussawalla. Jackson: University Press of Mississippi, 1987.

————. *The Enigma of Arrival*. New York: Vintage Books, 1988.

————. *A Writer's People: Ways of Looking and Feeling*. New York: Alfred Knopf, 2008.

Obama, Barack. *Dreams from My Father: A Story of Race and Inheritance*. New York: Three Rivers Press, 1995.

O'Connor, Flannery. *The Complete Stories*. New York: Farrar, Straus and Giroux, 1971.

Packer, ZZ. *Drinking Coffee Elsewhere*. New York: Riverhead Books, 2003.

Palumbo-Liu, David. *The Deliverance of Others: Reading Literature in a Global Age*. Durham, N.C.: Duke University Press, 2012.

Rich, Adrienne. *Diving into the Wreck*. New York: W. W. Norton, 1973.

Roth, Philip. *Conversations with Philip Roth*. Edited by George J. Searles. Jackson: University Press of Mississippi, 1992.

————. *The Facts: A Novelist's Autobiography*. New York: Penguin Books, 1988.

Rumi. *Unseen Rain: Quatrains of Rumi*. Translated by John Moyne and Coleman Barks. Boulder, Colo.: Shambhala, 1986.

Said, Edward W. *Culture and Imperialism*. New York: Alfred A. Knopf, 1993.

————. *Orientalism*. New York: Vintage Press, 1978.

Salter, James. *Burning the Days: Recollection*. New York: Random House, 1997.

Smith, Sidonie. *A Poetics of Women's Autobiography: Marginality and the Fictions of Self-Representation*. Bloomington: Indiana University Press, 1987.

Sun Tzu. *The Art of War*. Translated by Thomas Cleary. Boston: Shambhala Dragon Editions, 1988.

Thandeka. *Learning to Be White: Money, Race, and God in America*. New York: Bloomsbury, 1999.

Vogler, Christopher. *The Writer's Journey: Mythic Structure for Storytellers and Screenwriters*. Los Angeles: Michael Wiese, 1992.

Wallace, David Foster. *Consider the Lobster and Other Essays*. New York: Little, Brown, 2006.

Watt, Ian. *Conrad in the Nineteenth Century*. Berkeley: University of California Press, 1979.

Wilderson, Frank B., III. *Red, White & Black: Cinema and the Structure of U.S. Antagonisms*. Durham, N.C.: Duke University Press, 2010.

Wolff, Tobias. *This Boy's Life*. New York: Grove Press, 1989.

Wong, Shawn. *American Knees*. New York: Simon and Schuster, 1995.

Young, Kevin. *The Grey Album: On the Blackness of Blackness*. Minneapolis: Graywolf Press, 2012.